Carmelite Prayer

Carmelite Prayer

A Tradition for
the 21st Century

edited by Keith J. Egan

Paulist Press
New York/Mahwah, N.J.

Cover design by Sharyn Banks
Book design by Lynn Else

Library of Congress Cataloging-in-Publication Data

Carmelite prayer : a tradition for the 21st century / edited by Keith J. Egan.
   p. cm.
ISBN 0-8091-4193-0 (alk. paper)
   1. Carmelites—Spiritual life. 2. Contemplation—History of doctrines. I. Egan, Keith J., 1930-
   BX3203 .C38 2003
   248.8′942—dc21

2003008771

Published by Paulist Press
997 Macarthur Boulevard
Mahwah, New Jersey 07430

www.paulistpress.com

Printed and bound in the United States of America

Table of Contents

v

Contents

Dedication

We, the Carmelite Forum and our associates,* dedicate this book to our dear friend, collaborator, and source of much inspiration, Father Ernest E. Larkin, O. Carm. His life, ministry, and scholarship have greatly enriched our lives and those of countless others who have sought to live and pray more contemplatively.

> Donald W. Buggert, O. Carm.
> Kevin Culligan, O.C.D.
> Margaret Dorgan, D.C.M.*
> Keith J. Egan, T.O. Carm.
> Constance FitzGerald, O.C.D.
> Kieran Kavanaugh, O.C.D.
> Roland E. Murphy, O. Carm. (d.)*
> Steven Payne, O.C.D.
> Vilma Seelaus, O.C.D.
> John Welch, O. Carm.

Abbreviations

The Collected Works of St. Teresa of Avila, trans. Kieran Kavanaugh and Otilio Rodriquez. Washington, D.C.: Institute of Carmelite Studies. This publisher is cited as ICS. Abbreviations are supplied for frequently cited works of Teresa of Avila, John of the Cross and Thérèse of Lisieux.

Note the study edition of *The Way of Perfection*. ICS, 2000.

Vol. 1 (1976): *The Book of Her Life* . . . . .BL
Vol. 2 (1980): *The Way of Perfection* . . . . .WP
                   The Interior Castle IC
Vol. 3 (1985): *The Book of Her Foundations* . . . . . . .BF

The Collected Works of Saint John of the Cross, revised edition; trans. Kieran Kavanaugh and Otilio Rodriquez. Washington, D.C.: ICS, 1991. Below are abbreviations for commentaries. Letters are cited as Letter with number of the letter.

The Ascent of Mount Carmel . . . . .A
The Dark Night . . . . .DN
The Spiritual Canticle . . . . .SC
The Living Flame of Love .LF
The Sayings of Light and Love . . . . .SL

Story of a Soul: The Autobiography of Saint Thérèse of Lisieux, 3rd ed.; trans. John Clarke. Washington, D.C.: ICS, 1996.

Story of a Soul . . . . .SS

Albert's Way: The First North American Congress on the Carmelite Rule. Rome, Institutum Carmelitanum; Barrington, IL: Province of the Most Pure Heart of Mary, 1989.

Formula of Life (1206–1214) . . . . . Formula of Life

Carmelite Rule (1247) . . . . Rule

Foreword

In the "oldest preserved Christian document,"[1] St. Paul urged the Thessalonians to "Rejoice always, pray without ceasing, give thanks in all circumstances; for this is the will of God in Christ Jesus for you" (1 Thess 5:16–18). Paul the Apostle made a habit of giving thanks, and he connected gratitude and prayer, as did his admirer Teresa of Avila (BL.147). The Carmelite mystic reminded her daughters not to "be negligent about sharing gratitude" (WP. 2.10); she wrote to her friend Maria Bautista that "we must always be grateful for the good that is done for us."[2] In the spirit of Paul and Teresa and on behalf of the Carmelite Forum, and as editor of this book I wish to acknowledge with gratitude everyone who has contributed in so many ways to the publication of this book on Carmelite Prayer.

First of all, we gratefully remember Father Thomas Kilduff, O.C.D. (1907–1986), our fellow member and friend whose life was wholly dedicated to the dissemination of Carmelite spirituality. The Carmelite Forum cherishes and strives to continue Tom Kilduff's legacy.

An anonymous grant underwrote a meeting of the Carmelite Forum in the year 2000 in Tucson, Arizona, where first drafts of these essays were shared with each other and critiqued amid the hospitality of the Carmelites at Salpointe High School. The majority of the essays in this book were then presented in June of 2000 as lectures at the annual Summer Seminar on Carmelite Spirituality, which honored Father Ernest E. Larkin, O. Carm. The anonymous grant also defrayed some of the expenses involved in the preparation of the

1

essays for publication. The grant has been administered by the Center for Spirituality at Saint Mary's College, Notre Dame, Indiana. The Center for Spirituality has sponsored the Carmelite Forum's annual Summer Seminars in Carmelite Spirituality since the seminars began in1985. The Forum appreciates this grant and the sponsorship of the Center for Spirituality, now ably directed by Dr. Kathleen Dolphin, P.B.V.M. I completed work on the manuscript version of this book during the first half of a sabbatical awarded me by Saint Mary's College for which I am grateful. Editorial work was carried out in the hospitable environment of the Cushwa-Leighton Library at Saint Mary's College and its congenial and helpful staff.

The Carmelite Forum also thanks Kathleen Walsh, formerly an editor at Paulist Press, who welcomed and gave encouragement to the project in its initial stages, and we heartily thank Dr. Christopher Bellitto who with enthusiasm, professional expertise and editorial acumen has very ably guided this book to its final form. Our debt to Dr. Bellitto and the Paulist Press staff is immeasurable.

As the editorial work neared completion, Karen Shannon applied her splendid skills to the elimination of pesky computer glitches, and with a keen eye and generous spirit she expeditiously proofread the manuscript. I am grateful to her for her professional expertise and her dedication to the project.

I am also grateful to the other members of the Carmelite Forum for their magnanimous collaboration during the time that this book has been in gestation, and for their inspiration through the years. I wish that all the readers of this book could have the privilege of working with so gifted and committed a group of scholars whose lives of deep faith and knowledge of the Carmelite classics are truly inspiring. The editor and the rest of the Carmelite Forum have expressed on the dedication page their gratitude and admiration for their brother Carmelite, Father Ernest E. Larkin, whose lifetime commitment to Carmel and its heritage has been a wondrous gift to countless women and men, including ourselves. Father Ernest's life and contributions

2

are chronicled briefly in the final essay in this book. Since this book of essays represents the collaborative efforts of the Carmelite Forum, a few words are in order about this group of Carmelite scholars.

The Carmelite Forum

Over the last few decades there has been a rapidly growing interest in Carmelite Spirituality and Carmelite Prayer. The essays in this book are an attempt to respond to that interest. These essays have been composed by members of the Carmelite Forum and two of the Forum's associates, Margaret Dorgan, D.C.M., and Roland E. Murphy, O. Carm. Father Murphy died on July 20, 2002, the Carmelite feast of the prophet Elijah about whom he wrote much and well. His collaboration with the Forum will most certainly be missed.

The fourth centenary of the death of Saint Teresa of Avila was celebrated in Washington, D.C., at the Catholic University of America and elsewhere in the District of Columbia under the sponsorship of the Washington Province of the Discalced Carmelites. The lectures presented at Catholic University were published as *The Centenary of Saint Teresa*, volume 3 of *Carmelite Studies* (1984). This celebration honoring Teresa of Avila, saint and doctor of the church, clearly demonstrated a widespread and profound hunger in North America for the contemplative tradition of the Carmelite Order.

In recognition of this hunger, a gathering of Discalced Carmelites (O.C.D.) and Carmelites of the Ancient Observance (O. Carm.) was convened not long afterward at Whitefriars Hall, Washington, D.C. At this meeting the Carmelite Forum came into existence. Gathered for this initial meeting were Constance FitzGerald, O.C.D., Vilma Seelaus, O.C.D., Thomas Kilduff, O.C.D., Kieran Kavanaugh, O.C.D., Kevin Culligan, O.C.D., Ernest E. Larkin, O. Carm., John Welch, O. Carm., and Keith J. Egan, T.O. Carm. Subsequently Donald W. Buggert, O. Carm., and Steven Payne, O.C.D., became members of the Carmelite Forum.

At this first meeting, the Carmelite Forum endeavored to respond to the signs of the times which called for closer collaboration between the two branches of the Carmelite Order: the Ancient Observance and the Discalced Carmelites. They undertook to work together to disseminate the spiritual heritage of Carmel. Members of the Forum had witnessed how effectively the Jesuits had shared the Spiritual Exercises in the sixties and seventies with the many people who were eager to hear about the wisdom of Saint Ignatius of Loyola. It was time that more be done to acquaint Christians with the spiritual legacy of Carmel.

The charisms of religious orders are not the private property of their members; rather, their charisms are public graces, spiritual gifts intended to enrich the lives of Christians wherever and whatever their station in life. The spiritual traditions of religious communities, inspired by the Holy Spirit, exist not only for their members but for the benefit of everyone who seeks a deeper relationship with God. Carmelites the world over have recognized the challenge to share their tradition with others.

The deliberations at Whitefriars Hall that followed the Teresian centenary set the Carmelite Forum on a course that it still pursues—to explore the Carmelite Spiritual tradition and to share that tradition with Christians of North America so that there might be a more contemplative church. Over the last two decades members of the Carmelite Forum have introduced spiritual seekers in the English-speaking world to the Carmelite classics. These classics contain "inexhaustible wisdom" about human existence and about the journey to union with God in love. It has been the urgent desire of the Carmelite Forum that they might inspire a growing number of Carmelites and laity to undertake the ministry of Carmelite scholarship and spiritual guidance. Just as biblical, theological and liturgical scholars prepared the way for the Second Vatican Council, it is the hope of the Carmelite Forum that the heritage of Carmel may be readily accessible to all Christians who experience the call to pray more deeply and more contemplatively.

In 1985 the Carmelite Forum inaugurated a series of Summer Seminars on Carmelite Spirituality, hosted by the Center for Spirituality at Saint Mary's College, Notre Dame, Indiana. Over the years large numbers of laity, religious and clergy of differing faiths have gathered at Saint Mary's to study and pray with the Carmelite classics under the guidance of the Carmelite Forum. These seminars have explored the Carmelite Rule; the *Institution of the First Monks;* and the writings of Teresa of Avila, John of the Cross, Brother Lawrence of the Resurrection, Thérèse of Lisieux, Elizabeth of the Trinity, Titus Brandsma, Edith Stein and others.

Lectures and workshops from the summer seminars have been published as audio and video cassettes by Alba House Publishers of Canfield, Ohio, the Institute of Carmelite Studies and the Carmelite Institute. Both of the latter are in Washington, D.C. The members of the Carmelite Forum have published many articles as well as books that have originated at these summer seminars. These publications have benefited from the thoughtful responses of those who attended these seminars. A recent publication by the Carmelite Forum that originated in a Summer Seminar was *Carmel and Contemplation: Transforming Human Consciousness,* (volume 8) *of Carmelite Studies,* edited by Regis Jordan and Kevin Culligan (Washington, D.C.: Institute of Carmelite Studies, 2000).

Finally, in the name of the Carmelite Forum, let me say that it has been and continues to be a special privilege to share with Christians of every kind the wisdom of the Carmelite tradition, especially its tradition of contemplative prayer as it has been explored by the saints of Carmel, canonized and uncanonized. The Carmelite Forum believes that the Carmelite tradition can make a significant contribution to the transformation of a church that owes its members more guidance in prayer, especially the practice of contemplative prayer which leads to justice for the oppressed and an enduring peace for a civilization weary of war.

The Carmelite Forum has learned much not only from participants in the Summer Seminars but also from guest speakers who have joined them at the seminars as lecturers and workshop leaders. Besides Father Roland Murphy and Sister Margaret Dorgan, others who have enriched these seminars have been Dr. Dianne Traflet, the Rev. Allan Budzin, John Russell, O. Carm., Daniel Chowning, O.C.D., Michael Dodd, O.C.D., and Robert Stefanotti, O. Carm. The contributions of these scholars to the Summer Seminars are very much appreciated.

Finally, we, the Carmelite Forum, welcome readers of these essays as friends and companions on the journey to union with God in love, for as John of the Cross wrote to those whom he guided on the path to God: "When evening comes, you will be examined in love" (SL. 60).

Keith J. Egan

Notes

1. Raymond E. Brown, *An Introduction to the New Testament* (New York: Doubleday, 1997), 456–57.

2. *The Collected Letters of St. Teresa of Avila,* vol. 1; trans. Kieran Kavanaugh, O.C.D. (Washington, D.C.: ICS, 2001), Letter 153.5.

Carmel: A School of Prayer

Keith J. Egan

The human heart yearns for something, someone beyond its reach. Augustine of Hippo put it this way in his oft-quoted words: "Our heart is restless until it rests in you."[1] World religions attest to this universal impulse to pray. The desire to pray is a desire for God and is already prayer. Teresa of Avila wrote for her nuns that "in the measure you desire him, you will find him" (WP.26.3). In the Jewish-Christian tradition the instinct for prayer has been a response to God's initiative as a loving creator and redeemer. In the Christian tradition prayer is also a response to the Incarnation as an expression of divine love. In the words of the great doxology of the Eucharist, Christians respond to God's love through, with, and in Christ. Like the disciples, those who desire to pray look to Christ for instruction on how to pray: "Lord, teach us to pray" (Luke 11:1). One Christian school of prayer is the Carmelite tradition. As Father John Welch has written: "Carmel in the contemporary church stands for prayer. The original Carmelites and the saints of Carmel, known and unknown, were preoccupied with attentiveness to Mystery. From this attentiveness flowed identity, community, and service of the world. If the tradition of Carmel has anything to say to the modern world it is a word about prayer."[2] The essays in this book offer its readers some words about prayer in the Carmelite tradition.

The Carmelite Tradition

The Carmelite tradition goes back to the simple origins of the Carmelite Order when lay hermits banded together near the fountain of Elijah on Mount Carmel. Through the intervening years Carmelites have prayed, taught others to pray, and sometimes have written about prayer. Since the sixteenth century, Carmel has been widely perceived as a school of contemplative prayer, especially as the Carmelite tradition became well known through the writings of Teresa of Avila and John of the Cross. Carmelite prayer, it must be said, is not an esoteric or elitist tradition, despite the popular but not always accurate reputation of these two Spanish Carmelites. Contemplative prayer in the hands of Teresa and John moves toward simplicity. As Iain Matthew has written, prayer in the Carmelite mode "...contains an impulse towards simplicity."[3] It is a movement that invites the Spirit of God to take over the dynamics of the heart. Graced human effort is mere preparation for prayer that truly becomes prayer when God prays within us (Rom 8:26). Contemplative prayer is not a matter of human achievement but is God's gracious gift to a heart that struggles to be free so that it may be open to and filled with divine love.

Teresa was convinced that even vocal prayer can be contemplative. This woman whose life became a prayer could be adamant about this conviction: "...it may seem to anyone who doesn't know about the matter that vocal prayer doesn't go with contemplation; but I know that it does. Pardon me, but I want to say this: I know there are many persons who while praying vocally...are raised by God to sublime contemplation..." (WP.30.7). Carmelite prayer is contemplative in that one does with grace what one can do to ready oneself for union with God. Then one leaves all the rest up to God. If God desires that one's prayer be gifted in some special way, that is God's concern. What matters for the Carmelite is that she does what she can to have a "liberated heart" (A.1.4.6), where God's love can thrive, a space that God fills with love.[4] One's effort at prayer and one's detachment from whatever keeps one blind to God's love is a struggle to give God ample space in one's heart. Teresa sees that space grow as one becomes humble, detached from obstacles to God's love, and as one practices what she called the prayer of recollection.[5]

The phenomena too often popularly associated with mystics do not constitute holiness, and if anything these phenomena can be dangerous as they may easily lead to pride and distraction. In her usual direct approach, Teresa says it this way: "...there are many holy persons who have never received one of these favors; and others who received them but are not holy" (IC.5.9.16). John of the Cross knows what matters: "When evening comes, you will be examined in love" (SL.60). The goal of Carmelite prayer, as of all Christian prayer, is love of God and neighbor with the love of neighbor as *the* test of one's love of God. Such was the conviction of that insightful mistress of prayer, Teresa of Avila (IC.5.3.8).

The Word of God

Carmelite prayer is quite simply the many ways that Carmelites have prayed since those original lay hermits sought solitude on Mount Carmel. According to their Formula of Life, these hermits were to "meditate day and night on the law of the Lord unless engaged in some just undertaking," a practice rooted in Jewish tradition and in the prayer of the Christian desert.[6] The prayer book of these early hermits was simply the psalter.[7] The Carmelites have always prayed the psalms, and praying the psalms has taught them how to pray and has given them a language of prayer. In fact, as for all Christians, the Word of God, especially as announced in the liturgy, is the wellspring where the Carmelites have gone for guidance in prayer. Father Roland Murphy's essay in this book works off this tradition of praying the psalms.

From the beginning the Carmelite community was to celebrate Eucharist each day, when it was possible to do so. Along with the psalms, which they prayed in their cells, the early Carmelite hermits would have heard the Word of God proclaimed regularly at the Eucharist. Moreover, the quite simple Formula of Life given to the Carmelite hermits between 1206 and 1214 by Albert, Patriarch of Jerusalem, is a pastiche of biblical quotations and allusions.[8] The Bible must never be very far from one who prays in the Carmelite tradition.

The Prayer of Christ

Pledged by their Rule to live in "allegiance to Jesus Christ," Carmelites have looked to Christ as their teacher of prayer and, as John of the Cross reminded his readers, Carmelites must be aware that the Holy Spirit, the Spirit of Christ, is the principal guide in the spiritual life (LF.3.46). Jesus taught his followers to pray by word and example. The gospels show Jesus as a man of prayer and as a rabbi instructing his followers how to respond in prayer to a loving God. In the gospels one hears often of Jesus going off alone to be with his Father,[9] a habit to be reflected in a Carmelite's life. Indeed, all over the world Christians have prayed the Lord's Prayer, the prayer taught to the disciples by Christ. Much of Teresa's *Way of Perfection*, written in her inimitable style, is a commentary on the Lord's Prayer. At the close of this book, in which Teresa teaches her "daughters" to pray, she claims that the Lord's Prayer contains "the entire spiritual way" (WP.42.5). John of the Cross, often recognized as a mystic's mystic, could say that in the seven petitions of the Lord's Prayer is "embodied everything that is God's will and all that is fitting for us." John added that all prayer is, in fact, "reducible to the *Pater Noster*" (A.3.44.4), a conviction that runs through the whole Christian tradition with its proliferation of commentaries on the Our Father.

Important to Christians in the early church was the prayer of Jesus at Gethsemane. This event is described in the three synoptic gospels and is alluded to in the Gospel of John.[10] The prayer of Jesus in the garden was a favorite text for Teresa of Jesus.[11] To this writer at least, the collapse of the ministry of Jesus at Gethsemane is an illustration of John of the Cross's dark night experience.[12] Dark nights prepare the heart by emptying it of what does not belong there so that God's love can flow into the heart and become its lifeblood. Everywhere and always God seeks to come alive in the human heart. Carmelite contemplative prayer is a response to God's desire to be the dynamic energy of human existence. The prayer of Carmel has faith that "God is never absent, not even from a soul in mortal sin...." John of the Cross goes on to speak of the search for the hidden God who is never absent:

> What more do you want, O Soul! And what else do you search for outside, when within yourself you possess your riches, delights, satisfaction, fullness, and kingdom—your Beloved whom you desire and seek? Be joyful and gladdened in your interior recollection with him, for you have him so close to you. Desire him there, adore him there. (SC.1.8)

Jesus taught his apostles and disciples to pray, and they sought to pray as Jesus had prayed. So too the prayer and wisdom of Christ shapes Carmelite prayer. John of the Cross tells his readers what God says: "Fasten your eyes on him alone because in him I have spoken and revealed all and in him you will discover even more than you ask for and desire" (A.2.22.5). "...[F]ix your eyes only on him and you will discern hidden in him the most secret mysteries, and wisdom, and wonders of God..." (A.2.22.6). Perhaps no one has ever been more emphatic than Teresa that all prayer, mystical and otherwise, must be rooted in the humanity of Christ (BL.22; IC.6.7.6). Teresa wanted her sisters to be focused on Christ: "Fix your eyes on the Crucified and everything will become small for you" (IC.7.4.8). To its very core Carmel's life and prayer are centered on Jesus the Christ.

Carmelite prayer is also the prayer of the whole Christ, the Body of Christ, the church. Their Rule of 1247 called Carmelites to ecclesial prayer: daily celebration of the Eucharist, communal recitation of the divine office[13] besides meditation "day and night on the law of the Lord." The Carmelite tradition is an ecclesial heritage with a call to pray and to love out of this heritage. Thérèse of Lisieux discovered for herself this ecclesial calling: "Yes, I have found my place in the Church and it is You, O my God, who have given me this place; in the heart of the Church, my Mother, I shall be *Love*" (SS.194). John of the Cross wrote to a young woman advisee: "...what need is there in order to be right other than to walk along the level road of God and of the Church" (Letter 19).

The prayer of Carmel is then rooted in Christ, shaped by the holy scriptures and lived within the church and is oriented to a contemplative stance before God, waiting for God to do God's work so that one may be transformed into union with God in love. The ways of praying in the Carmelite tradition are varied according to times and circumstances but always contemplative, seeking God and union with God in love. The Carmelite who prays in imitation of Christ and with the church does so with a pervasive consciousness that the Carmelite Order from the beginning has been devoted in a special way to Mary, the Mother of Jesus, to whom the chapel of the first Carmelite hermits was dedicated. The scapular worn by Carmelites is a sign of this Marian devotion and dedication. Carmelite prayer occurs with an appreciation of Mary's unique role in the lives of Carmelites down through eight centuries, when they have been known as the brothers and sisters of Our Lady of Mount Carmel.[14]

The varied ways of praying within the Carmelite tradition can be learned from the women and men who have composed Carmelite classics that carry much wisdom about the journey to union with God in love.

Carmelite Classics

Carmelite prayer is the prayer of known and unknown Carmelites who have raised their hearts and minds to God during the last eight hundred years. Would that we were able to gain access to the inner life of these Carmelite women and men. However, access to the inner life of countless Carmelites of the past largely eludes human inquiry. The intimate relationship between these Carmelites and God belongs to the realm of sacred mystery, the *un no sé qué* (I don't know what) of John of the Cross (Poem 12). Edith Stein has said it this way: "No human eye can see what God does in the soul during hours of inner prayer. It is grace upon grace."[15] But, now and then the veil has been drawn back so that one may sense something of what has transpired between God and these sisters and brothers of Mary, the Mother of Jesus.

Those who commune with God in the depths of their hearts sometimes possess a special gift for expressing something of that experience. Thomas Aquinas called this gift the "grace of speech."[16] Such was the gift of Teresa, John, and Thérèse, as well as other Carmelites. Teresa, the great storyteller of God's love, reports often on what God's presence has been like for her and not infrequently breaks into explicit prayer in her writings:

> O greatness of God! How You manifest Your power in giving courage to an ant! How true, my Lord, that it is not because of You that those who love You fail to do great works but because of our own cowardice and pusillanimity. Since we are never determined, but full of human prudence and a thousand fears, You, consequently, my God, do not do Your marvelous and great works. (BF.2.7)

Moreover, Teresa realized that she had received the grace of speech. The Lord, she said, "taught me the manner of explaining it [her prayer experience]" (BL.16.2). John of the Cross's mystical poetry is a manifestation of what occurred in the "deep caverns" of his heart where he had been touched by God's love. John wrote that his poem, "The Spiritual Canticle," was "composed in a love flowing from abundant mystical understanding" (SC. Prologue, 2). Thérèse's *Story of a Soul* is all about a God who has led a timid and fearful young woman to spiritual maturity, to a life of "confidence and love."[17] These and other Carmelites have revealed something of the mystery of prayer, the mystery of their hidden life as Edith Stein was fond of calling what went on in the depths of one's being.[18] The three doctors of the church, Teresa, John, and Thérèse, and other Carmelites, have composed classic texts that contain wisdom for those who desire to pray more contemplatively. These Carmelite classics are a rich resource for anyone who wishes to enter wholeheartedly into that fullness of love "for which we were created" (SC.29.3).

The Religious Classic

A classic is a person, event, or text that has inexhaustible, enduring, or timeless meaning. Some speak of a classic's excess or surplus meaning which, out of its abundance, speaks anew to generation after generation. Religious classics carry the meaning of a religious tradition; they stamp a tradition with specific characteristics. When religious classics are neglected, a tradition slips into superficial expressions that fail to offer substantial wisdom about how to live a tradition. But classics require interpretation. They need to be understood and mined for meaning in each succeeding age.

The Carmelite Forum came into being in the wake of the four-hundredth anniversary of the death of Teresa of Avila, which occurred in 1982. Members of the Forum realized that the Carmelite classics were not being shared effectively and broadly enough with those who sought to lead a deeper spiritual life. From its inception the Forum, in its summer programs and writings, has stressed the reading and interpretation of the Carmelite classics as a way of making the Carmelite heritage more accessible. The goal was and is to make it possible for more people to become conversation partners with the

Carmelite tradition, especially through its classics. This book of essays is an effort to share interpretations about contemplative prayer gained by members of the Carmelite Forum through their study of Carmelite classics.

Carmelite classics, like all classics, contain wisdom about human existence. At the beginning of the third millennium, the Carmelite classics offer guidance about how the church and Christianity may become more contemplative, that is, how Christians may embrace their common humanity with the awareness that to be fully human one does what one can to live in the presence of a loving God.

Members of the Carmelite Forum have engaged in the interpretation of Carmelite classics using contemporary methods such as those proposed by scholars like Hans-Georg Gadamer, Bernard Lonergan, David Tracy, and Sandra Schneiders.[19] These scholars have made our age more conscious of the need to become conversation partners with the great religious classics and of the need to engage in the interpretation of these classics. In the telling phrase of Pope John XXIII, classics are to be interpreted in the context of "reading the signs of the times," so that religious classics do not become museum pieces but rather sources of wisdom about human existence. Interpretation of the classics requires that one ask of the classics what they have to say to this age about living more contemplatively in a culture of distraction and anxiety.

Scholars have engaged in the interpretation of religious classics by examining (1) "the world behind the texts," that is, the historical and literary situation in which the classic text was composed, examining what went into the production of the text; (2) "the world of the text," that is, the questions that need to be addressed to the text: What is the truth of this text and what does it reveal about serious issues of human existence?; and (3) "the world before or ahead of the text." It is in this final phase of interpretation that the transformation of consciousness mostly occurs. This last phase in the process brings one into the spiritual terrain of interpretation: what does this text say about ultimate values? How shall one integrate the wisdom of the text into one's world view, into one's spiritual horizons, into one's relationship with God? In this final phase of interpretation the reader finds that because she can trust the text, she can abandon herself to it, letting the text shape her consciousness about God and the way to union with God in love.

The work of interpretation may seem like an esoteric exercise to be left to the experts and the specialists. Indeed, there is much work for the professional exegete to do in the interpretation of classical texts. But the classics are not meant for an elite few, certainly not the Carmelite classics. Most of the Carmelite classics were written for the benefit of quite ordinary Carmelites who sought a deeper relationship with God. They were not composed merely for the erudite. Teresa of Jesus wrote for the women who in great numbers had flocked to her newly founded monasteries but who had little or no formal education. John of the Cross wrote for the same women as well as for friars and laity who wanted to pray and live more contemplatively. In school-like notebooks Thérèse, with very little formal education, wrote in simple, straightforward language for the nuns in her monastery what became a bestseller, the *Story of a Soul*. Specialists have something to share with readers of the Carmelite classics. However, the purpose of scholarly interpretation is to aid others in becoming able conversation partners with the classics. In fact, the aim of the essays in this book is to share with others some of the fruits of interpretation garnered by the Carmelite Forum. It is hoped that these explorations of the Carmelite classics will be an invitation to many to join in the task of interpreting Carmelite classics so that Carmel may truly be in this new millennium a School of Prayer that reaches out to all who want to pray more deeply.

The Carmelite classics explored in this book are principally from the hands of Teresa, John, and Thérèse, Carmel's doctors of the church, but also from others like the modern Carmelite, Edith Stein. These authors by no means exhaust the Carmelite canon. As is clear from the essays, the Formula of Life (1206–1214) and the Carmelite Rule (1247) and the *Institution of the First Monks* (before 1391) are classical documents that have shaped the spiritual landscape of Carmel. There are important Carmelite authors who appear incidentally in these essays, like Titus Brandsma, who deserves to be better known. Concentration in this book on the three Carmelite doctors of the church should not lessen the importance of texts by other Carmelites who have enriched the Carmelite tradition with their writings. The following Carmelites come to mind: Blessed John Soreth, Venerable John of Saint Samson, Brother Lawrence of the Resurrection, Blessed Elizabeth of the Trinity, Jessica Powers, and many others.[20]

The Journey Within

"Prayer," as T. S. Eliot has written, "is more / Than an order of words."[21] Not a little of what we learn from the Carmelite classics is by way of metaphor and image, like the images in the poetry of John of the Cross: dark night, living flame, fire of love, bride and bridegroom. Much of the imagery in the writings of Teresa and John is derived from the Song of Songs. Bridal language became part of the Carmelite tradition through the agency of Teresa of Jesus and John of the Cross. Since their day, the Song of Songs has become a classic text within the Carmelite canon. To understand the Carmelite tradition after Teresa and John, it is necessary to become conversant with the Song of Songs and its interpretation in the Christian tradition. The latter, begun by Origen and enlarged by the likes of Bernard of Clairvaux, became a fountain for God-talk by Teresa of Jesus and John of the Cross. Teresa and John brought bridal mysticism into the Carmelite tradition and with it a fiery passion for God.[22]

Transforming union with God is indescribable. "What God communicates to the soul in this intimate union is totally beyond words. One can say nothing about it, just as one can say nothing about God himself that resembles him" (SC.26.4). Yet, there is a simple sacramental principle upon which Carmelite prayer rests: God is within. Carmelite prayer is a call to make a journey to the center of one's being. Teresa's *Interior Castle* is built upon the awareness of the presence of God within the human person. Teresa taught her sisters this foundational truth of Carmelite prayer so that they may journey into the depths of the *Interior Castle*. She writes that those who seek to pray contemplatively should

> ....consider the Lord as very deep within their souls...[and that]...the glorious St. Augustine speaks about this, for neither in the market place nor in pleasures nor anywhere else that he sought God did he find Him as he did when he sought Him within himself. Within oneself, very clearly, is the best place to look; and it's not necessary to go to heaven, nor further than our own selves; for to do so is to tire and distract the soul, without gaining as much fruit. (BL.40.6; cf. WP.28)

John of the Cross expresses this principle in the following words:

> Oh, then soul most beautiful among all creatures, so anxious to know the dwelling place of your Beloved so you may go in search of him and be united with him, now we are telling you that you yourself are his dwelling and his secret inner room and hiding place. There is reason for you to be elated and joyful in seeing that all your good and hope is so close as to be within you, or better, that you cannot be without him. (SC.1.7)

Thérèse Martin also knew well Carmel's tradition of going within to find the Lord. She writes:

> I understand and I know from experience that: *'The kingdom of God is within you.'* [Lk17:21] Jesus has no need of books

or teachers to instruct souls; He teaches without the noise of words. Never have I heard Him speak, but I feel that He is within me at each moment; He is guiding and inspiring me with what I must say and do. I find just when I need them certain lights which I had not seen until then, and it isn't most frequently during my hours of prayer that these are most abundant but rather in the midst of my daily occupations. (SS.179)

To pray in the Carmelite tradition is to be aware of the inner divine presence that beckons one to be mindful of and responsive to that presence as the bread of life.

Conclusion

This brief introduction to Carmel as a School of Prayer cannot do justice to this charism in the Christian tradition. Barely has the surface been skimmed, nor can all its various expressions be explored in so short a space. On the other hand, the intent of this introductory chapter is to invite readers to explore themes of Carmelite prayer with authors of the essays in this book, but more importantly the aim of this chapter is to urge readers to become interpreters themselves of the Carmelite classics. These classics hold Carmel's wisdom about prayer and life, realities that are never to be separated. What is left to do in this introduction is to try to summarize briefly, albeit inadequately, some characteristics of Carmelite prayer. Once again, one must remind oneself that Carmelite prayer is Christian prayer shaped by the Word of God, rooted in Christ, celebrated in the liturgy, and expressed in just living. The emphasis on contemplative prayer in the Carmelite tradition can never make the mistake that one who so prays can be blind to injustice, oppression, or poverty. Elijah the prophet has been from the earliest days when Carmelites settled on his mountain a key inspiration for Carmelite life and prayer. The experience of prayer in Carmel has by its prophetic orientation a call to justice. Ernest Larkin, to whom this book of essays has been dedicated, has written:

> We need to be activists who pray and pray-ers who do justice....I write as a Carmelite, and Carmelite theory starts with prayer and moves to action. But while Carmel emphasizes the inner life, it is wholly committed to peace and justice too. "The work of justice," the superior general of the Carmelites wrote in a recent circular letter "must be an integral part of our preaching of the gospel and inform everything we do." Prayer and justice are a both/and dyad, never either/or.[23]

The special characteristic of Carmelite prayer, since the beginning, has been its contemplative orientation; that is, this prayer tradition is a call to journey into God's loving presence within. Carmelite prayer is not for the sake of experiences but for the sake of loving union with God. The prayer of Carmel is simple loving attentiveness to God present within. This prayer is always humble and as unpretentious as the anonymous beginnings of the order on Mount Carmel. Teresa of Jesus claims that this contemplative prayer is akin to what takes place in human friendship: "...mental prayer in my opinion is nothing else than an intimate sharing between friends; it means taking time frequently to be alone with Him who we know loves us" (BL.8.5). Teresa does not mean to imply casual, friendly chatter, but she is speaking of serious conversation between deeply committed friends. Moreover, Teresa wants one to know that this inner prayer calls one "to be alone with" Jesus Christ with the realization that this Christ loves the one who prays. That is how Teresa prayed and exhorted her sisters to pray.[24] Thérèse would want to add that we should learn to pray with "confidence and love" (SS.259), for to search for God within takes trust in the God who is love.

The Carmelite tradition says that one prepares for this contemplative prayer by doing what one can to grow in purity of heart for the pure of heart "will see God" (Matt 5:8). Purity of heart is "nothing less than the love and grace of God. The pure of heart are called blessed by our Savior (Matt 5:8), and to call them blessed is equivalent to saying they are taken with love, for blessedness is derived from nothing else but love" (DN.2.12.1). Carmelite asceticism, whether it be that of the Carmelite Rule or of John of Cross, is for the sake of what John of the Cross calls "freedom of the heart for God" (A.320.4).[25] The human struggle to be free is a prelude to God's liberation of the heart so that God's love may find a space in which to abide. "God is love, and those who abide in love abide in God, and God abides in them" (1 John 4:16). With a liberated heart that knows God's love, one can respond to God with love, and one can then love others in the way that others deserve to be loved. Carmelite prayer is all about letting God create within one a magnanimous loving heart.

Notes

1. Augustine, *Confessions*, trans. Henry Chadwick (Oxford University Press, 1992), 1.1.1.
2. John Welch, *The Carmelite Way: An Ancient Path for Today's Pilgrim* (New York/Mahwah: Paulist Press, 1996), 75.
3. Iain Matthew, *The Impact of God: Soundings from St. John of the Cross* (London: Hodder & Stoughton, 1995), 145.
4. Ibid., Part III: Space.
5. Keith J. Egan, "The Foundations of Mystical Prayer: Teresa of Jesus," *Medieval Religious Women*, vol. 2: *Peaceweavers*, eds. Lillian Thomas Shank and John A. Nichols (Kalamazoo, Mich.: Cistercian Publications, 1987), 331–44.
6. Formula of Life, 7. On the roots of this practice, see Keith J. Egan, "Contemplative Meditation: A Challenge from the Tradition," *Handbook of Spirituality for Ministers*, vol. 2, ed. Robert J. Wicks (New York/Mahwah: Paulist Press, 2000), 445–48.

7. Kees Waaijman, *The Mystical Space of Carmel: A Commentary on the Rule;* trans. John Vriend (Leuven: Peeters, 1999), 98–100. See James Boyce, "The Liturgy of the Carmelites," *Carmelus* 42 (1995), 15.

8. Giovanni Helewa, "The Word of God and the Rule of Carmel," *The Rule of Carmel: New Horizons* (Rome: Il Calamo, 2000), 21–44.

9. Mark 1:35; Luke 5:16; 6:12; 9:18, 28; 11:1 (Lord Teach Us to Pray); see Luke 22:41–46.

10. Mark 14:26–42; Matt 26:36–46; Luke 22:39–46; John 12:20–32; 17:1–26.

11. See BL.9.4; 29.4; WP.26.5; 28.4; 30.2; 32.6; IC.6.7.10–11; Meditations on the Song of Songs 3.10–11; Letter 304.2

12. On the collapse of the ministry of Jesus, see David Stanley, *Jesus in Gethsemane: The Early Church Reflects on the Suffering of Jesus* (New York/Mahwah: Paulist Press, 1980), chapter 4.

13. Boyce, op. cit., 15.

14. Emanuele Boaga, "Devotion to Our Lady at the Beginnings of Carmel," *Mother, Behold Your Son: Essays in Honor of Eamon R. Carroll, O. Carm.*, eds. Donald Buggert, Louis P. Rogge, Michael J. Wastag (Washington, D.C.: Carmelite Institute, 2001), 81–101.

15. Edith Stein, *The Hidden Life; Hagiographical Essays, Meditations, Spiritual Texts,* The Collected Works of Edith Stein; vol. 4, ed. L. Gelber and Michael Linssen, trans. Waltraut Stein (Washington, D.C.: ICS, 1992), 6.

16. *Summa theologiae* 2.2.177, 1. Note that in article 2 Thomas Aquinas restricted women to the private presentation of the gift of speech.

17. SS.259.

18. Stein, op. cit., see index, entry: hidden.

19. Hans-Georg Gadamer, *Truth and Method;* rev. ed. (New York: Continuum, 2000 for 1989); Bernard Lonergan, *Method in Theology* (New York: Herder and Herder, 1972); David Tracy, *The Analogical Imagination: Christian Theology and the Culture of Pluralism* (New York: Crossroad, 1981), chapters 3–7; Sandra M. Schneiders, *The Revelatory Text: Interpreting the New Testament as Sacred Scripture;* 2d ed. (Collegeville, Minn.: Liturgical Press, 1999).

20. For an historical overview of authors and texts in the history of Carmelite prayer see Redemptus M. Valabek, *Prayer Life in Carmel* (Rome: Carmel in the World, 1982).

21. "Little Gidding," *Four Quartets.*

22. For the contribution to the understanding of the Song of Songs by a modern Carmelite, see Keith J. Egan, "A Carmelite Master of the Song of Songs," *Master of the Sacred Page: Essays and Articles in Honor of Roland E.*

Murphy, O. Carm., eds. Keith J. Egan and Craig Morrison (Washington, D.C.: Carmelite Institute, 1997), 91–108.

23. Ernest E. Larkin, "Contemplative Prayer as the Soul of the Apostolate," *Handbook of Spirituality for Ministers*, vol. 2, ed. Robert J. Wicks (New York/Mahwah: Paulist Press, 2000), 458.

24. See Kieran Kavanaugh, "How to Pray: From the Life and Teachings of Saint Teresa," *Carmel and Contemplation: Transforming Human Consciousness*, Carmelite Studies, 8, eds. Kevin Culligan and Regis Jordan (Washington, D.C.: ICS, 2000), 115–35.

25. See Keith J. Egan, "The Symbolism of the Heart in John of the Cross," *Spiritualities of the Heart*, ed. Annice Callahan (New York/Mahwah: Paulist Press, 1990), 130–42.

2

The Spirituality of the Psalms

Roland E. Murphy, O. Carm.

This title calls for an explanation. We know what the Psalms are, and when we pray them we are in a spiritual mode. But the term *spirituality* is daunting of its various meanings. It could designate a second-order, more or less objective, presentation of the spiritual values discovered in Israel's prayers. Many studies have been written from this point of view, illustrating the various types and motifs in the psalter.[1] That is a very important dimension to our topic. However, the definition of spirituality remains difficult to determine. I adopt the definition of John O'Donohue: "What is spirituality? It is the unfolding and articulation of the divine dimension in experience."[2] If we apply this definition to the Bible, we can say that the Psalms (and other portions) trigger in the reader an experience that captures a divine dimension. I presume that the experience of the psalmist is appropriated and made our own, as we read the text; it fills our consciousness and is stored in our memory. O'Donohue warns that spirituality is not to be separated from the experience in which the divine presence is perceived. He stresses the role of the imagination, which "incarnates the vital threshold where the human and the divine are co-present. A concept of spirituality which recognizes the centrality of the imagination offers an inclusive hospitality to all areas of experience and, consequently, a more rounded portraiture of the diversity of divine presence."[3] Moreover, I wish to argue that this experience derives directly from the literal historical sense of the text, which is at least approximately attainable.

Emphasis on experience and imagination is not something new. Rebecca Weaver entitles an article about John Cassian's approach to the Bible: "Access to Scripture: Experiencing the Text."[4] She describes Cassian's interpretation as "an interaction between the sacred text and the sanctified heart." In that interaction each could be said to indwell the other. The text gained admission into the heart as the interpreter read it, memorized it, and meditated on it. At the same time, the heart came to inhabit the text as the interpreter sought to experience through imagination and action the world the text described. "A theoretical description of Cassian's method would indicate that he agreed with the traditional paradigm of the four senses, the historical, allegorical, tropological, and anagogical, that found literary expression in a famous medieval couplet.

> *Littera gesta docet, quid credas allegoria,*
> *Moralis, quid agas, quod speras, anagogia.*

In effect, the last three are separated from the historical; they alone convey the spiritual meaning. The traditional example is famous: Jerusalem. It can be understood as the city, the church, the moral progress of the soul, the heavenly Jerusalem (eschatological meaning). The failure of the ancients to recognize a religious thrust to the literal (historical) sense did not prevent them from a very existential understanding of the encounter between the reader and the text, but it is difficult for the modern reader to absorb their approach. The tidy medieval couplet leaves much to be desired. The fatal mistake is the limiting of the spiritual sense to the allegorical and the other levels. There is no denial that moral and eschatological meanings appear in many texts. But these can best be reached *through* the literal historical sense. A direct experiential encounter with the Word is what O'Donohue describes and it is particularly appropriate to reading the psalter. The spiritual thrust of a psalm can doubtless be illustrated in several ways. For example, one can analyze the literary forms that convey the movement and mood of various Psalms. These engage the readers and invite them to identify with the psalmist. I will illustrate that approach, and then choose a prominent theme or attitude, namely trust, that is reflected throughout the psalter. But first the depth of the spiritual is to be sounded on the basis of the literal historical sense.

The direct style of language leaps out to even a casual reader of the psalms. One cannot remain indifferent to the summons to utter the praise of the Lord: "O come, let us sing to the LORD, let us make a joyful noise to the rock of our salvation! For the LORD is a great God, and a great King above all gods" (95:1, 3). One is really compelled to worship, or else drop the Book of Psalms and go about other business. Or, "I waited patiently for the LORD; he inclined me and heard my cry. He drew me up from the desolate pit, out of the miry bog" (40:1–2). We have all been there, and if not, we know some who have earnestly appealed for such deliverance. We need not have the troubles of the psalmist spelled out for us; we can fill in the "desolate pit" with the desperate lot of many a human being. Or we can be caught up sharply by the reality of death: "You turn us back to dust, and say, 'Turn back, you mortals.' For a thousand years in your sight are like yesterday when it is past" (130:3). And then there is the intensely human reminder given to God: "If you, O LORD, should mark iniquities, Lord, who could stand?" (130:3). These few examples are warm human experiences that do not really need comment. But there are other affairs in the psalter, allusions, proper names, and so forth, which call for some kind of realistic explanation. Is Zion or Bashan, geographical terms, readily intelligible to the average person? It is not that geography, per se, is all that important; it is what stands behind it, the symbolism of certain words, or the associations which they call up to the ancient but perhaps not to us.

Biblical Literacy

The match-up between the reader and the Word depends partly on biblical literacy, that is, the ability to resonate to specific biblical ideas. For example, unless the concept of Zion/Jerusalem is more than a geographical designation, there will be no vital experience. For this one must appreciate Zion, with the Temple and the Ark, as the center of divine presence for Israel. The Lord could not be imaged, but dwelt invisibly in the Temple, where his footstool, the Ark, was guarded by cherubim. Psalm 132 recalls two "oaths" in idealistic fashion: David's alleged oath to find a home for the Lord to dwell in, and the oath of the Lord that stands behind the promise to the dynasty of David and the choice of Zion. Some specific issues of the Israelite world view have to be appreciated. Thus the Israelites would journey to Zion "to see the face of God" (e.g., Ps 42:2–3). At the same time there is the paradoxical counterpoint that to see the face of God entails death. No one who sees God can live: see Moses in Genesis 33:10; Isaiah in 6:5. Those statements underscore the infinite distance between the human and the divine. The elusive presence of God is a full dimension of the divine as Israel experienced the Lord.

In the biblical world view the Lord is the prime responsible agent of all that occurs. There was a particular bond between sin and suffering. Adversity was judged to be a part of divine displeasure, a punishment for sin. Hence the predominance of laments that challenge the Lord: "Why?" "How long?" and so on. Of course, such complaints are part of our repertoire as well. God is judged, in the modern as well as the ancient world, by human standards of "justice" that fall short of the Mystery. The attitude to death is generally one of acceptance and resignation (Eccl 2:16; 9:10–12 is exceptional in tone). But death is uppermost in biblical thought. The death that "hurts" is the living death, the non-life that afflicts the living. Death and Sheol are envisioned metaphorically as powers that pursue human beings; hence the psalmist speaks frequently of the grave, the pit, the residence of shades who have died and inhabit Sheol, where there is no possibility of a *loving* contact with God (e.g., Ps 30:3, 9). The mystery of suffering, which still plagues us, received no easy solution. To the extent that one experienced non-life, to that extent one was in Sheol or the nether world.

The biblical world of metaphor differs from the modern. This is an inevitable but not insuperable difficulty. It calls for a poetic response from the reader. In a bold article Karl Rahner wrote: "And so it is true that the capacity and the practice of perceiving the poetic word is a presupposition of hearing the word of God. The poetic word and the poetic ear are so much part of man that if this essential power were really lost to the heart, man could no longer hear the word of God in the word of man. In its inmost essence, the poetic is a prerequisite for Christianity."[6]

Fortunately, the biblical symbols are not difficult to understand; with a minimum of effort one can react positively to them. It is perhaps more difficult for Christians to deal with the vengeance and violence that appears in many psalms. How is one to react to the words and experience of the psalmist (or other biblical writers, in fact)? As recently as 1970 a Roman liturgical directive recommended that Psalms 58, 83, and 109, along with certain parts of several psalms be omitted.[7] This unconscionable censorship has led to their disappearance in "prayer" books. A very limited hermeneutic, to say the least, lies behind this move. It fails to recognize the human need to see divine justice at work, a need found in both testaments. Although the censorship is well meant, it betrays a superior and moralistic attitude, as if violence and vengeance were not part of Christian existence. Is prayer supposed to consist of pious thoughts, with no relationship to reality? The sad fact is that Christians can fail to confront the vicious reality in their lives, and remain blind to the vengeance and violence that lurk in their own hearts. These psalms should be turned *against* whoever prays them, challenging them concerning the violence and vengeance that mark their existence. It is ironic that such a directive could be given in the most violent of Christian centuries. The church fathers had their own hermeneutic to deal with whatever difficulties they found in the Bible, but they never eliminated passages from their *contemplation*.

Another example of a crippling "superior and moralistic attitude" is a common failure to understand the Torah, or Law of Israel. What is meant by the Law? The Hebrew term *torah* means instruction or teaching, and is applied also to the Pentateuch because of the large body of legislation extending from Exodus 20:1 to Numbers 10:11. In Jewish tradition it is expanded to include the oral torah, the interpretation that comes from the time of Moses and extends to the written codification of the Mishnah in the second century A.D. and the later Talmud (Babylonian and Palestinian). The Hebrew division of the Bible is Law, Prophets, and Writings (where the Book of Psalms is placed), expressed in the acronym *Tanakh*. Because the "five books of Moses" were formed as a unit early in the postexilic period, they came to be fundamental to Jewish self-understanding. But this is often countered by a Christian misunderstanding because of a shortsighted interpretation of the New Testament, especially the unhappy phraseology of "Law and Gospel." Anyone who prays the Psalms should come to them without the prejudicial phraseology of "Law and Gospel." Anyone who prays the Psalms should come to them without prejudice against "law." The opening Psalm is not a prayer, but a torah Psalm, in which the writer holds up constant meditation on the Law of the Lord as the way to go. It serves as a flagstaff to the psalter. The Psalms that the Israelites addressed to God are now seen as God's revelation of self to his people. Dedication to the Torah is not legalism. There are many examples of enlightened legislation, such as the attitude to the *gerim* or strangers, for example, Leviticus 19:10, 33–34. But more important is the understanding of the Law as revelation of the divine will and hence an occasion of joy, as reflected in Psalm 19:7–11 and also in the longest Psalm, 119. Again, the Torah is celebrated as a delight, a source of life, "sweeter than honey" (19:10), an object of "love" (119:113, 127). It designates the revelation of God's will as the path to follow. There is much here that spirituality can ponder and expand. As so often, a knowledge of the Old Testament on its terms can purify and intensify Christian ideals.

The 1993 Document from the Biblical Commission

The Pontifical Biblical Commission, now constituted of biblical scholars, issued a lengthy document entitled, "The Interpretation of the Bible in the Church."[8] The scholars described the literal historical interpretation as "indispensable," but many other approaches were recognized. These included the traditional, such as the typological and allegorical, and there was also an acknowledgment of the insights of sociology and anthropology that are associated with liberation, feminism, deconstruction, and reader response. The document describes the strengths and weaknesses of the latter views which have become popular in recent times. There is a recognition that any literary work can have more than one meaning. This characteristic is intrinsic to a written text that continues its journey through history and hence is subject to renewed interpretation. Biblical exegesis in the patristic and medieval periods may be termed precritical (as opposed to historical critical), but that does not mean that it was uncritical. Origen, Augustine, and John Cassian were sophisticated interpreters of the biblical word, even though their vantage point differs from ours. Their predilection for interpreting the Old Testament almost only in the light of New, their fondness for allegory and typology, are not shared by moderns. By and large, we prefer an interpretation closer to the literal sense. Hence we take this point of view in our approach to the Psalms. We propose that our access to the Psalms, and hence their "spirituality," is better served by the recognition and appropriation of the literal sense, which is essentially open-ended. This is in tune with the emphasis placed on actualization.

Actualization

The idea of actualization is a reminder that the 1993 document was written originally in French. *Actualiser* means to make something *actuel*. It conveys the notion of discovering what the text has to say to the modern age—how does the biblical message apply to present circumstances? While it presupposes the literal historical sense of the text, it goes beyond it to consider the Bible in the light of current issues, such as poverty, the situation of women, and so on. The process is ongoing. Through long historical periods the Bible has been interpreted in light of later revelation. The approach of the patristic age centered on holding together the two Testaments and on understanding Christ in terms of the revelation made to Israel. At the beginning, the Old Testament was the only Bible. But the role of the Old Testament in the time after Christ is different from the purpose it had in explaining Christ to the first believers. While those interpretations form part of the ongoing and living tradition of the church, there are new issues which call for a different actualization of the biblical text.

Is it possible to link the spirituality of the Psalms to a basic attitude? We have argued above for a spiritual experience deriving directly from the literal sense. The variety of moods reflected in the psalter are manifold: praise, thanksgiving, nostalgia, wise instruction, complaint, anger, vengeance, and so on. These can be held together, or at least can be seen to rest upon a fundamental religious stance—in a word, *trust*. This point does not rest upon the frequency of the word, it designates an atmosphere. The many literary genres represented in the psalter are helpful characterization of the individual Psalms. But with all this variety, there is a certain air of confidence and trust that is hardly ever lacking. Even the genre of complaint finds room for the motif of trust. This motif goes beyond a hope that the Lord will be pleased with the prayer or give an answer to the psalmist's request. It is an atmosphere, an ambience from which the Psalm arises. Why talk to the Lord if there is no existing relationship?

On whom can one depend? Even the most desperate pleas, which might seem to lack all hope, have a quality of trust. Psalm 88 (and to a certain extent, Psalm 39) is the sharpest example of despair:

> O LORD, God of my salvation,
>> when, at night, I cry out in
>>> your presence,
>> let my prayer come before you;
>>> incline your ear to my cry.
> For my soul is full of troubles,
>> and my life draws near to Sheol....
> O LORD, why do you cast me off?
>> Why do you hide your face
>>> from me?...
> You have caused friend and
>> neighbor to shun me;
>>> my companions are in darkness. (88:1–3, 14, 16, 18)

Despair? A failure to trust? Not so. There is the basic primal trust in God, manifested simply by calling out in prayer, even within the experience of what is considered to be divine wrath. The fundamental assurance of the promise to the fathers, Abraham, Isaac, and Jacob, and to Moses in the Sinai covenant (Ex 34:6; cf. Ps 103:7–13) prevails. Trust, even at the knife's edge of despair, is a healthy reminder of the many other occasions when confidence and reliance upon the Lord find expression.

As a motif, the note of trust is sounded not only in cries for help, but also in songs of praise and thanksgiving which record the fulfillment of the trust the psalmist or the people have demonstrated. Psalm 23 seems to be everyone's favorite portraying the Lord as a good shepherd, a frequent metaphor long before the application to Christ in John 10, and also as a host who provides a rich meal, long before the episode of the loaves and fishes. Several Psalms are best categorized as simply prayers of trust: 11, 27:1–6, 62, 121, 131. Psalm 27 may be considered a lament, but the note of trust is so strongly expressed that it carries the lament to another level: "The Lord is my light and my salvation; whom shall I fear?" Noteworthy are the metaphors which characterize these motifs: light and salvation (27:1); rock and salvation, mighty rock and refuge (62:2,7–8). This confidence qualifies the future, but it rests upon the past experience of the Lord's intervention in favor of his people. One can rely on the Lord always: "Trust in him at all times, O people; pour out your heart before him; God is a refuge for us" (62:8). Psalm 130, the famous *De profoundis*, is permeated with serene confidence, trusting that the Lord will not mark sins, or otherwise no one could stand, and at the end the psalmist *waits* for the Lord and even assures Israel of full redemption from sin.

This basic attitude can be contrasted with other approaches to the psalter. The superscriptions to the Psalms give a particular level of meaning. They are the Psalms of David, and some dozen of these seventy-three Psalms have been interpreted in the light of specific events in the life of Israel's most famous king. This approach is common in Jewish tradition, as the superscriptions to several Psalms testify. Christians may prefer to allegorize the Psalm, or to find a typology (e.g., Christ as the good shepherd for Psalm 23). The sermons of St. Augustine, his so-called *Enarrationes*, are noted for this. Such approaches, although favored especially in antiquity, are not easily adopted by modern readers. In most cases they call for shifts away from or at least beyond the movement intrinsic to the Psalm, as when the details of David's life obscure a personal experiential thrust (e.g., Psalm 51, the famous *Miserere*, which reaches the spiritual depths of any sinner). It may be argued that the experience of God that is expressed by the psalmist, apart from the detail alleged in the superscription, is more appealing and ultimately more in tune with modern prayer style. The literal historical critical approach is not locked into the past, and even if it can only approximate the original sense, it yields deeper and more psychological levels. This is true for most of the Psalms—songs of praise, thanksgiving, and lament. In some cases, the reader may need a modicum of biblical literacy to understand what is at issue (e.g., Psalms 48 and 87; why is Zion glorified?), but no one will fail to experience the emotions and desires in these prayers. In general, the Psalms are open-ended, expansive; they can easily fit in with the spiritual condition of anyone who is willing to pray them. They evoke universal human experience, and the spiritual meaning can be expanded, if need be, to suit a post-biblical context. This does not make them less appealing or adaptable to Christians; they speak the universal language of humanity. For Christians who recognize the continuity between the Testaments, both the historical and the present meanings can be honored.

At the same time, the use of the psalter or other biblical books must be guided by the dialectic that is inherent in the Word. Any reading of the text is selective to some extent. The biblical trust in the Lord might at first sight appear to be merely a spiritual nostrum. That is why we analyze Psalm 88; it is in tension with easy recourse to the Lord. Ultimately that is the reason why no censorship of the tough Psalms is to be practiced. Along with continuity there is also tension. For example, the sentiments concerning the nature of sacrifice vary widely even within a Psalm, as in Psalm 51:18–19 (cf. also 40:6–8) and 51:15–19. There are many other examples of tension. The experience behind the advice given in Psalm 37 is quite serene. But the same problem (envy over the prosperity of the wicked in Ps 37:7–9) nearly toppled the writer of Psalm 73:2–3, who finally persevered to the end with the help of God's right hand and counsel (73:23–24). There are many such tensions within the entire Bible.

Spiritual Preparation

It would be foolhardy to claim that the spirituality of the Psalms can be appropriated by the saint, but not the sinner. These prayers are clearly the aspirations of a people that readily admitted its sinfulness, and hence they are appropriate for the modern reader. However, Christian tradition emphasizes another aspect to praying the Psalms. From the time of John Cassian (fifth century) to the late Jesuit theologian, Bernard Lonergan, there is an emphasis on the subjective attitude of the reader of Scripture. Lonergan called for a "conversion" of the interpreter in pursuing theology, including the interpretation of the Word.[9] John Cassian insisted on spiritual preparation.[10] While his *Conferences* were primarily geared to the monastic life, and were the fruit of his living with the ancient monks of the desert, his views have a taste of the modern in that they reach out to experience. Abbot Nesteros urges him to read the Scriptures with the same diligence with which he pursued secular studies; then the secular will yield to the spiritual (XIV:13). At the end of XIV:14 the abbot insists on purity of heart: "It is impossible that anyone whose soul is not pure, can acquire spiritual knowledge, no matter how diligently he applies himself in study." When Germanus, the companion of Cassian, contests his point of view, the abbot replies that without this requisite one cannot reach the heart of Scripture or penetrate the mysteries of its spiritual meanings. He goes on in XIV:16 to quote Psalm 119:1–2 to the effect that a blameless life is mentioned *before* the teaching of the Lord; it is only by such a priority of values that one reaches the heart of divine revelation. The abbot can see two reasons for failure in teaching the Scriptures (XIV: 18–19): the teacher fails to experience what they communicate, or the learner is wicked and hard of heart. It is by way of exception that one who is wicked can teach others with any profit to them. The situation of those who read the Bible is somewhat paradoxical. On one hand, spiritual discipline is needed to prepare for the reading; on the other hand, spiritual experience accompanies and is the fruit of such reading.

Conclusion

I have sketched briefly both a modern and an ancient approach to Scripture: experiencing the Word through the direct literal sense, and a traditional view consisting of the four levels associated with John Cassian and others. In a sense, these approaches come together in emphasizing the spiritual, although their paths differ. The experience of God is the goal for both as it is for the reader of these lines: "articulation of the divine dimension in experience."

It is fitting, in view of honoring Father Ernest Larkin, O. Carm., who has enriched us all by his studies on prayer, that we ask if there is a particularly Carmelite nuance to praying the Psalms. We have no reason to think that Carmelites of old approached the Psalms any differently than their contemporaries. We do know that there are echoes of the Psalms, and other parts of the Bible, in the Rule. Perhaps the most conspicuous allusion is the phrase *meditantes in lege Domini die nocte*, meditating on the law of the Lord day and night, in the first chapter of the Rule, which echoes Psalm 1:2. In the modern era the Carmelite family adopts the daily liturgical prayers, which incorporate the Psalms. As far as I know, there is no evidence of a specific Carmelite tradition existing outside of the general tendency of the church at a given period. While the 1993 document of the Biblical Commission is open to more than one approach, its emphasis on the role of the literal historical sense and its actualization is to be welcomed. For it puts us in direct contact with the text, which can be immediately applied.

Notes

1. The classic study of the century is *Die Psalmen*, ed. J. Begrich (Göttingen: Vandenhoeck & Ruprecht, 1933) by Hermann Gunkel, who set the tone for later research. A popular presentation can be found in R. E. Murphy, *The Psalms Are Yours* (New York/Mahwah, N.J.: Paulist Press, 1993). A revised version of the latter is *The Gift of the Psalms* (Peabody, Mass.: Hendrickson, 2000).
2. Cf. John O'Donohue, "Spirituality as the Art of Real Presence," *The Way: Supplement* (1998), 85–101, see 87.
3. Ibid., 88–89.
4. Cf. *Interpretation* 52 (1998), 367–79; the following quotation is from 367.

5. The couplet is attributed to Augustine of Dacia (13th century): "the letter (or literal sense) teaches fact, the allegorical what you are to believe, the moral (or tropological) what you are to do, the anagogical (or eschatological) what you are to hope for." See the basic study of H. de Lubac, *Medieval Exegesis: the Four Senses of Scripture;* trans. Mark Sebanc (Grand Rapids: Eerdmans, 1998), 1, 8, 115.

6. K. Rahner, "Poetry and the Christian," *Theological Investigations,* vol. 4 (Baltimore: Helicon, 1966), 357–67; see 363.

7. The document is the Apostolic Constitution, *Laudis canticum,* of November 7, 1970, promulgating the revised book of the Liturgy of the Hours. An English translation can be found in *Documents on the Liturgy 1963–1979* (Collegeville, Minn.: Liturgical Press, n.d.), 114, #3561. For an analysis of specific psalms and verses, see W. L. Holladay, *The Psalms Through Three Thousand Years* (Minneapolis: Fortress, 1996), 304–11.

8. The document was written in French and is reproduced in *Biblica* 74 (1993), 451–528. The English translation is in *Origins* 23/29 (Jan. 6, 1994), 499–524. English text and commentary are to be found in J. A. Fitzmyer, *The Biblical Commission's Document "The Interpretation of the Bible in the Church": Text and Commentary;* "Subsidia Biblica 18" (Rome: Biblical Institute, 1995).

9. Cf. Bernard Lonergan, *Method in Theology* (New York: Herder and Herder, 1973), especially 242–43; 267–93.

10. A critical edition, Latin with French translation, of the conferences of John Cassian appears in volumes 42, 52, and 64, *Sources chrétiennes* (Paris: du Cerf, 1955–59). See also an English translation: John Cassian, *The Conferences,* trans. Boniface Ramsey, "Ancient Christian Writers 57" (New York/Mahwah: Paulist Press, 1997).

3

The Solitude of Carmelite Prayer

Keith J. Egan

So I say now that all of us who wear this holy habit of Carmel are called to prayer and contemplation. This call explains our origin; we are descendants of men who felt this call, of those holy fathers on Mount Carmel who in such great *solitude* and contempt for the world sought this treasure, this precious pearl of *contemplation*. (IC.5.1.2)[1]

Carmelite Spirituality is a richly woven tapestry whose warp and woof change over time to accent now one hue, then another. This Carmelite tapestry, like Joseph's coat, is multicolored with rich fibers running this way and that. Some fibers are so integral to an authentic Carmelite charism that, were they eliminated, the tapestry would no longer be true to the Carmelite tradition. Unthinkable is Carmelite life without Mary. What would Carmelites do without the inspiration of Elijah? Carmel's various ministries, whether preaching, teaching, or the all-important ministry of the contemplative life, are crucial to the variations that occur in Carmel's spiritual tapestry. Even more incomprehensible is Carmelite life without solitude. Solitude lay at the heart of the original charism of Carmel and has been restored whenever new life has been breathed into Carmelite spirituality. When great figures in Carmel's tradition have articulated their understanding of Carmel's way of life, they have inevitably retrieved solitude as crucial to the authenticity of Carmelite prayer. The quotation from Teresa of Jesus at the heading of this essay shows how strong was Teresa's conviction that the recovery of solitude was crucial to her reform of the Carmelite Order.

Carmel's staying power in the church's religious traditions may well rest on its insistence that solitude has a unique place in its way of life and prayer. At the very heart of human existence is the challenge to be a person and at the same time to be in relationship with others. That is the paradox of solitude and community. Two modern philosophical systems put the emphasis at opposite ends of the spectrum. Marxism comes down on the side of community, while existentialism favors the autonomy or freedom of the person. Keeping the poles of this paradox, solitude and community, in creative tension, is the challenge of every human person, of the human community, and is a special concern of the Carmelite tradition. Were there space in this essay, one might inquire in what way the paradox of solitude and community reflects the three persons and one nature of the Trinity and the unity of two natures in one person of the Incarnation. Or one might explore how celibacy can create within one a holy solitude. These explorations must wait for another day.

In Carmelite spirituality solitude is in creative tension with community and with the ministries undertaken by community. I suggest that a crucial factor in the attraction of so many religious seekers to the Carmelite charism is its ongoing struggle to live creatively this paradox of solitude and community. From the beginning Carmel gave a special place to solitude but always as a solitude within community. Living the dynamic of solitude within community is Carmel's mission in the church, its perennial challenge, its key to ongoing reform and its way of challenging its members to stand in mindfulness before the living God even as some Carmelites serve the apostolic needs of God's people. Solitude, shaped variously in differing eras, has been a decisive factor in the life of prayer for anyone who is called to pray within or with the Carmelite family. One way to track the evolution of Carmelite prayer is to trace how solitude was configured at different moments in Carmel's history, especially by classic figures in its tradition like the three Carmelite doctors of the church, Teresa, John and Thérèse.

Solitude in the Carmelite Tradition

The solitude of the original Carmelites was integral to their "allegiance to Jesus Christ."[2] This phrase from the prologue to the Formula of Life sees Carmelite life as an imitation of Christ and as an "...obedience to His way of life depicted in the Gospels, remembered in the tradition...."[3] The earliest Carmelites were to imitate the Jesus who was in the habit of going aside to pray, to be alone with God, his Abba (Luke 5:16).[4] The Carmelite charism thus focuses on a central issue of human existence and at the same time imitates a habit of Jesus whom Carmelites by their rule were pledged to follow. From their first location on Mount Carmel the Carmelites had inherited a desert spirituality which prized solitude. The desert dweller Abba Moses once said: "The man who flees and lives in solitude is like a bunch of grapes ripened by the sun, but he who remains amongst men is like an unripe grape."[5]

The first Carmelites were conscious that they had settled in a land made holy by the presence of Jesus, who often sought solitude, and in a land made sacred by the monks of the deserts whose very name, monk, means to be alone. A modern interpreter of Carmel's prayer, Kilian J. Healy, has written that "...the tradition of Carmel has always been to live a life of solitude, silence and mortification in order to be continually occupied with God....To be occupied with God (*vacare Deo*); this is the spirit of the Order...."[6] This solitude is for the sake of being alone with God so as to experience the transforming power of God's love. The thesis of this essay is that Carmelite prayer has grown and matured creatively whenever solitude has been nurtured. Solitude here does not mean the completely eremitic life where one lives totally alone. The Carmelites have never espoused a life divorced from community; in fact, in 1247 they expanded the communal aspects of their life so as to identify with the fraternity of the friars. Carmelite solitude has always been for the sake of inner solitude, a habit of deep inner mindfulness of the presence of a loving God. Physical solitude is for the sake of solitude of the heart or, as John of the Cross would say, for the sake of poverty of spirit, an emptiness to be filled by God's love. Carmelite prayer depends on the retrieval of a solitude that is faithful to the original charism of Carmel and at the same time is shaped by the signs of the times. Without discernment in each age, Carmelite prayer would not be ecclesial and contemporary. In every era the Holy Spirit shapes the life of the church and its religious communities according to a design that can be seen as an ongoing epiclesis. This is a calling on the Holy Spirit to weave the threads of the Carmelite tapestry according to God's will.

Carmelite solitude has been and is lived in various manifestations, that is, in one way by cloistered Carmelite nuns, in another by apostolic Carmelite sisters, then again by the friars and in other ways by lay Carmelites and by anyone who turns to Carmel for inspiration. As Saint Paul taught, every charism is for the sake of the whole community (1 Cor 12). Carmel's paradox of solitude and community is a gift to be shared with all who seek to live attentively in God's presence.

It is impossible to report in a brief essay the whole story of Carmel's retrievals of solitude during the eight hundred years of the order's existence. I shall indicate only some special moments in that history that illustrate the connection between solitude and Carmel's life of prayer. These moments reveal how Carmelites have lived according to the aphorism *vacare Deo*, being open to God's presence, "continually occupied with God," as Kilian Healy translates the phrase.[7] John of the Cross's Spanish for *vacare Deo* has been translated into English as "free for God" (SC.7.6). Solitude makes one free for the guidance of the Holy

Spirit, who, as John of the Cross wrote, is the soul's "principal guide"(LF.3.46). This solitude is what Bernard of Clairvaux and John of the Cross have referred to as the wine cellar of the Holy Spirit, using the imagery of the Song of Songs. This wine cellar is where one is anointed by the Holy Spirit and where, in the mixed metaphor of the Middle Ages, elephants can swim and lambs can paddle.

The Carmelite Formula of Life

One first encounters Carmel's call to solitude in its earliest document, the "formula of life," which describes the original lifestyle of the hermits on Mount Carmel. The Carmelite Order had its origins about 1200 A.D. on Mount Carmel in a ravine two and a half miles south of the modern city of Haifa at the Wadi' ain es-siah. The lay hermits who settled in this ravine near the fountain of Elijah knew full well the significance of this lovely location that faces the beautiful blue waters of the Mediterranean Sea. These hermits sought church approval for their simple way of life from Albert, Patriarch of Jerusalem, who presented them between 1206 and 1214 with their formula of life. This formula, in a slightly revised form, became their Rule in 1247. The formula or, more precisely, letter is a description of a small community of hermits with each hermit having his own cell separated from the others. Besides a weekly meeting about their way of life, the hermits gathered for daily Eucharist when this celebration was possible. Solitude, silence[8] and simplicity were the hallmarks of a life that included manual labor. The life of the hermits entailed spiritual combat so well known to the desert dwellers of early Christian monasticism and for which the Carmelite was to "put on the armor of God." Each hermit was to "...remain in his cell, or near it, meditating day and night on the law of the Lord and keeping vigil in prayer unless occupied with other lawful duties." A persuasive case has been made that the first Carmelites prayed the Psalms rather than recited the hours of the divine office.[9] After all, the prayer book of the medieval hermit was the psalter. The early Carmelites were to avoid some of the well-known excesses of the ancient desert by practicing *discretio* (discernment) about spiritual matters. The formula of life was an invitation to solitude and unceasing prayer, not a charter for heroic ascetical exploits.

Prayer among the first Carmelites was simple, contemplative and carried out in a solitude supported by community. This prayer was shaped in the solitude of the wine cellar of the Holy Spirit. No pre-scribed methods of prayer appear in the formula of life, as has been the norm in the Carmelite tradition. A life of prayer in the desert tradition undoubtedly led to an intensification of prayer that later would be described as mystical. There are no reports of the prayer of the lay her-mits at the Wadi' ain es-siah. It is reasonable, however, to conjecture that, in the silence and solitude of Mount Carmel, some of these hermits enjoyed that prayer of desert dwellers described by John Cassian as "...fashioned by the contemplation of God alone and by fervent char-ity, by which the mind, having been dissolved and flung into love of him, speaks most familiarly and with particular devotion to God..." and which "leads them by a higher stage to that fiery and...wordless prayer which is experienced by very few."[10] Kees Waaijman, a Dutch Carmelite scholar, has written a lively recent commentary on the Carmelite Rule. The title of his commentary, *The Mystical Space of Carmel*,[11] reveals the contemplative and mystical capacity of the Carmelite Formula of Life and the subsequent Rule. The Carmelite hermits, whose Formula of Life was a guarantee of solitude, appeared on the scene when a move-ment of medieval eremitic life was coming to an end and the mendi-cant way of life was about to begin. This mendicant event had far-reaching effects on Carmelite life and prayer.

Carmelites Become Friars

Carmel's origins occurred when the Latin Kingdom of Jerusalem was under constant threat by enemy forces that would soon make life impossible for the Latins in the Holy Land. By 1238 some of the Carmelites were migrating to the West and found themselves in places like Cyprus, Sicily, England and France. When they got to Europe, the hermits of Mount Carmel encountered the phenomenon of the friars. The friars were everywhere and were attracting recruits in extraordinary numbers. Dominic and Francis had turned traditional religious life on its head. In place of the stability of the monks, the friars were mobile and international. Along with the personal poverty of the monks, the friars adopted corporate poverty. The friars streamlined the monastic liturgical hours. Perhaps most revolutionary of all, the friars began to evangelize the expanding urban centers of Europe. To prepare for this ministry the friars entered the universities so that they might prepare their members to bring the gospel to the large numbers of poorly instructed Christians in Europe. With their move into the universities the friars became student orders, with each of their foundations a feeder for specialized student houses in various provinces.

The first Carmelite foundations in Europe were eremitic, but it soon became evident that this lifestyle was out of sync with the taste of the friars' patrons and with the sensibilities of young recruits eager to throw in their lot with the enormously popular mendicant orders. In 1247 the Carmelite Formula of Life became an official Rule, and the Carmelite hermits slipped into the ranks of the friars. The Carmelites quickly acted like friars and turned with haste to make foundations in cities like London, Cambridge, Oxford, Paris and Bologna. The papally approved revision of the Formula of Life entailed only slight verbal changes in the text but the implications for solitude and prayer were telling. The changes not only allowed the Carmelites to settle in non-eremitic sites (towns), but the time of silence was shortened. The Carmelites now gathered in a common refectory and recited the canonical hours. While the once eremitic Carmelites now lived the more communal life of the mendicants, they had a legacy of solitude that had to be woven into the newly shaped

Carmelite tapestry if the Carmelites were to remain faithful to their original charism. The Carmelite historian, Father Joachim Smet, believes that the transition from an eremitic to a mendicant order was more gradual and less abrupt than I have described this change. Father Smet's interpretation extends the eremitic character of the Carmelites beyond 1247 and therefore puts additional emphasis on solitude after this date.[12]

The demands prompted by Carmelite participation in the evangelization of Europe's towns altered the way solitude could be lived. This ecclesial call to evangelization recast the more simple paradox of solitude and community into a tension between solitude and ministerial community, a community called upon to serve the neighbor through preaching, teaching and spiritual guidance. The stillness, quiet and solitude experienced on Mount Carmel were no longer possible. Hence it was inevitable that the prayer of the Carmelite friars would also be altered.

The change from hermits to friars, an alteration of the original Carmelite charism, did not occur without opposition. First of all, the Carmelites encountered the general opposition to friars that was mounted during the second half of the thirteenth century by bishops and secular clergy who saw the friars as intruders into their ministry of evangelization. Within the Carmelite Order, Nicholas the Frenchman, prior general from 1266 to1271, scolded his brothers in no uncertain terms for fleeing to the cities instead of remaining faithful to solitude: "You who flee solitude and spurn the consolations it has to offer, would you hear how the Lord has shown by his words the high esteem in which he holds it [solitude]?" Nicholas proceeded to eulogize solitude as practiced from Abraham to Jesus, and he reminded his brothers that their predecessors had, though *rarely*, preached what they had reaped "in solitude with the sickle of contemplation."[13] However, neither external nor internal opposition deterred this recently minted mendicant order from a commitment to evangelization.

At the very time they were undergoing opposition, certainly by 1281, probably earlier as their Constitutions could have dated from 1247, the Carmelites were telling their young members that the order had a long tradition of being "true lovers of solitude for the sake of contemplation." That significant statement about solitude in the prologue of their Constitutions was retained in the Constitutions for centuries. Here is the longer context of this quote from the *rubrica prima*, a charter for young Carmelites contained in the Constitutions:

> Since some of the younger brothers in our order seek when and how our order began but in truth do not know how to respond, we wish to answer them with the following written words: bearing witness to the truth, we say that from the time of the prophets Elijah and Elisha who dwelt devotedly on Mount Carmel, holy fathers of the Old and New Testament praiseworthily lived there in ever continual holy penitence on that same mountain as *lovers of solitude for the sake of contemplation.*[14]

As early as 1281, if not three decades earlier, the Carmelites had composed a mission statement for the young that gave pride of place to solitude, a solitude for the sake of contemplation. The Carmelites were also becoming more and more conscious of what was implied by their having been founded on Elijah's mountain. To look toward Elijah and Elisha for their inspiration was to become aware of the prophetic dimensions of their solitude and prayer.

A New Vision of Carmel's Mystical Tradition

It was only as the thirteenth century came to an end that the first Carmelite doctors of theology came on the scene and only in the second quarter of the fourteenth century that the Carmelites began their literary tradition in earnest. There are no notable records of the prayer tradition of the Carmelites until the fourteenth century. Then toward the end of that century a very crucial work appeared that made explicit the mystical character of Carmelite life and prayer. Felip Ribot (d. 1391), provincial of Catalonia, put together a set of documents that he not only edited but much of which he seems to have composed himself. This collection of documents is known as the *Ten Books about the Institution and Special Events of Carmelite Religious.* In one of the books in this collection, the *Institution of the First Monks*, Ribot laid out quite explicitly the goals of Carmelite life and attributed a mystical orientation to Carmelite spirituality that he grounded in the solitude of Elijah the prophet.

The *Institution* became a widely read document throughout the order and had a decisive impact on the subsequent Carmelite tradition. A case has been made that Teresa of Avila and John of the Cross were familiar with this text. The following passage from the late fourteenth century *Institution* resonates, I believe, with the teachings of the two Spanish Carmelite mystics. This excerpt from the *Institution* explicitly characterizes Carmelite prayer as rooted in solitude and oriented toward mystical experience.

> The prophet of God, Elijah, was the chief of the monks, from whom the holy and ancient order took its origin. For it was he who, desirous of greater progress in the pursuit of divine contemplation, withdrew far from the cities and, despoiling himself of all earthly and mundane things, was the first to adopt the holy and solitary life of a prophet which he had established at the inspiration of the Spirit.
>
> The goal of this life is twofold. One part we acquire, with the help of divine grace, through our efforts and virtuous works. This is to offer God a holy heart, free from all stain of actual sin.... The other part of the goal of this life is granted as the free gift of God: namely, to taste somewhat in the heart and to experience in the soul, not only

after death but even in this mortal life, the intensity of the divine presence and the sweetness of the glory of heaven.[15]

The Carmelite search for identity had been clouded by the anonymity of the order's origins. Their founding on Mount Carmel and the lack of a known founder led the Carmelites to look to Elijah as their ideal and even as their "founder." The archetypal figure Elijah provided them with a typology for their solitude and from the end of the fourteenth century specified in a more conscious way the mystical orientation of their prayer.

No one alleges that gifted mystical experience as described by Teresa of Avila in the fourth through the seventh dwelling places of her *Interior Castle* is a human achievement. The mystical contemplation of Teresa and John is always a special or infused gift. But the Carmelite tradition as reinforced by Ribot and subsequent Carmelite teachers asks for a preparation and readiness to be open to this gift in whatever form the gift may come. Karl Rahner has prepared our age to understand the grounding of the mystical life in the sacraments of Baptism and Eucharist. Rahner's ordinary mysticism reveals, however, a continuity between the usual or ordinary gifts of grace and those special gifts granted by God to those whom God has chosen for the special gift of infused mystical prayer. What we learn from Rahner is that there is a greater continuity between ordinary, everyday mysticism and God's specially gifted awareness of the presence of God.[16] The call to solitude in the Carmelite tradition is a call to find ways of prayer that allow for a contemplative stance before God. Then God brings about whatever God's love seeks for the good of the person and the community.

Religious orders, like the church itself, became aware from the fourteenth century on that reform was sorely needed throughout the church and within the religious orders. Some reforms floundered as mere schemes of reorganization. From Saint Paul until the twelfth century successful reform focused on a return to the biblical symbolism of the human person as created in the "image and likeness of God."[17] An openness to the Holy Spirit by listening to the Word of God was the way to return to this fundamental notion of reform, which was the struggle of late medieval reform movements. The *Institution's* focus on Elijah's solitude, the liberation of the person from sin and disordered attachments and the consequent openness to union with God in contemplation gave direction to various reforms in Carmel during the fifteenth and early sixteenth century. Whatever success the late medieval reforms attained stemmed from the renewal of a more contemplative spirit among the Carmelites and from calls for authentic solitude on behalf of contemplation.

Blessed John Soreth

A key medieval Carmelite reformer, John Soreth, prior general from 1451 to 1471, called urgently for a return to solitude and a renewed regard for the cell, the separated cell of the Formula of Life and the Rule. As Titus Brandsma wrote, Soreth was "lavish in his praise of solitude."[18] Moreover, Soreth officially welcomed for the first time women as Second Order Carmelites,[19] an innovation that had a momentous impact on the Carmelite tradition of prayer. It is among the cloistered Carmelite women that the ideal of solitude in community from the original charism continues as a special witness to the whole church and to the rest of the Carmelite Order. Soreth would be a major figure in Carmelite history had he done nothing else but create the opportunity for the initiation of Second Order Carmelites. But, this energetic and saintly prior general had other goals and achievements. He raised the sights of the late medieval Carmelites to an awareness that they must not neglect solitude nor forget their vocation to contemplative prayer, that is, prayer open to God's transforming presence. Soreth knew that solitude and contemplative prayer had been the lot of the Carmelites since the days of the hermits on Mount Carmel. The challenge then and now is for a fruitful solitude that leads to living attentively in the presence of God, whether that prayer be mystical or quite ordinary, whether in the cloister or the classroom, in the pulpit or one's cell, whether in service of the poor or in pursuit of one's work in the world, whether as a lay Carmelite or as a Carmelite religious.

Teresa of Jesus

There were other late medieval reforms in the Carmelite Order but none of them had the far-reaching and long-lasting effects of the reform initiated in the sixteenth century by the Spanish Carmelite Teresa of Avila. Teresa and her collaborator, John of the Cross, not only influenced the Carmelite tradition, but they had a decisive influence on subsequent Christian spirituality and mysticism. The church has recognized the significance of their teachings for the whole church by declaring John a doctor of the church in 1926 and Teresa as the first woman doctor of the church in 1970.

Key to Teresa's reform was her conviction that the Monastery of the Incarnation where she entered and had lived for some twenty years was too crowded and busy for the solitude and contemplative prayer that she came to consider integral to Carmelite life. When Teresa began to found monasteries for women, she intended for the sake of solitude that there be only thirteen nuns in each new foundation. That number rose to twenty when Teresa discovered that the larger number was necessary so that a monastery could support itself.[20] Teresa's ideal of solitude was inspired by her vivid image of the first Carmelites on Mount Carmel. In the quotation with which this essay began, Teresa connected solitude, prayer and contemplation, a solitude for the sake of prayer and contemplation. Teresa discovered this original Carmelite emphasis on solitude in the lives of those whom she called the "holy fathers on Mount Carmel."[21] The remembrance of Carmel's origins shocked the imagination of Teresa into action, action that sought to restore for the women and men of her reform the original solitude of Carmelite life.

When Teresa prepared to make her first foundation, she consulted among others the Dominican Pedro Ibáñez. Teresa said of this Dominican that, from then on, "he dedicated himself much more to prayer and withdrew to a monastery of his order where there was much solitude so that he could practice prayer better" (BL.33.5). Teresa thus connected solitude with growth in prayer. She wrote that the nuns of her first foundation, San José at Avila, "...must always have as their aim: to be alone with Him alone" (BL.37.29).

Teresa's program for her nuns, once they had entered one of her "dovecotes" (BL.14.3; BF.4.5), was that they get to know themselves well, that they be detached from whatever distracted them from God, that they be friends with one another and that they practice often during each day what she called the prayer of recollection. This form of prayer, described in chapters 28 and 29 of *The Way of Perfection*, was a going within to find God in the solitude of the heart. This prayer of recollection resembles, in essence, forms of modern contemplative prayer like Centering Prayer and John Main's Christian Meditation.[22] This prayer of recollection was not a detailed method of prayer but a way of fostering a contemplative awareness of Christ's presence and was meant by Teresa to be a preparation for gifted or passive recollection. Teresa knew well that God's special presence in contemplation is all God's gift, but it was her conviction that her nuns were called to prepare themselves for this gift. Teresa renewed the Carmelite tradition by making Carmel's women and its friars heed the call to solitude so that they may meditate "day and night on the law of the Lord" (Rule 7). Teresa made sure that her sisters were aware of the blessings of enclosure, which she referred to as a "...living in the running streams of their Spouse." She added with undisguised humor that these sisters may not "...recognize the great favor God has granted them in choosing them for Himself and freeing them from being subject to a man who is often the death of them and who could also be, God forbid, the death of their souls" (BF.31.46).

John of the Cross

John of the Cross shared Teresa's convictions about the primacy of solitude in Carmelite life. When Teresa of Jesus invited the then John of Saint Matthias to join her in the reform of Carmel, he was intrigued, but John warned Teresa that she must act quickly. He told Teresa that he had been thinking about transferring to the Carthusians. John clearly desired greater solitude, but he promised Teresa that he would remain a Carmelite "...as long as he wouldn't have to wait long" (BF.3.17). John was a friar in a hurry, eager to find greater solitude and thus to become more contemplative. Throughout his life John relished solitude. Less than two and a half months before he died, John wrote to Doña Ana del Mercado y Peñalosa, for whom he wrote *The Living Flame of Love* and for whom he acted as a spiritual guide: "Yet I plan to return here [La Peñuela] immediately, for I am indeed very happy in this holy solitude." About a month before he wrote that letter, John had written to Ana that "...the life of the desert is admirable."[23] Of prayer and solitude John wrote: "Our prayer should be made either in the concealment of our inner room (where without noise and without telling anyone we can pray with a more perfect and pure heart...) or, if not in one's room, it should be made in the solitary wilderness, and at the best and most quiet time of night, as he did [Luke 6:12]" (A3.4.44).

Physical solitude in the Carmelite tradition is always for the sake of the inner, spiritual solitude where one encounters God in the depths of one's being. John calls this spiritual solitude spiritual poverty, emptiness, nakedness. John admonishes the spiritual guide to lead souls "...into greater solitude, tranquillity, and freedom of spirit. He should give it latitude so that when God introduces it into this solitude it does not bind..." the soul. John added that when the soul frees itself of all things and attains to emptiness and dispossession concerning them, which is equivalent to what it can do of itself, it is impossible that God fail to do his part by communicating himself to it, at least silently and secretly. It is more impossible than it would be for the sun not to shine on clear and uncluttered ground. (LF. 3.46)

John of the Cross is the poet and spiritual guide of inner solitude. Listen to his verses about solitude and then to his comments on this stanza:

She lived in solitude,
And now in solitude has built her nest;
And in solitude he guides her,
he alone, who also bears
in solitude the wound of love.

John's commentary reads:

The Bridegroom continues the explanation of his happiness over the blessing the bride has obtained through the solitude in which she formerly desired to live. This blessing is a stable peace and unchanging good. When the soul has become established in the quietude of solitary love of her Bridegroom...she is settled in God, and God in her, with so much delight that she has no need of other masters or means to direct her to him, for now God is her guide and her light. He accomplishes in her what he promised through Hosea: *I shall lead her into solitude and there speak to her heart* [Hos 2:14]. In this promise he reveals that he communicates and unites himself to the soul in solitude.

To speak to the heart is to satisfy the heart, which is dis-
satisfied with anything less than God. (SC.35.1)

John of the Cross saw the experience of union with God in love
as the ultimate experience of solitude. What was once active with-
drawal or the practice of contemplative meditation was now for the
soul the "...perfect solitude in which she reaches union with the
Word" (SC.35.4). The emptiness, the nothingness is now filled with
the All who is God.

John of the Cross relished solitude, but he was a friar and a
priest who preached to the poor, heard confessions, was intensely
active in the administration of his order, worked with his hands and
devoted himself most of all to a far-flung ministry of spiritual guidance. John traveled extensively in a day when travel was utterly
exhausting and time consuming. John integrated the apostolate of the
friar with the solitude and contemplative spirit of a Carmelite rooted
in the order's original charism. John found God in solitude but also in
action on behalf of others and in creation as well. The discovery of
God's presence everywhere made it possible for him to assure other
God-seekers that "...if anyone is seeking God, the Beloved is seeking
that person much more" (LF.3.28). Through God's gift of contemplation John of the Cross combined his much prized solitude with a life
of intense ministry. Not as a Carthusian but as a Carmelite, John of
the Cross fit Jerome Nadal's description of Ignatius of Loyola as "a
contemplative in action." John of the Cross's poetry, his commentaries on that poetry, his sayings, his letters are all the work of a sin-
gle-minded friar who wrote so that others may benefit from his
experience of the journey to God, a journey on which he experienced
the desolation of darkness but also the presence of the Holy Spirit as
the Living Flame of Love. Solitude, prayer, contemplation were all for
the sake of love, the love of God and the love of neighbor which Jesus
had placed at the center of the lives of his followers. The writings of
John of the Cross are an invitation to let God liberate one from self-

absorption so that one may be united through love with God. John saw this liberation taking place through the dark nights, which are always for the sake of light and love. Dark nights restore one's capacity for loving God and creation as both are meant to be loved (DN.2.9.1). These dark nights enhance one's capacity for appreciating the beauty of God and the beauty of creation. John once broke forth in this joyous prayer "...your very beauty will be my beauty, and thus we shall behold each other in your beauty" (SC.36.5).[24]

John of the Cross is the poet of the journey from solitude to a heart filled with the Holy Spirit, to a contemplation that is an inflow of love. The poem, "The Living Flame of Love," which John says represents his deepest experience of God concludes with these lines: "...and in your sweet breathing / filled with good and glory, / how tenderly you swell my heart with love!" Solitude becomes loving communion with the Triune God.

Desert Houses

The Discalced Reform of the Carmelite Order, shaped by Teresa of Jesus and John of the Cross, was truly a classical moment in the history of Christian Spirituality. This reform has cast in sharp relief the Carmelite charism whether it be the paradox of solitude and community of the first Carmelites, or the evolution of the charism as solitude in ministerial community, the ministry of cloistered Carmelite nuns or the contemplative prayer of lay Carmelites. In a word, solitude has a place in every scheme of Carmelite life. No matter their lifestyle, Carmelites are called to make a habit of being alone with God.

The Discalced Reform creatively recaptured the intent of the original Carmelite charism of solitude with the establishment of desert or hermitage houses which attracted Carmelites who wished to honor the formula of life's injunction to meditate day and night on the law of the Lord. The Discalced friar Thomas of Jesus (1564–1627) conceived the idea of desert foundations and established the first desert house in 1592 at Bolarque in Spain. These "holy deserts" flourished in the seventeenth and eighteenth centuries, and this design for the solitary life is once again a reality among Carmelites of all stripes.[25]

The Touraine Reform

The sixteenth century Discalced Reform of Carmel resulted in the birth of a new branch of the order in 1593. Not long after that separation, the friars of the older branch, who are known as Carmelites of the Ancient Observance, began a reform of their own that has had a long-lasting impact on Carmelite life. This Reform occurred in the midst of the dynamic mystical revival of early seventeenth-century France. It took its name from the seminal friary of Touraine and, like the Reform of Teresa and John, had as its goal the restoration of a more contemplative life. The Touraine Reform also established desert or hermitage houses attached to friaries but their hermitages were not as widespread as the Discalced Carmelite deserts. The constitutions of the Touraine Reform had the following provision for houses of solitude: "We ordain that in every province there be one eremitic convent, remote from cities and the noise of people, where some of us may live under strict cloister, wholly dedicated to the contemplation of heavenly things and to the practice of holy solitude."[26] The desert houses of both branches of the order, in the past and presently, are a unique witness to solitude as a core value of Carmelite life.

Best known among the early members of the Touraine Reform was the blind brother Venerable John of Saint Samson (1571–1636) whose ministry of spiritual guidance shaped the lives of numerous novices within this reform movement. Of this blind brother, Joachim Smet writes that "with the exception of its saints, Brother John of St. Samson is the greatest mystic the Order produced."[27] The Touraine

Reform illustrates an important aspect of prayer. While Carmel has never insisted on a particular method of contemplative prayer, the tradition in its various eras has read the signs of the times to determine what approaches to prayer were the best ways to practice contemplative prayer in a given time. Among the followers of the Touraine Reform, aspirative prayer or recurring mindfulness of God's presence was distinctive.[28]

This is the same era in which the Discalced Carmelite Brother Lawrence of the Resurrection (1614–1691) practiced a ministry of spiritual guidance which is remembered by the title of the treatise, *The Practice of the Presence of God*, and which is now read widely by peoples of many faiths.[29]

Toward the end of the seventeenth century the Discalced Reform and the Reform of Touraine lost not a little of their mystical orientation when anti-mystical sentiment erupted in France. In fact, a general antipathy toward mysticism has held sway in the church from then until the last quarter of the twentieth century. That loss of a contemplative, mystical orientation during the anti-mystical era left the Carmelite Order and many others with an overly ascetical spirituality that often led to a Pelagian approach to prayer when prayer is perceived as a human work, not God's. The contemplative life seemed during that era reserved to the few with no appreciation of a "Universal Call to Holiness."[30]

Thérèse of Lisieux

On October 19, 1997, Pope John Paul II named Thérèse Martin the third woman doctor of the church and the third Carmelite to be so declared. One is named a doctor of the church because one is not only a person of profound holiness but because one has significant teaching for the whole church.[31] Thérèse holds a special place in the interpretation of Carmelite prayer. Named for Teresa of Jesus, Thérèse of Lisieux became an astute interpreter of John of the Cross, whose writings she got to know at about age seventeen. She imparted to her novices and left for posterity a simple message about life and prayer. This young woman who became a Carmelite at fifteen knew from an early age that she wanted to follow two of her siblings into the Carmelite monastery at Lisieux. She also knew that this choice involved a journey into solitude. In April of 1897, the year she died, Thérèse wrote to Maurice Bellière about the inspiration that Joan of Arc had been for her. She said that "...instead of voices from heaven inviting me to combat, I heard in the depths of my soul a gentler and stronger voice, that of the Spouse of Virgins, who was calling me to other exploits, to more glorious conquests, and into Carmel's solitude."[32] In 1895 Thérèse had written in her notebook that she was "enjoying Carmel's solitude" (SS.114).

The solitude of this Carmelite nun who died prematurely at twenty-four did not lead to extraordinary *phenomena* but nonetheless to profound contemplative prayer. To all appearances hers was a very ordinary, everyday mysticism akin to that described by Karl Rahner. Yet, Thérèse's prayer led to an uncommon wisdom about life. This has been called her "little way," a way of going about one's daily tasks with love and confidence in God and fully conscious of God's presence. When her community feared that she might die alone some night without the ministrations of a priest, her confident response was that "everything is a grace."[33] Here was extraordinary faith born of the contemplative prayer of a young woman who was having a hard time believing in a blessed eternity.

Filled with the gift of wisdom, Thérèse became a modern exponent of the Carmelite charism, which she lived simply and faithfully amid day-to-day tasks. In her, as it always had been in the tradition, the solitude of Carmel was geared toward love of God and love of neighbor. In the year before she died, Thérèse described the discovery of her calling: "...in the excess of my delirious joy, I cried out: O Jesus, my Love...my *vocation*, at last I have found it....MY VOCATION IS LOVE!" (SS.194). During the last eighteen months of her life Thérèse endured terrible suffering. More devastating than anything else was loss of her assurance about the reality of heaven, her "night of nothingness." Added to this prolonged spiritual agony was the relentless and ruthless advance of the tuberculosis that finally took her life on September 30, 1897. This youngest doctor of the church shows how the simple solitude of being alone before the living God makes possible love of God and love of neighbor.

Edith Stein and Titus Brandsma

Before I conclude this essay, I want to mention briefly two Carmelites from modern times who have illustrated the crucial role of solitude in their journey to God. Edith Stein's life was filled with very divergent and complex realities: Jewess, nonbeliever, philosopher, special assistant to the philosopher Edmund Husserl, Catholic convert, educator, feminist, Carmelite nun, martyr, canonized saint (1998) and, as of October 2, 1999, co-patroness of Europe. Despite this collage of identities, Edith Stein sought solitude before and after her entry into Carmel.

In 1935 Edith made explicit the connection of solitude with her Carmelite vocation. Alluding to the example of the prophet Elijah, she wrote: "To stand before the face of the living God, that is our vocation." Stein added that the entire meaning of the Carmelite way of life is contained in the rule's challenge that "all are to remain in their own cells..., meditating on the Law of the Lord day and night and watching in prayer, unless otherwise justly employed."[34]

Edith Stein brought together many paradoxes in her life, none more so than her integration of the life of the mind and the life of the spirit, intellectual pursuits and spiritual solitude. John Paul II in his encyclical on *Faith and Reason* (#74) reveals his admiration for Edith Stein's integrated life.

Titus Brandsma was a Dutch Carmelite friar, philosopher, exponent of Carmelite mysticism, ecumenist, faculty member and Rector

Magnificus at the Catholic University at Nijmegen, journalist, adviser to Dutch Catholic journalists and to the Dutch bishops, and finally, a martyr at Dachau in 1942. Throughout his life, Titus Brandsma showed a profound appreciation for solitude as the foundation of Carmelite life. He expressed this conviction in poetry composed as a Nazi prisoner. In his cell at the Scheveningen prison, he concluded his poem, "My Cell," with lines that reveal a Carmelite aware that even this terrible solitude brought him intimacy with Jesus: "For, Jesus, you are at my side; / Never so close did we abide. / Stay with me, Jesus, my delight, / Your presence near makes all things right."[35]

Conclusion

What shall one say after this brief excursion into the recurring role of solitude in the lives of Carmelite witnesses to a life of prayer? First of all, solitude is not mere separation from others. Before all else, solitude means living in God's presence so that one may grow in love of God and love of neighbor. Solitude consists in doing whatever it takes to let God take over one's heart, because "in this solitude...the soul is alone with God" (SC.35.5). For some this means the solitude of a cloistered life, for others it may be the faithful practice of con-templative prayer in the midst of intense apostolic ministry. For lay women and men who find an affinity with the Carmelite tradition, solitude may mean making time to practice Centering Prayer or Christian Meditation.[36] In the spirit of Elijah, Carmelite prayer, nur-tured in solitude, transforms the way one sees reality and creates in one a prophetic imagination that does not tolerate injustice.

Notes

1. Emphasis added.
2. The Formula of Life, prologue: "Obsequium [Jesu] Christi,"quoted from the Vulgate Bible, 2 Cor 10:5.

3. Kees Waaijman and Hein Blommestijn, "The Carmelite Rule as a Model of Mystical Transformation," *The Land of Carmel*, eds. Paul Chandler and Keith J. Egan (Institutum Carmelitanum: Rome, 1991), 69. On imitation of the humanity of Christ in the Middle Ages see Giles Constable, *Three Studies in Medieval Religious and Social Thought* (Cambridge: Cambridge University Press, 1995), 169ff.
4. See also Luke 6:12; 9:18, 28; 11:1 and Luke 22:41–46; Mark 1:35.
5. *The Sayings of the Desert Fathers*, rev. ed., trans. Benedicta Ward (Kalamazoo, Mich.: Cistercian Publications, 1984), 140.
6. Kilian Healy, *Methods of Prayer in the Directory of the Carmelite Reform of Touraine* (Rome: Institutum Carmelitanum, 1956), 80.
7. Ibid.
8. Silence was, of course, an important element of the Formula of Life and the Rule but in this essay is presupposed within the consideration of solitude.
9. Kees Waaijman, *The Mystical Space of Carmel: A Commentary on the Carmelite Rule*, trans. John Vriend (Leuven: Peeters, 1999), 98–99.
10. John Cassian, *The Conferences*, trans. Boniface Ramsey (New York/Mahwah: Paulist Press, 1997), 340, 345: Ninth Conference, XVIII, 1 and XXV, 1.
11 Waaijman, op cit.
12. Joachim F. Smet, "The Carmelite Rule After 750 Years," *Carmelus* 44 (1997), 21–47, especially 39–47.
13. Nicholas the Frenchman, "The Flaming Arrow *(Ignea Sagitta)*," trans. Bede Edwards, *The Sword* 39 (1979), 27.
14. Emphasis added. My translation is of the Latin text in *Medieval Carmelite Heritage: Early Reflections on the Nature of the Order*, ed. Adrianus Staring (Rome: Institutum Carmelitanum, 1989), 40–41.
15. A critical edition of the *Institutio Primorum Monachorum* is being prepared by the Australian Carmelite Paul Chandler. The above translation is his.
16. Donald Buggert, "Grace and Religious Experience: The Everyday Mysticism of Karl Rahner," *Master of the Sacred Page*, eds. Keith J. Egan and Craig Morrison (Washington, D.C.: Carmelite Institute, 1997), 189–218.
17. Cf. Gerhart Ladner, *The Idea of Reform* (Cambridge: Harvard University Press, 1959).
18. Titus Brandsma, *Carmelite Mysticism: Historical Sketches* (Darien, Ill.: Carmelite Press, 1986, originally, 1936), 39.
19. A designation long used for cloistered Carmelite nuns.
20. BF, 1.1. See note 2, p. 415, of BF.

21. Besides IC.5.1.2, see, for other comments by Teresa about the first Carmelites on Mount Carmel, BF.17.8; 28.20; 29–33.
22. See elsewhere in this book: Ernest Larkin, "The Carmelite Tradition and Centering Prayer/Christian Meditation."
23. Letter 31 and 28 of *The Collected Works of St. John of the Cross.*
24. See Keith J. Egan, "Dark Night: Education for Beauty," *Carmel and Contemplation—Transforming Human Consciousness,* eds. Kevin Culligan and Regis Jordan, Carmelite Studies 8, (Washington, D.C., ICS, 2000), 241–66.
25. Paul-Marie de la Croix, "Déserts," *Dictionnaire de Spiritualité,* Tome 3, columns 534–39. In the various branches of the Carmelite Order, "desert houses" or hermitages have once again been established.
26. Joachim Smet, *The Carmelites,* vol. 3, part 2 (Darien, Ill.: Carmelite Spiritual Center, 1982), 426.
27. Ibid., 438.
28. Healy, op. cit. Chapter VI: "Aspirative Prayer, or the Exercise of the Presence of God."
29. Lawrence of the Resurrection, *The Practice of the Presence of God,* trans. Salvatore Sciurba (Washington, D.C.: ICS, 1994).
30. Dogmatic Constitution on the Church, # 40, *Vatican Council II, Constitutions, Decrees, Declarations;* rev. ed., ed. Austin Flannery (Northport, N.Y.: Costello; Dublin, Ireland: Dominican Publications, 1996).
31. See Keith J. Egan, "The Significance for Theology of the Doctor of the Church: Teresa of Avila," *The Pedagogy of God's Image,* ed. Robert Masson (Chico, Calif.: Scholars Press, 1982) 153–71.
32. Thérèse of Lisieux, *General Correspondence;* vol. 2, trans. John Clarke (Washington, D.C.: ICS, 1988), Letter 224, p. 1085.
33. Thérèse of Lisieux, *Her Last Conversations,* trans. John Clarke (Washington, D.C.: ICS, 1977), 57, 293.
34. Edith Stein, "On the History and Spirit of Carmel," *The Hidden Life,* trans. Waltraut Stein (Washington, D.C.: ICS, 1992), 1–6.
35. Translation by Joachim F. Smet, O. Carm.
36. See the essay by Ernest Larkin, chapter eleven in this book.

4

New Wine: Jesus, Carmelite Prayer, and Postmodernity

Donald W. Buggert, O. Carm.

In the Prologue of the Carmelite Rule given to the hermits of Mount Carmel between 1206 and 1214, Carmelites are called "to walk in the footsteps of Jesus Christ." Then the Rule spells out in eighteen brief chapters and an Epilogue how Carmelites are to do this. The Rule of Carmel is thoroughly Christocentric. So also is its understanding of prayer. Indeed, within the Rule it is understood that through silence, solitude, penance, fasting, and above all through meditating upon the law of the Lord, the recitation of the psalms, and the eucharistic meal, the first hermits of Carmel were to be transformed into Christ. This Christocentrism of the Rule is highly kenotic or decentering, patterned on the self-emptying of Jesus coming to completion in his own suffering and death.[1]

Teresa of Avila and John of the Cross are two of Carmel's paramount expositors of Carmel's kenotic or decentering Christocentrism. For both, the humanity of Jesus is central to their understanding of transformation into Christ and hence to their understanding of the journey to God-Father. For both, this Christocentrism is focused on the role of the humanity of Jesus in prayer, even in the highest stages of contemplative prayer.[2]

The noted Marian scholar, Eamon R. Carroll, O. Carm., points to Teresa of Avila as "one of the all-time great defenders" of the Rule's injunction to follow Jesus, *in obsequio Jesu Christi.*³ For Teresa, the humanity of Jesus remains the sole gate through which we must enter if we desire "his sovereign Majesty to show us great secrets" (BL.22.6). No one image can exhaustively express for Teresa the centrality of Christ in prayer. Rejecting a totally apophatic mysticism and wanting to keep prayer solidly anchored in humanity and corporeality, Teresa speaks of Christ as friend, companion, brother, support, model, the way—but also the master, teacher, and the bridegroom into whom one is transformed in prayer. It is through meditation and contemplation on and imitation of the mysteries of Christ's life, especially his passion and death, that one is more and more transformed through love into Christ.

So too for John of the Cross the humanity of Christ remains central in the journey of prayer. All prayer is in and through the Incarnate Word. As with Teresa of Avila, John invokes many images to portray Jesus' essential role in prayer. He is the model (especially in his suffering and death), brother, companion, teacher, the one who reveals the Father, and in whom the Father gives all to the soul, and, finally, the spouse with whom one is united in spiritual marriage. In this union, the soul is so transformed into the divine that it becomes deified insofar as this is possible during earthly existence.

The challenge to Carmelites and those who pray in the Carmelite tradition in our day is that they not merely repeat the tradition and its great masters. This tradition and these masters like Teresa and John lived in another world, at another time. Mere repetition makes for irrelevance. Rather the challenge for the contemporary Carmelite tradition is to retrieve and renew the centrality of Jesus in life and prayer for our time. How might we depict or characterize our time? Many refer to it as the period or era of postmodernity. What is postmodernity and what does it mean to be postmodern?⁴

Postmodernity

Postmodernity refers to the spirit or mentality that describes modern Western culture. Postmodern is its adjectival form. Although the term postmodern was not used until the 1930s in reference to architecture and the arts, and became popular only in the 1970s, the phenomenon goes back to the late nineteenth century and Friedrich Nietzsche (d. 1900). Nietzsche attacked both the haughty rationalism of modernity with its pretense that it knows the stable meaning inherent in an objective and stable world and its attempt to manipulate and control this world for what it conceived to be human ends. Nietzsche's nihilism challenged the very idea of intrinsic, stable meaning, and the human person as the autonomous or self-constituting subject who grasped this meaning. With Nietzsche the world of stability became the world of flux, with no Archimedean point outside the flux. Everything was now up for grabs, caught up in and by the eternal flux, including the seemingly autonomous subject supposedly impervious to and above the flux.

Postmodernity, therefore, must be understood first in terms of that to which it is a reaction, namely modernity. Modernity is that cultural epoch whose roots go back to the English philosopher and scientist, Francis Bacon (d. 1626). Bacon marks the beginning of the Age of Reason, or the Enlightenment, the mother and matrix of modernity. For Bacon, knowledge is power. Such a view leads to modernity's attempt to alter and control the physical universe and eventually human behavior. Since knowledge is power, knowledge can also be used to privilege some and exclude others, especially the weak.

With Descartes' search for absolutely certain truth, the individual self and its consciousness became the autonomous, rational subject, that is, the center of reality and the foundation for all truth and certitude. While Kant proclaimed the conscious self as an autonomous, *universal* subject, always and everywhere the same, a self who stood outside the flux of time and history and above all traditions, and hence could serve as a ground for universal truth and morality.

What characterizes modernity, therefore, is its emphasis upon the individual self, the individual self as rational, as knower, the individual knowing self as always and everywhere the same, hence the self as a transcendental self with universal reason, a reason that transcends particularity and hence is the basis for true, certain, universal knowledge. This is the autonomous self. As Grenz notes: "The centrality of the autonomous self…became the chief identifying characteristic of the emerging modern era."[5]

Accompanying this anthropology of the autonomous self is a view of the world. Everything that exists has its own intrinsic, stable meaning or intelligibility, which can be grasped by the transcendental, knowing subject. Since the world is characterized by intrinsic intelligibility, and since the human mind is now enlightened, that is, freed from the shackles of the past, especially religion, it can know, subdue, and transform the world for its own purposes. Hence, modernity is characterized by unlimited optimism about inevitable progress. There is no end to that which humans can accomplish in this orderly universe with its objective, intrinsic rationality. Again, it is a celebration of individual autonomy and freedom.

Then came Nietzsche! With Nietzsche not only was God dead, an event that had occurred earlier in the nineteenth century with Feuerbach, but with the death of God came also the death of meaning and the self-constituting, transcendental, autonomous self.

What is postmodernity? Whatever else it may be, "it embodies a rejection of the Enlightenment project…and the philosophical assumptions upon which modernism was built."[6] Of course as a reaction to the rationalism and quest for intrinsic, stable meaning characteristic of modernity, postmodernity by definition cannot be defined. If it could be defined, it and its definer would escape the flux that is reality. Hence, postmodernity represents a spectrum of attitudes and/or positions.[7] Not every postmodern thinker would share all points on the spectrum. Nonetheless there are four interrelated traits that are typically postmodern and which are of interest here. What are these typically postmodern traits?[8]

First, there are the decentering of the self and the death of the subject. Postmodernity, especially as articulated through deconstructionist philosophers like Michel Foucault, Jacques Derrida, and Jean-François Lyotard, takes seriously the radical historicity of the person or self. It challenges the haughty claims or epistemic hubris of modernity's reason and replaces it with a more chastened view of reason's prowess and with a good dose of "gnoseological humility" (Scanlon). The self is not an autonomous, self-constituting universal reason that exists above and outside the flux of history and culture, unaffected by language, traditions, and narratives. Hence modernity's self or subject, which had been the center of reality and the Archimedean solid ground of universal truth, is itself caught up in the flux and hence radically "decentered." It is a self that is constituted by language, traditions, narratives, and relationships—relationships to others, and to the natural environment.

Second, there are the death of logocentrism and the consequent rejection of the metaphysics of presence. The consequence of this decentering of the self or the death of the subject is the death of logocentrism and the rejection of the metaphysics of presence (Derrida), that is, the modern notion of stable meaning intrinsic to an already given universe, meaning apart from the language that constructs it, not merely packages or represents it. There is no intrinsic meaning, no meaning in itself, no meaning and hence no world apart from language, from the text. Hence there is no objective, universal truth.[9] The status quo has been replaced by the *fluxus quo*.[10] Hence, postmodern philosophers maintain a much more practical approach to truth. "Truth consists in the ground rules that facilitate the well-being of the community in which we participate."[11]

Third, there is the death of metanarratives and the irruption of alterity. If there is no universal, objective truth, then there are no metanarratives or grand narratives (Lyotard). Metanarratives are universalizing worldviews or ideologies that claim to know the whole of reality and history, or *the* meaning of reality and history, and so attempt to block out and vanquish heterogeneity and difference embedded in other, possibly competitive worldviews. Modernity's metanarratives too often exclude and leave no room for that which postmodernity celebrates, particularity, difference, diversity, and otherness. Postmodernity resists "more of the same" (Foucault). For postmodernity, there is no single worldview, no all encompassing, universally valid explanation. Postmodernity declares "war on totality" (Lyotard) and lives with many narratives, many traditions, many versions of truth, and with cultural diversity. Thus postmodernity entails radical relativism and pluralism.

Postmodernity is especially concerned with alterity, the turn toward the other (Emmanuel Levinas), so often ignored, leveled, or oppressed by modernity's autonomous subject and its metanarratives. For Lyotard and others, the abandonment of metanarratives means the encounter with the other. Who is this other?

> The other…is the suspect, the deviant, the path not taken, the darkness, the chaos, standing over against the surety and clarity of the subject's chosen practice. It is the female to the male, the black to the white, the East to the West, the native culture to the representative of the Raj, the homosexual to the heterosexual.[12]

Fourth, there is universal emancipation. While modernity proclaimed freedom, in fact, its emphasis upon the autonomous subject and its exclusionary metanarratives often lead to social and political oppression. In the name of freedom, modernity curtailed freedom by privileging those with power and voice. Postmodernity, in its decentering of the self and its metanarratives, claims to be the herald of an inclusive human emancipation.

I would summarize postmodernity as the cultural *geist* that is quite comfortable with ambiguity and open-endedness, which, with Pascal, knows more through the heart and imagination than reason alone can know, and which looks for relationality and complementarity primarily through the acceptance of the other. Given this description of postmodernity, how might we understand the centrality of Jesus in Carmelite prayer today?

Carmelite Prayer and Postmodernity

As we saw above with Teresa and John, Jesus, especially the kenotic Jesus, was central to prayer because he was the model or way, the teacher, and the goal of prayer. Postmodernity's emphasis on radical historicity challenges us to return to Jesus himself, the pre-Paschal Jesus, to ascertain how this Jesus can be central to Carmelite prayer today as model, teacher, and goal.

In returning to the pre-Paschal Jesus we see that Jesus was both model and teacher of prayer. He encouraged his disciples to pray his own prayer, the Abba prayer, Our Father, who art in heaven. Central to this prayer, as one would expect, is the invocation: your kingdom come. To appreciate truly the prayer of Jesus, the prayer which he gives to us as both model and teacher of prayer, we must first see it within the context of that which constitutes the heart and center of Jesus' consciousness and ministry of word and deed, and that is the kingdom or reign of God. "The reign of God is near at hand, repent and believe the good news," Jesus proclaims (Mark 1:15). Everything else that Jesus preaches or does is a spin-off of this basic proclamation of the inbreaking of God's reign, the heart of Jesus' own prayer. For Jesus, all is of one piece: his prayer, his ministry of word, his ministry of deed.[13] All is centered in the reign of God. What is this reign of God which Jesus proclaims? Or, more precisely, who is this reign?

The biblical symbol of the reign of God, the *malkuth Yahweh*, reaches back to the beginning of the monarchical period (c.1000

B.C.E.) and refers to Yahweh's past and present mighty rule over creation and history. The motif is picked up by Israel's prophets for whom Yahweh's mighty rule becomes an eschatological or end-time reality. On that day Yahweh will be fully manifested and rule victoriously over his creation and human history. Creation and history will enjoy the paradisal peace intended for them by God in the beginning. When Yahweh rules definitively over his creation, the lame will walk, lepers will be cleansed, the blind will see, the deaf will hear. Beginning around 165 B.C.E. the reign of God brings about a new heaven, a new earth, a new creation, and a new age. This is the period of apocalyptic expectations. Yahweh, in order to be fully manifest and victorious over his creation, will have to bring this creation and history, as we know it, to a definitive end and bring forth a new age, a new creation. It is in this period of apocalyptic expectation that the understanding of personal resurrection arises in Jewish thinking. The resurrection of the dead becomes the sure-fire sign that the end is here and Yahweh is now ruling.

What therefore is the reign of God which Jesus proclaims? The reign of God (*malkuth Yahweh*) is in the first place the reigning God. It is Yahweh himself, Yahweh as Yahweh will be in the end when Yahweh fully rules and is victorious over his creation and salvation. The reigning God is the God of the absolute future, the God of salvation, the God who will be all in all (1 Cor 15:28). We must remember that the God of Jesus, the Abba to whom he prays, is the Yahweh of Israel. And this Yahweh is a God who, unlike the God of Greek thought who is absolutely immutable and hence has no history, is only fully God when he fully reigns. And that is in the end! This God is a God whose name, Yahweh, is a promise, the promise "to be there with you" (Exod 3:14). The only God Israel knows and confesses is Yahweh, the saving God, the God whose mighty creative and transformative power or Spirit (*ruach*) has always yet new and surprising things to do in order that God may be here with us and bring about his definitive saving presence and reign, when all will be returned to him and he will be all in all.

The *malkuth Yahweh* which Jesus proclaims is this definitively ruling, saving God of the end times, the God of the absolute future, the God of surprises who continually pours new wine. With this God one never knows what's up next. With this God, the verdict is never in. This God is more absent than present because this God is the God of the absolute future whose power or spirit comes at us in the present from the future to pour new wine and draw us beyond every past and present into his own absolute future. This God, as the God of the absolute future, does not stand outside of or over and against time and history with their many particularities, narratives, and cultures. This God is the God who takes up, sums up, and thus fulfills the many nations with all their distinctiveness and plurality. This is the God whose reigning Judeo-Christianity, in its metanarrative of the reign of God, calls the goal of history. It is this God, the God of the absolute future, the God of surprises, the God who continually pours new and at times shocking wine, whom Jesus proclaimed and made present in his words (proverbs and parables) and deeds.

It was because of his experience that the definitive inbreaking of the reigning God was now occurring in and through him that Jesus turned especially to those who were considered marginalized or outcasts in his day: public sinners, tax collectors, lepers, demoniacs, women, children. He not only associated with these excluded ones, he broke bread with them and in so doing included them in the inbreaking of God's reign. The compassion of Jesus' God knew no boundaries. All were included. All were within the pale of God's eschatological forgiveness celebrated and made present in Jesus' parables and table-fellowship meals. The only ones excluded were those who excluded others, a certain group of Pharisees who had very clear guidelines (the law) as to who was included and who excluded, who is just and who not, with whom one could eat and with whom not. For Jesus even the detested Samaritan is included and hence is our neighbor; even the profligate son who became a swineherd remains our brother and hence is included at the banquet. In fact, for Jesus the forgiveness and compassion of his God now reigning through him and his ministry of word and deed seemed to go out especially to these marginalized and outcasts, the ones excluded by the Pharisees and chief priests, but included by the God of Jesus. "Truly, I tell you, the tax collectors and the prostitutes are going into the kingdom of God ahead of you" (Matt 21:31).

Indeed, Jesus is the one in whom Yahweh's final reigning power and reality is now beginning to break into history. He is God's last or eschatological prophet, the agent of the reigning God. He is the sacrament and prolepsis (anticipation) of the reigning God himself.[14] As such he is the new wine that the old wineskins of legalistic Judaism could not contain. With Jesus and the inbreaking reign of his Father, everything is stood on its head: the last becomes first and the first last, the humbled are exalted and the exalted humbled, the uninvited are present while the invited guests are absent, the darnel turns out to be the wheat and the wheat the darnel. With the inbreaking of the reigning God in Jesus and his ministry, everything was up for grabs! Again, prostitutes and tax collectors are entering the Reign of God before the chief priests and elders. The tax collector goes home justified and the law-keeping Pharisee does not.

The question now is: how might this Jesus with his reign-of-God prayer, his reign-of-God ministry of word and deed, relate to our postmodern era in terms of its four traits outlined above, if there is some sort of a compatibility or fit between the Jesus who prays that Yahweh's reign come and as its prophet and sacrament makes this reigning God of the endtimes now present? Then, indeed, Jesus not only can remain model and teacher of prayer for us today, but perhaps our postmodern *geist* may help us to see anew, or perhaps to see truly for the first time (Marcus Borg), the radical nature of this new wine that Yahweh poured in and as Jesus of Nazareth. Perhaps our postmodern *geist* can sensitize us to aspects of Jesus into which we must be transformed if he is to be not only model and teacher but also goal of prayer. How might the Jesus whom I have described briefly above react to our postmodern era? I suspect that Jesus of Nazareth would feel much more comfortable and much less threatened by the postmodern *geist* than many of his disciples who pray his Abba prayer, who look to Jesus as model and teacher of prayer, and who hope to be transformed through prayer into him. Let us take a look at the four traits of postmodernity outlined above to see how Jesus with his reign-of-God experience might relate to the postmodernity of our times.

Jesus and Postmodernity

The first trait is the decentering of the self and death of the subject. These themes of course are central to Jesus' challenge to repent or convert. Because the reigning God is now at hand, we are called to turn around and accept the good news. What good news? The good news that the compassion, mercy, and love of Yahweh (who is a promise to be with us) are now breaking into history in their fullness in the person and ministry of Jesus. Because of the inbreaking, in and through Jesus, of the God of the absolute future, those who would follow him are to deny themselves and take up their cross as he will do (Mark 8:34). If they attempt to save their lives, they will lose them, whereas if they lose them for the sake of the good news, they will save them (Mark 8:35), for unless the grain of wheat falls to the earth and dies, it remains just a grain of wheat, but if it dies, it produces much fruit (John 12:24–25). They are to drop their nets immediately (Mark 1:18), sell all that they have and give it to the poor (Mark 10:21); they are to take nothing on their journey but a staff only, neither wallet, nor bread, nor money (Mark 6:8). They are to love Yahweh with all of their heart and soul and mind and strength and their neighbor as themselves (Mark 12:30), and they are to do good to those who hate them and bless those who curse them (Luke 6:27–28).

This is the kenotic, decentered existence which Jesus himself lived and to which he calls his followers, as Paul so well realized: "Let the same mind be in you that was in Christ Jesus, who, though he was in the form of God, did not regard equality with God as something to be exploited, but emptied himself, taking the form of a slave..." (Phil 2:5–7).

For Jesus, the reign of God or the God of the absolute future, is totally decentering. One finds one's self not in one's self but in the God of the absolute future. And that is why Jesus calls for such total trust and abandonment to that God. His followers are not to worry about their lives, what they are to eat or wear. They are to be like the birds of the air who do not sow or reap or gather into barns but who are fed by their heavenly Father, or like the lilies of the field that neither toil nor spin but not even Solomon in all his glory was arrayed as one of these (Matt 6:25–30).

The Jesus way is the way of living according to the reign of God, and that way is one of radical kenosis or decentering, a theme central to Carmelite prayer as we saw above. The disciple of Jesus is not the self-constituting, autonomous self of modernity but the self who finds him/herself in the God of the absolute future. Unless the grain of wheat be buried and die, it remains just a grain of wheat.

The second trait of postmodernity discussed above is the death of logocentrism and the consequent rejection of the metaphysics of presence. With postmodernity there is no status quo but only the *fluxus quo*. Stable and fixed meaning has evaporated, is absent more than present. Being is more concealed than revealed (Heidegger). The last word is not yet in and hence, given also the decentered self, gnoseological humility is called for.

Of course this trait of postmodernity resonates extremely well with the apophatic tradition of mysticism.[15] The very word mysticism comes from the Greek verb *muein*, to keep silence. Mystics are not those who know but those who do not know, who have abandoned the effort to attain to God through knowing and have been taken up (passive voice) to God through love. Mystics know little but love much.[16] And mystical prayer is the doing of love.[17] As Sanders rightly claims, "...mystical union is precisely not the immediacy of presence."[18] The cry of the great mystics is let God be God. How fitting are the words of David Tracy: "God enters postmodern history not as a consoling 'ism' but as an awesome, often terrifying hope-beyond-hope. God enters history again not as a new speculation—even a modern Trinitarian one!—but as God. Let God be God becomes an authentic cry again."[19] Mystics do not speak of possessing absolute truth or having God and God's will figured out and nailed down.

This is exactly Jesus' position. Let God be God. Even for Jesus, the reign of God, the God of the absolute future, is always yet ahead of him. The reign has not yet fully come, is not yet fully present. The God of the absolute future is still outstanding. And so Jesus prays: thy kingdom come. The Yahweh of Jesus is not a God merely of the past or the present but a God who has yet new things to do, new wine to pour, who has yet to fully reign and hence be fully God, for God is not all in all until God fully reigns.

Because the God of Jesus is a God always yet ahead with new and surprising things to do, with yet new wine to pour, Jesus spoke of God not through clear and distinct concepts but by means of parables, those shocking metaphors extended into little stories. The God of the parables, because he is the God of the reign, is never the God whom we would have ever figured out or anticipated but always the God who turns things upside down, who plays not by our rules but by his rule of incomprehensible love. And that is why the parables are scandalizing metaphors that turn our world upside down with their unanticipated endings. No wonder Jesus runs afoul of at least a certain group of Pharisees, who have God and God's will tied down, for whom God is no longer the God of surprises, the eschatological God who is beyond all our *theo-logos*, God-talk. For Jesus, the prophet of

God's reign, history is not closed; the last word is not yet in, for the last word is God's reign. Jesus would have no problem with the death of logocentrism and the metaphysics of presence. If one's God is the reigning God of the absolute future, you can have only a *fluxus quo*. Things are no longer black or white, settled and determined, for this God with his wily Spirit can jump out at you from the future quite unexpectedly with shocking new wine to pour. With his God of the absolute future, it could be no other way. Only this God in his absolute future could be the center. All else, including meaning and truth, would have to be decentered and become ecstatic, or out-standing. Only a God like the God of Greek metaphysics, the absolutely immutable God who has no history of being God for us, could reduce the *fluxus quo* to the status quo, the divine absence to the divine presence.

The third characteristic of postmodernity considered above is the death of metanarratives and the irruption of alterity. Metanarratives are those universalizing stories or worldviews that allow no other worldview and hence exclude the other, those who see things differently. There is no question but that Jesus' vision and proclamation of the reign of God is a metanarrative. The symbol of the reign of God, as used by Jesus, as well as by the prophets and the apocalyptic seers before him, is a universalizing symbol. The reigning God of the absolute future creates everything, lures everything back to himself through his Spirit, and promises to be the fulfillment of all. Nothing escapes this reigning God. There is no God beside him or any narrative of any other God that can stand alongside his story. For his story, Yahweh's his-story is all encompassing. There may be other gods and other stories of gods, but they have mouths that speak not, eyes that see not, ears that hear not (Ps 115). So it seems, alas, that Jesus and postmodernity part ways. Or do they? Perhaps Jesus' meta-narrative precisely because it is so unique, so truly meta, is not just one story among other stories, one totalizing schema among other totalizing schemata. Perhaps Jesus' metanarrative precisely because it deals with the God who is a promise, who will be all in all only in the absolute future, is a metanarrative that does not exclude other meta-narratives but includes all other metanarratives by summing them all up and bringing them into completion. Jesus' metanarrative of the God of the future no more excludes than does Jesus' God, Yahweh. Yahweh is not the bad infinite attacked by Hegel that cannot contain the finite because it itself is part of the finite. Yahweh includes all because he brings all to completion in his own absolute future or reign. Again the God of Jesus' metanarrative is not the God of Greek philosophy, the totally other God, who is infinitely opposed to the finite and thus quickly becomes himself finite. The God of Jesus is not the status quo opposed to the *fluxus quo*, which always horrified Greek sensibilities. The God of Jesus is himself found in the *fluxus quo* and is its fulfillment.

And so Jesus' metanarrative does not exclude other narratives. No wonder, therefore, that we see in Jesus' own ministry such an irruption of alterity, of the turn towards the other, the marginalized or outcast: the lepers and lame, the blind and the deaf, the prostitutes and the tax collectors, the hungry and thirsty, the naked and sick, the stranger and the imprisoned. Jesus and his God had no problem with all these who were marginalized by the distorted narrative of the Judaism of Jesus' time. For Jesus, precisely because of the all-encompassing, universal-izing nature of his God and that God's compassion, the excluded became included. The sinners ended up sitting at the table with the just, and in fact in the places of honor. Jesus too would have problems with metanarratives that vanquished the other. But his metanarrative would not allow that to happen.

Finally, we turn to the fourth trait of postmodernity, universal emancipation. Since for Jesus there really is no other, and since no one is excluded and all are included, all are equal in God's eyes and hence set free. His Father's love, which goes out to and embraces all just, as his rain falls on the just and the unjust (Matt 5:46), breaks down all barriers and divisions that privilege some and enslave others.

Jesus is depicted by Luke as actually interpreting his ministry as one of proclaiming liberty to captives and release to prisoners (Luke 4:18). Because he could mediate to others an experience of the love and compassion of his God, Jesus had the uncanny ability to make people feel good about themselves and break their bondage. No wonder he comes to be called redeemer or liberator, the one who sets free.

Jesus proclaimed and made present the reign of God. In doing so he was God's final or eschatological prophet, the prophet of the reigning God. He was in his person and his ministry of word and deed the sacrament and foretaste or prolepsis of the reigning God himself. This Jesus prayed: thy kingdom (reign) come. And he urged his followers to do likewise. In doing so, he serves as a model and teacher of prayer. But, he is to be not only model and teacher, but also goal. Those who pray thy kingdom come, if they pray it honestly and authentically, will be transformed into that Jesus, the eschatological prophet, the sacrament of God's reign.

To pray Christocentrically so as to be transformed into the Jesus who is the prophet of God's reign is to be swept off one's feet and drawn up into the experience of the reigning God that Jesus had and made a reality for others. It involves response to the inbreaking of God's reign into one's life, as Jesus responded. It involves living according to the reign of God. One cannot separate thy kingdom come from being a doer of that kingdom. To respond to this inbreaking reign of God is to repent, to become decentered, which results in a committed reign of God praxis in favor especially of the excluded, the other. This praxis is a worldly praxis and a world-transforming praxis, since the reign of God is to encompass all of creation, heal it, restore it, and fulfill it. Too often prayer, even prayer which claims to be Christocentric, is just prayer, the prayer of one not swept up by the experience of the reigning God. Such prayer can quickly become the prayer of the opulent and bourgeoisie, a prayer legitimized by a God and Jesus who are not the reigning God and his prophet, but the God of the status quo.

If Jesus is to be the center of Carmelite prayer in the postmodern era, we must allow the traits of postmodernity to enable us to see Jesus again and anew, perhaps even for the first time. The Jesus about whom I have written here is, I believe, a Jesus who would feel somewhat comfortable with many postmodern thinkers. Undoubtedly he would try to sweep them off their feet with his reign-of-God vision. And he, with his grand metanarrative, may well end up taking the prize for being the greatest deconstructor of them all for he remains always the new wine poured into wineskins ever old.

Notes

1. See my analysis of the Christocentricity of the Rule in "Jesus in Carmelite Spirituality," *The Land of Carmel*, eds. Paul Chandler and Keith J. Egan (Rome: Institutum Carmelitanum, 1991), 91–107.
2. See Donald Buggert, *The Christocentricism of the Carmelite Charism* (Melbourne: Carmelite Communications, 1999), 21–30.
3. Eamon R. Carroll, "The Saving Role of the Human Christ for St. Teresa," in *Carmelite Studies* 3 (Washington, D.C.: ICS, 1984), 133.
4. The literature on postmodernism and its challenge to contemporary theology is immense. For a clear introduction to postmodernism see Stanley J. Grenz, *A Primer on Postmodernism* (Grand Rapids, Mich.: Eerdmans, 1996). For the dialogue between postmodernity and contemporary theology see Paul Lakeland, *Postmodernity: Christian Identity in a Fragmented Age* (Minneapolis: Fortress, 1997); David Tracy, *On Naming the Present: God, Hermeneutics, and Church* (Maryknoll, N.Y.: Orbis, 1994); Michael Scanlon, "The Postmodern Debate," in *The Twentieth Century: A Theological Overview*, ed. Gregory Baum (Maryknoll, N.Y.: Orbis, 1999), 228–37; Michael Scanlon, "Theological Studies at the Threshold of the Third Millennium: An Overview," in *Proceedings of the Theology Institute of Villanova University* 30 (1998), 1–29.
5. Grenz, 79.
6. Ibid., 81.
7. Sallie McFague includes among the characteristics of postmodernity "a greater appreciation for nature, a recognition of the importance of language to human existence, a chastened admiration for technology, an acceptance of the challenge that other religions present to the Judeo-Christian tradition an apocalyptic sensibility, a sense of the displace-

ment of the white, Western male and the rise of those dispossessed due to gender, race, or class, perhaps most significantly, a growing awareness of the radical interdependence of life at all levels and in every imaginable way." *Metaphorical Theology* (Philadelphia: Fortress, 1982), x–xi.

8. Obviously I am not here attempting to give an exhaustive treatment of that which constitutes postmodernity. Nor am I in any way claiming to be in agreement with all that goes under the rubric of postmodern. But there are certain traits of postmodernity which open up possibilities for fruitful dialogue with Christian theology and that may help us to retrieve in a new key for our day the centrality of Christ in Carmelite life and prayer.

9. This postmodern relativizing of truth is only reenforced by twentieth century science with Einstein's relativity theories, Niels Bohr's quantum mechanics, and Werner Heissenberg's principle of indeterminacy or uncertainty principle. The objectivity of modernity's science is itself no longer scientifically possible, since the scientist him/herself is part of the flux!

10. Tracy, *On Naming the Present*, 16.

11. Grenz, 7.

12. Lakeland, 31.

13. For Jesus, as for any Jewish prophet, the later debates within Christian theology and spirituality regarding the contemplative life versus the life of ministry or the active life, the mystical versus the prophetic would be nonsensical. Among other difficulties with such dichotomies is that they rest on a Christology which quickly leaves the pre-Paschal Jesus behind. See my article "The Contemplative as Iconoclast: The Countercultural Nature of Contemplation," *Carmel and Contemplation: Transforming Human Consciousness*; eds. Kevin Culligan and Regis Jordan (Washington, D.C.: ICS, 2000), 53–75.

14. In his being raised by the Father, Jesus becomes fully identified with the reigning God. He is, in Origen's words, the *autobasileia*, the reign itself. Hence because of his resurrection he is called Lord, Christ, Savior, Son, High Priest, Spirit-Sender.

15. For Derrida's own interest in this apophatic tradition, see the above-mentioned articles by Scanlon. Derrida is of course the deconstructor par excellence of the metaphysics of presence.

16. Along the same lines Theresa Sanders writes with reference to John of the Cross: "The last step of the spiritual journey, a journey of and within the structures of signification, is allowing oneself to be subsumed into the very disintegration of those structures. It is letting go of comprehension and the desire for presence, letting go of meaning itself, and

offering the whole of oneself to what one is not." "Remarking the Silence: Prayer After the Death of God," *Horizons* 25 (1998), 214.

17. As John Duns Scotus maintained, God is the *cognoscibile operabile*, the knowable-doable. God is known only by the doing of love. See Scanlon, "The Postmodern Debate," 235.

18. "Remarking the Silence," 213.

19. *On Naming the Present*, 43.

5

Jesus Christ in Carmelite Prayer

Margaret Dorgan, D.C.M.

Jesus Christ, the Alpha and Omega of Carmelite Prayer

In the spirituality of Carmel, prayer begins and ends with Jesus Christ. All that takes place from the first desire to pray up to the final goal of transforming union is rooted in Jesus Christ. He is the God-given model for prayer, the redeemer who leads one out of the quagmire of barren self-centeredness onto a path of freedom and exhilarating fulfillment in union with God.

In taking human nature, Jesus embraces all humanity in each one's specific humanity. One who is like us lifts us up in our very earthiness. We do not cease to be citizens of this planet, but in Jesus, everything that we are is raised to a new dimension of existence through him. By his invitation we are called to become what he is, a child of God. The wonder of this glory makes his followers eager to offer the riches of their lives in Christ to others. Sure of the treasures to be found in him, they are always reaching out to say "Look what we have in such abundance. We want you to have it too." Teresa of Avila shines as a seller of spiritual goods. No one has more persuasive enthusiasm than *La Madre*. She writes in the *Way of Perfection*, "A good means to having God is to speak with His friends, for one always gains very much from this" (WP.7.4). Teresa is such a friend who describes the stages of prayer which lead us to "supreme happiness for having found repose and because Christ lives in it" (IC.7.3.1).

John of the Cross, with the enthusiasm of an inspired poet, declares, "There is much to fathom in Christ, for he is like an abundant mine with many recesses of treasure, so that however deep individuals may go, they never reach the end or bottom, but rather in every recess find new veins with new riches everywhere" (SC.37.4). To John, each one of us is called to plumb the mysteries of the incarnation uniquely, for "...however numerous are the mysteries and marvels that holy doctors have discovered and saintly souls have understood in this earthly life, all the more is yet to be said and understood" (SC.37.4). That more is for every prayer to explore and feed upon. Jesus reveals himself to the incarnated reality I am as to no other. In the love song we begin to sing together, the harmony between lover and beloved moves one into new longing and new fulfillment. Words and melody point to deeper wonders that defy expression.

In nineteenth-century France, Thérèse of Lisieux, echoing the certainty of her Spanish forebears, points to the spiritual heights each one of us can hope to reach. "Ah! If all weak and imperfect souls felt what the least of souls feels, that is, the soul of your little Thérèse, not one would despair of reaching the summit of the mount of love. Jesus does not demand great actions from us but simply *surrender* and *gratitude*" (SS.188).

Yielding our whole being to Christ is not to lose anything but to gain all. Over and over again, Teresa underlines the importance of Christ's humanity to succor the limitations of our own humanness and to open up for us the plenitude God wills to give us in the mysteries of the Incarnation. "And I see clearly...that God desires that if we are going to please Him and receive His great favors, we must do so through the most sacred humanity of Christ, in whom He takes His delight....we must enter by this gate...on this road you walk safely.

This Lord of ours is the one through whom all blessings come to us" (BL.22.6–7).

Time takes on a new dimension because the one who is eternal has embraced all the ongoing moments from the beginning of the world. The incarnate one touches the human race in each member's personal journey onward. Blessed Elizabeth of the Trinity writes that Christ wills that where He is we should be also, not only for eternity, but already in time...."[1]

In each instant, we meet Christ who once smelled the air, felt the wind upon his face, shivered in the cold and perspired in the hot noonday sun. Now in me, he embraces all my human experience. With every happening, I encounter a friend who shares what I am undergoing and is always concerned for my welfare.

Identification with the Incarnate God

In the narrative of Jesus' thirty-three years, much attention is given to the beginning, the babe in a manger. Then St. Luke shows Jesus in the Temple just before he becomes a teenager. Afterwards the gospels describe the events of his public life. We can also ruminate on what has not been reported. There must have been times when Jesus laughed. Surely humor, the special gift that comes from the union of a physical body with a spiritual soul, enlivened walks along the Sea of Galilee. Wouldn't Peter's often awkward grasp of a situation make for comedy? Look at Zacchaeus up the sycamore tree. We know the serious exchange that took place. But Jewish wit—that marvelous talent to provoke merriment and mirth—must have showed itself at such times. Prayer is more than strict solemnity. Reverence mixes with familiarity as we take all our human emotions to one who felt them in his lifetime.

Especially the agony of human pain reaches out to find strengthening in the chapters of the gospel that tell of Christ's suffering, the certainty that our death is not an end but only a passage. Christ's human Risen Life gives us comfort and assurance that we too will rise in glory. Thus we ponder all Jesus' earthly moments from birth to his ascension and link them to our own.

Contemplative Orientation for the Young

Prayer can establish a foundation in a child's life from its first awakening to what is around it. To show a picture or a statue of Jesus and of Mary, to urge the child to repeat their names, to tell stories adapted to the developing imagination is to nourish a hungry mind and heart. Liturgical events, church gatherings, feast days are celebrations that feed emotions. A child who is encouraged to pray in the earliest years will have images and thoughts that focus the young intelligence and can easily lead into happy silence, a peaceful wonder. Today's world is constantly offering stimulation to children so that the ability to settle into awe can be blocked or sadly centered on fantasy figures.

Yet there are favored children today who would understand Thérèse's answer at the Abbey school when she was eleven. Her teacher asked her what she did on free afternoons. "I told her I went behind my bed in an empty space," and that "...I think about God, about life, about ETERNITY..." (SS.74).

If prayer begins early enough in an atmosphere where vocal prayer is an ordinary part of the day, like the blessing at meals and turning to God in everyday needs, the first dark night may not be necessary since, as John of the Cross explains, this night is an adjustment. Meditation, which helps to quiet an older mind and introduces thoughts of spiritual realities, does not have the same work to do. If the younger boy or girl is in contact with religious symbols, pictures, and tales, and if spontaneous prayer is heard often, then the task of meditation may be already accomplished. Simplified prayer becomes the normal contact with God.

Though Scripture tells us little about it, we can ponder Christ's so-called hidden life. We know Jesus was a teenager. What was he like? Surely his mother took notice when his voice changed. Did his foster father smile to see a beard begin to show on his cheek? How did he move through the decade of his twenties?

In our modern world, these years of passage into maturity are especially problematic. Jesus, the companion of young people, can be friend and confidant, reliving his youth with girls and boys growing into adulthood. His body underwent the physical changes that mark these years. Teenagers can bring him their hopes and anxieties, trusting in his empathy as a fellow traveler along a course with which he is familiar. Do we ponder enough how truly human Jesus was and is for us today? Teresa speaks to Christ with a blunt directness: "Since You possess our nature, it seems You have some reason to look to our gain" (WP.27.3).

Prayer in the beginning years of life helps to establish a habit that will be a source of strength and encouragement as body and psyche develop. When children and adolescents become accustomed to the companionship of Jesus in all the ups and downs of their days, they have someone to turn to who understands fully what they are going through. This turning to Jesus is true prayer. At any point in our lives we can begin what Teresa describes as "looking at Him." We are taking the first step on a path of awareness of Christ. She writes, "I'm not asking you to do anything more than look at Him. For who can keep you from turning the eyes of your soul toward this Lord, even if you do so just for a moment if you can't do more? ...your Spouse never takes His eyes off you....In the measure you desire Him, you will find Him. He so esteems our turning to look at Him..." (WP.26.3).

Gazing on Jesus

When we move our gaze to Jesus, we find that his eyes are on us, wholly concerned with whatever occupies us.

Teresa advises us to seek him according to what we are undergoing, to match our feelings with an event in his life that called forth the same kind of human response in him. "If you are joyful, look at Him as risen. If you are experiencing trials or are sad, behold Him on the way to the garden..." (WP.26.4–5)

The adjustment is all on the part of Christ. He will always meet us where we are, stooping to our lowliness. Teresa asks only that we shift from giving sole attention to our daily concerns and glance at him, a glance she hopes will become a more steady gaze. "Draw near, then, to this good Master with strong determination to learn what He teaches you..." (WP.26.10).

Going Within

This is the start of a process that takes us inward to find there a sanctuary where we meet our God in all that transpires. Teresa explains how we mute the exterior voices we have been listening to, no longer absorbed in pursuing the profits and pleasures our external world is always offering us. And if we are ardent consumers of such goods, we stop to realize we are at the same time being consumed by what we seek with so much energy. Now a different kind of seeking is arousing our minds and hearts. We bring Jesus into our ordinary affairs and also pause at times to give our whole attention to him through extended prayer. We focus on one who is always focused on us. This quieting-down spills over into the rest of our daily existence.

Teresa tells us: "Life is long, and there are in it many trials, and we need to look to Christ our model..." (IC.6.7.13). And she says that "He reveals Himself to those who He sees will benefit by His presence. Even though they fail to see Him with their bodily eyes, He has many methods of showing Himself to the soul..." (WP.34.10).

For Teresa, the most Blessed Sacrament is the supreme revelation of God, a sure presence of Christ that nourishes us in communion through our very bodies. She seems to congratulate God for finding a way so simple and so available. "Beneath that bread He is easy to deal with," she says, and urges us, "Be with Him willingly; don't lose so good an occasion for conversing with Him as is the hour after having received Communion....If you immediately turn your thoughts to other things,...and take no account of the fact that He is within you, how will He be able to reveal Himself to you?" (WP.34.10). She goes on, "Though He comes disguised, the disguise...does not prevent Him from being recognized in many ways, in conformity with the desire we have to see Him" (WP.34.12).

Moved by Desire

Desire is the force that moves us. Longing pushes us forward in our quest for God. John of the Cross affirms that "God does not place his grace and love in the soul except according to its desire and love." (SC.13.12) Teresa rejoices in Jesus' desire for us. He is "...our Companion in the most Blessed Sacrament; it doesn't seem it was in His power to leave us for even a moment." (BL.22.6)

Thérèse reflects on the sacramental presence, which through communion deepens the dwelling of God within us: "It is not to remain in a golden ciborium that He comes to us *each day* from heaven; it's to find another heaven, infinitely more dear to Him than the first: the heaven of our soul, made to His image, the living temple of the adorable Trinity!" (SS.104). Partaking of Christ in the sacred bread and wine deepens our ongoing communion with him afterwards. Teresa, looking back on her life, declares that "...in seeing You at my side I saw all blessings" (BL.22.6).

Christ opens our eyes to find the sacramental dimension in created beings everywhere. John of the Cross explains how Jesus "...took on our human nature and elevated it in the beauty of God, and consequently all creatures, since in human nature he was united with them all" (SC.5.4). John says that "since creatures gave the soul signs of her Beloved and showed within themselves traces of his beauty and excellence, love grew in her and, consequently, sorrow at his absence" (SC.6.2). Prayer feeds on the revelation of Christ in nature, sometimes murmuring the words of the psalms that celebrate creation. A hillside, a body of water, a rural pathway can take us to scripture passages that incorporate them. We are led to gospel incidents that hold our minds in quiet attentiveness. Thérèse writes that "...it is especially the *Gospels* that sustain me during my hours of prayer, for in them I find what is necessary for my poor little soul. I am constantly discovering in them new lights, hidden and mysterious meanings" (SS.179). We never abandon this kind of reflection, though gradually we need less input from meditation to stir our hearts and to settle into a loving silence before God. A single word or phrase shuts down the noise. Then at times a compelling stillness beckons. We respond to its bidding gladly.

John of the Cross invites us to this inward hush, which in prayer blocks out all the external voices soliciting our notice. "The Father spoke one Word, which was his Son, and this Word he always speaks in eternal silence, and in silence must it be heard by the soul" (SL.100).

Today many forms of silencing techniques are offered in the spiritual marketplace. Human consciousness can undergo a training in mental practices that move it into a more passive mode. This is a natural process and one with recognizable benefits. Our wide-ranging imagination is lured inward; analysis and planning come to a stop. A very cut-down diet is imposed on all our thinking.

When we pray, this pulling in of the attention also takes place, yet, with an important distinction. Christian prayer is primarily a *relationship* with one who calls us to intimacy, inviting us to believe in him. John of the Cross depicts the pray-er who "longs for union [with the Bridegroom]..." (SC.1.2). John rejoices with that happy person: "There is reason for you to be elated and joyful in seeing that all your good and hope is so close as to be within you or, better, that you cannot be without him. 'Behold,' exclaims the Bridegroom, 'the kingdom of God is within you'" [Luke 17:21] (SC. 1.7). What draws us is a living person, Jesus Christ, who called himself the Way. With Jesus our companion who provides a map for us, we do not walk on side roads that use up our energy without advancing us.

Living Our Prayer

Authentic prayer affects our moral understanding and gives strength for virtuous behavior. Teresa in her straightforward manner, declares, "Fix your eyes on the Crucified....How is it you want to please Him only with words?" Teresa adds that "...it is necessary that your foundation consist of more than prayer and contemplation. If you do not strive for the virtues and practice them, you will always be dwarfs" (IC.7.4.8–9). Our praying should spill over into our actions, leading us to a more accurate appraisal of circumstances and what they call for. Prayer helps to establish virtue as a habit that does not stand still but grows. Detachment from our false self and its demands gives way to a greater recognition of the needs of others and the response God is asking of us. We become more sensitive to the requirements of social justice and to environmental concerns. It does not mean that virtue always becomes easier although, as with any habit, it is more spontaneous. But the willingness to respond virtuously increases, and the recognition of failure in virtue is more acute. We become less defensive of actions that do not respond to grace.

Prayer in the New Millennium

"But, we have the mind of Christ" (1 Cor. 2:16). Yes, but not fully. In every age, Christ speaks with a fresh voice. We are far more aware in our contemporary world of the needy and helpless. Christ appeals to us in the homeless and in the marginalized. Since the sixteenth century of Teresa and John, the Church has had to face issues that the European culture of their time hardly dealt with. That many philosophies have challenged our understanding of Christian faith has forced us to wrestle with questions earlier centuries rarely considered. The legacy of the Enlightenment, as one example, has made us ponder the claims of reason, the rights of the individual, the values embodied in a democratic system. Feminism in its various forms raises the issue of the treatment of women in past ages and in our own. We have been made to examine more closely what was taken for granted.

We turn to scripture and find there meanings not previously uncovered. The mind of Christ is not a closed book but one we are constantly reading as time moves forward. Jesus Christ is the Truth but our vision is too nearsighted to take in the fullness he expresses. The church fathers used the philosophies of Plato and Aristotle to explain doctrine. The church in Ireland happily embraced Christianity without cutting itself off from its Celtic heritage. Today we are in contact with spiritual systems that can expand our own limited understanding. Close at hand, we see the vision of Native Americans. Farther away, practices from the Far East invite our consideration. If we treat other systems only as adversaries, we shut off the possibility that they can awaken us to new dimensions in the deposit of faith. At the same time, we evaluate what is offered and see its implications as measured by our Christian legacy.

We turn to the Holy Spirit, who empowers and enlightens us, to recognize what is according to the mind of Christ. In prayer, for example, we are aiming at something different from a species of altered consciousness, which can entice and sometimes deceive.

Margaret Dorgan

Prayer Becomes More Simple

The tendency, as prayer matures, to need less cognitive input for arousing the heart has particular attraction in our hectic contemporary world. We are drawn to what calms our mental faculties. Special attention is given to spiritual exercises that foster this development. In previous times, pray-ers often had no encouragement to leave meditation practices and could grow weary of their repetition. Yet every technique needs to be weighed in order to test when it is appropriate. With proper timing, simplifying our prayer can release us from the burden of too much thinking. We are drawn to a serene attentiveness that focuses on some aspect of divine mysteries. When our praying needs less input from the mind, we do not compel it to think but neither do we starve it. Very little mental food is nourishing, and spiritual techniques like Centering Prayer, Christian Meditation, the Jesus Prayer, and Mindfulness lead it into deeper peace where God awaits.

Teresa always urges gentleness, no forcing. "Taking it upon oneself to stop and suspend thought is what I mean should not be done...." She tells us that in regard to "...this effort to suspend the intellect...labor will be wasted..." (BL.12.5). She warns against a kind of mental coercion to empty ourselves of thoughts in order to achieve a held absorption. St. Teresa was familiar with this experience in herself and in others, based on a too-demanding cut-down of outside stimuli, that could lead to quietism. "To be always withdrawn from corporeal things...is the trait of angelic spirits, not of those who live in mortal bodies....How much more is it necessary not to withdraw through one's own efforts from all our good and help which is the most sacred humanity of our Lord Jesus Christ" (IC.6.7.6).

In prayer, we assess our inner atmosphere to determine how much mental content helps us to pray. Many variables affect our need: fatigue, physical pain, the pressure of external events. God can lead us to the passive mode of contemplation; on this path we move forward with Jesus. John of the Cross tells us that "...you will discern

92

hidden in him the most secret mysteries, and wisdom, and wonders of God..." (A.2.22.6).

Prayer that Purifies and Illumines

This path of contemplation is a way of purification and illumination. "The gate entering into these riches of God's wisdom is the cross, which is narrow and few desire to enter by it, but many desire the delights obtained from entering there" (SC.36.13). Contemplative prayer causes an experience of interior darkness, which is actually an excess of light overpowering our very human faculties. This light that darkens is a positive inflowing of God which we, however, experience as loss—though not entirely. The pray-er raised to contemplation will recognize fresh strengths even while being more acutely aware of personal weakness. New powers of perception discern with remarkable clarity what leads to God and what does not lead to God. There will be an immersion in darkness and sometimes confusion about oneself; but in dealing with others, light penetrates to the reality of a situation and its ramifications.

Inner purification wrestles with wounded human nature in order to heal it. The pain forces one to cry for a savior. In this world of time, many forms of suffering assail us. Disappointments, loss of material resources, physical agony, the death of loved ones—these tragedies come into our lives like unwelcome visitors, sometimes unexpected and always unwanted. This burden of earthly misery becomes allied to our spiritual purification, a purging that leads us deeper into the experience of Christ.

Teresa comforts us as she did herself with the reflection: "There is no trial that it wasn't good for me to suffer once I looked at You as You were, standing before the judges. Whoever lives in the presence of so good a friend...who went ahead of us to be the first to suffer, can endure all things. The Lord helps us, strengthens us, and never fails; He is a true friend" (BL.22.6).

John of the Cross turns to the Epistle to the Colossians (2:3): "In [Christ] are hidden all treasures and wisdom," and John comments: "The soul cannot...reach these treasures if...she does not first pass over to the divine wisdom through the straits of exterior and interior suffering. For one cannot reach in this life what is attainable of these mysteries of Christ without having suffered much..." (SC.37.4).

In an extremity of pain, Thérèse cries out: "Do not believe I am swimming in consolation; oh, no, my consolation is to have none on earth. Without showing Himself, without making His voice heard, Jesus teaches me in secret" (SS.187). Elizabeth of the Trinity wants to use all the negativity of human living and turn it into something positive. "My weaknesses, my dislikes, my mediocrity, my faults themselves tell the glory of the Eternal!...If I take up this cup crimsoned with the Blood of my Master and...mingle my blood with that of the holy Victim, it is in some way made infinite...."[2] One who is eternal has endured, as we do, the drop by drop experience of pain with each moment moving on to the next, which carries its own fresh measure of sorrow.

Suffering is never enclosed in its own anguish. Faith and hope leap forward to the divine recompense granted for every instant of agony here below. Elizabeth finds comfort in the realization that "He [Christ] wants to associate His Bride in His work of redemption and this sorrowful way which she follows seems like the path of Beatitude to her, not only because it leads there but also because her holy Master makes her realize that she must go beyond the bitterness in suffering to find in it, as He did, her rest."[3]

But such rest is not easily come by, and for many of us, *rest* will be too consoling a word. Of all human experience, pain and loss in their devastating diminishment can make us doubt the merciful love of our creator. Why, why, why rises in our throats. We feel ourselves trapped in our agony. Prayer in the desert of our sorrow can only long for what had been and is no more. Pain is what I undergo in my terrible isolation. Who else can feel what breaks my body or breaks my heart?

Thérèse tried to answer those questions for her sister Céline: "Doesn't He [Jesus] see our anguish, the weight that is oppressing us?...He is not far; He is there, very close. He is looking at us and He is *begging* this sorrow, this agony from us. He needs it for souls and for our soul."[4] We are never alone, for one who is both divine and human enters into what we undergo, experiencing with us the excruciating pain and urging us to make use of it to reach out to others. We ask that the fire of pain consuming our substance be applied to relieve the terrible coldness someone is enduring. In Jesus, we are all brothers and sisters, one family caring for every member. Then my sorrow is not what cuts me off, but rather a bridge to the agony endured by a grieving sibling.

Thérèse understands that one who was destined for crucifixion felt the burden of apprehension and dread. "It is very consoling to think that Jesus, the Strong God, knew our weaknesses, that He trembled at the sight of the bitter chalice, this chalice that He had in the past so ardently desired to drink."[5]

Prayer in the intensity of pain, in the misery of betrayal and destruction, moans and wails. Demonic voices incite us to doubt the good news proclaimed by Christ, telling us it is only a counterfeit assurance meant to deceive us. Doubt gnaws at the foundation of a relationship grounded in love. Beyond the tragedies in our own smaller world, we ask: How could a merciful God who sent the divine Word to take on a Jewish body, allow the Holocaust of six million Jews? Why are there plagues, the slaughter of innocent children, weather disasters that wipe out whole communities? Prayer does not mean the absence of questions, but rather probing them in the obscurity of faith, sinking into the abyss of mystery where we feel there is no foothold to steady ourselves. The depths of human misery call out for a redeemer who assures us "I will not leave you orphaned. I am coming to you" (John 14:18); "...your pain will turn into joy" (John 16:20); "...your hearts will rejoice, and no one will take your joy from you" (John 16:22).

But what if these words sound in the heart like a beautiful message of long ago that no longer convinces the mind? Thérèse describes her Night of Faith: "[Jesus] permitted my soul to be invaded by the thickest darkness, and that the thought of heaven, up until then so sweet to me, be no longer anything but the cause of struggle and torment....One would have to travel through this dark tunnel to understand its darkness" (SS.211–12).

John of the Cross describes such purification as part of the ascent up the mystic mountain to transforming union. Spiritual climbers will encounter storms that shake their inmost being. The tempests will rage according to the personal purification needed. They will fit my personality exactly. "All is meted out according to God's will and the greater or lesser amount of imperfection that must be purged from each one. In the measure of the degree of love to which God wishes to raise a soul, he humbles it with greater or less intensity, or for a longer or shorter period of time" (DN.1.14.5).

A God who becomes incarnate is united to every member of the human race in a new connectedness, which is fellowship. Prayer worships a transcendent divine being, but in Christ the pray-er also finds God on a level of intimacy that has submitted to our own existential boundaries. My subjection to change, human pleasure, and disappointment are now familiar to my God. John writes of "...the deep mysteries of God's wisdom in Christ, in the hypostatic union of the human nature with the divine Word, and in the corresponding union of human beings with God, and the mystery of the harmony between God's justice and mercy with respect to the manifestations of his judgments in the salvation of the human race. These mysteries are so profound...because of the depths of God's wisdom in them" (SC.37.3).

This wisdom is imparted by degrees as prayer advances. Some on the journey forward will have visions of "Christ, or a saint, or His most glorious Mother" (IC.6.8.6), as Teresa describes them. "The Lord leads each one as He sees is necessary....sometimes God leads the weakest along this path. And so there is nothing in it to approve or condemn" (IC.6.8.10).

Prayer in the Bridal Tradition

Prayer, being a movement of the heart, reaches for imagery that depicts the closest union of the lover with the beloved. Spousal and bridal symbolism abound in scripture and in the writings of mystics. John of the Cross describes the yearning of the lover still tied to this world: "...the soul, enamored of the Word, her Bridegroom, the Son of God, longs for union with him through clear and essential vision. She records her longings of love....Through this love she went out from all creatures and from herself, and yet she must suffer her Beloved's absence, for she is not freed from mortal flesh as the enjoyment of him in the glory of eternity requires" (SC.1.2).

In the Spiritual Canticle, Jesus the Bridegroom and the bride/soul speak to each other in words that mix supplication with praise for what is being accomplished. The goal is spiritual marriage where "...the Bridegroom reveals his wonderful secrets to the soul as to his faithful consort....He mainly communicates to her sweet mysteries of his Incarnation and the ways of the redemption of humankind, one of the loftiest of his works and thus more delightful to the soul" (SC. 23.1).

Teresa considers Christ's life on earth and sees every separate incident as taking place for her benefit: "Now I see, my Bridegroom, that *You are mine*....You came into the world for me; for me You underwent severe trials; for me You suffered many lashes; for me You remain in the Most Blessed Sacrament...."[6]

In using marriage similes for spiritual union, writers mirror the customs of their time, as Teresa does in describing the step-by-step progression from the initial meeting of a couple through further acquaintance to the engagement that leads to nuptial vows. The love relationship with Jesus the Bridegroom reflects the familiar pattern of an earthly progress in human love.

In the Romantic period of nineteenth-century France, with its high emotional overtones, bridal imagery is especially prevalent as we see with Thérèse of Lisieux and Elizabeth of Dijon, although it is often used in an almost exclusive manner for vowed religious. John of the Cross's commentary *The Living Flame of Love*, however, was written for a widow, and John is explicit elsewhere: "Each holy soul is like a garland adorned with the flowers of virtues and gifts, and all of them together form a garland for the head of Christ, the Bridegroom" (SC.30.7).

United with Christ, through him and in him, we have unique access to the other two persons of the Trinity. In fellowship with Jesus, we make contact with the inner life of the divine Three in their eternal relationships. Each of the divine Persons becomes an object of worship and love in the divine singularity that makes Father, Word, and Holy Spirit. God "...has given us a new birth into a living hope through the resurrection of Jesus Christ from the dead, and into an inheritance that is imperishable, undefiled, and unfading..." (1 Pet 1:3–4).

John of the Cross in his commentary *The Living Flame of Love* says this: "The Blessed Trinity inhabits the soul by divinely illuminating its intellect with the wisdom of the Son, delighting its will in the Holy Spirit, and absorbing it powerfully and mightily in the unfathomed embrace of the Father's sweetness" (LF.1.15). Commenting on a later stanza, John adds that "...the soul loves through the Holy Spirit, as the Father and the Son love each other, according to what the Son Himself declares through St. John: 'That the love with which you have loved me be in them and I in them'" (John 17:26 [LF.3.82]).

The pray-er has climbed to the peak of the mystic mountain after many trials and interior purification. Now "...God favors [the soul] by union with the Most Blessed Trinity, in which she becomes deiform, God through participation....No knowledge or power can describe how this happens unless by explaining how the Son of God attained and merited such a high state for us..." (SC.39.4–5).

For us—Jesus is always *for us* from the first turning to him in prayer, *for us* as we advance along the passive way of contemplation in darkness or walk a more active path. At the end of the journey, all the difficulties encountered, the struggles to keep going, the exhaustion endured are forgotten in the wonder of what is communicated. There at the summit of union, "...in the taste of eternal life which it here enjoys, it feels the reward for the trials it passed through....It feels not only that it has been compensated...but that it has been rewarded exceedingly. It thoroughly understands the truth of the promise made by the Bridegroom in the Gospel that He would repay a hundredfold (Matt 19:29). It has endured no tribulation or penance or trial to which there does not correspond a hundredfold of consolation and delight in this life..." (LF.2.23).

Blessed Elizabeth of the Trinity asks the Holy Spirit to come upon her "...and create in my soul a kind of incarnation of the Word: that I may be another humanity for Him in which He can renew His whole mystery."[7] Each one of us, unlike any other—a true created original and in the purpose of our existence—is called into time to show forth the wonders of Christ as no one before and as no one after.

Thérèse, whose little way takes hold of all the ordinariness of everyday life, explains the basis for her confidence and hope: "...[Jesus] teaches us that it is enough to knock and it will be opened, to seek in order to find, and to hold out one's hand humbly to receive what is asked for" (SS.257). She writes in capital letters about "...PRAYER which burns with a fire of love. And it is in this way, [the saints] have *lifted the world*; it is in this way that the saints still militant lift it, and that, until the end of time, the saints to come will lift it" (SS.258).

Notes

1. Elizabeth of the Trinity, *I Have Found God; Complete Works,* vol. 1; trans. Aletheia Kane (Washington, D.C.: ICS, 1984), 94.
2. Ibid., 149.
3. Ibid., 147.
4. Thérèse of Lisieux, *General Correspondence,* vol. 1 (1877–1890); trans. John Clarke (Washington, D.C.: ICS, 1982), Letter 57, pp. 449–50.
5. Ibid., vol. 2 (1890–1897), Letter 213, p. 1042.
6. *Meditations on the Song of Songs,* 4.10, *The Collected Works of St. Teresa of Avila,* vol. 2; trans. Kieran Kavanaugh and Otilio Rodriguez (Washington, D.C.: ICS, 1980).
7 Elizabeth of the Trinity, op. cit., 183.

6

Contemplation and the Stream of Consciousness

Kieran Kavanaugh, O.C.D.

The primary complaint of people about their prayer is distractions. What should we do about them, about our minds, as T. S. Eliot writes, "Distracted from distraction by distraction / filled with fancies and empty of meaning"?[1] The advice found in books often leads people to think they must exert themselves to eliminate distractions during prayer, or that certain practices will help them eradicate these nuisances. But I once heard another kind of advice given in answer to this question: "Welcome to planet earth." Although that comment was meant to hit the mark, people are still likely to think to themselves, "There must be someone out there, some guru, who can direct me to another space, unpolluted by distractions." This predominant problem has led me to deal with some pressing questions about the nature of distractions, those pests running back and forth to clot the free flow of prayer. In this essay, then, I propose to draw out what I hope will provide some useful insights from Carmelite classical authors and from recent discoveries and reflections on the workings of our minds.

First, I will focus on some of the teachings found in Teresa of Avila and John of the Cross about distractions in prayer and then compare them. Next, I will consider these in the light of certain theories presented by some modern investigators of consciousness and educe a few conclusions about the reality of a prayer mired in distractions.

Teresa's Teachings

To take Teresa first, her general term *mental prayer* no longer conveys well what she had in mind. Today the word *mental* has a number of connotations that foil the immediate grasp of her meaning. For Teresa, mental prayer includes love and friendship as essential elements. Not only thought is present in this prayer but also emotion, will, memory, and imagination.

What Teresa teaches is that when we begin to pray, knowing through faith that Christ is always looking at us, we should place ourselves in his presence, keep him present by speaking to him, asking him for what we need, complaining to him in our labors, and being glad with him in our enjoyments. We must be with Christ, she insists, relate to him, and enjoy his presence. This is something any of us can do through our own efforts and abilities. Any thinking should be done as a means toward entering into this relationship or communion of friendship with Christ.

But to pursue a relationship of this sort with Christ, whom we cannot perceive through our senses, can hardly come easily. In a bustling world and the excitements of every day, prayer can seem boring or a waste of time, or the source of nothing but useless distractions. Teresa herself admits that the mind fills up with noisy thoughts.

In the development of her experience of prayer, Teresa observed that when she made the effort to enter within herself in what she calls the prayer of recollection (a turning inward to the presence of Christ in the soul's depth), different degrees of recollection seemed to unfold. Then she noticed, as well, that in this very recollection a subtle change took place in which the recollection was aided by a sense of being drawn passively into an inner quiet that did not come from her efforts or submit to her desires. This was the initial stage of passive prayer, of what she calls the supernatural.

Teresa's Terms and Descriptions

In trying to explain the many active and passive elements of prayer, Teresa used the terms she found in the books she read and the sermons she heard. People today, not surprisingly, find it difficult to connect with her terminology and divisions, terms that originated with the ancient and medieval philosophers. Observing the different forms of life activity, these philosophers deduced that, since we can do certain things, we have distinguishable powers for such activities. The external and internal senses are means by which we function at the level of both the sensory and material creation. We can easily conclude that since we are able to see and hear and picture things to ourselves, we have powers, or faculties, for doing such things. But we also have universal ideas, that is, we know the classes that things belong to as particular instances of that class. These ideas or concepts are abstract, imperceptible to the senses. Thus, the reasoning goes, we have other faculties in order to deal with objects imperceptible to the senses, objects like animal, humanity, truth, goodness, beauty.

Psychology for these philosophers is principally concerned with the study of human beings. The analysis of the parts or faculties of the human soul is an analysis of the properties of human nature. But in modern times, psychology has turned its focus away from the faculties to consciousness itself.

Going back to Teresa, to her image of the castle as a tool for explaining the life and development of prayer, she observes that God dwells in the center of the soul and desires to bring its faculties back to this center where the soul will find the Holy Trinity and be united through Christ with our triune God.

In our human efforts to practice the prayer of recollection, Teresa teaches that, though the faculties will keep going far afield, we must keep calling them back and refocusing them on their center. In the passive recollection the Lord, like a meek shepherd, with a whistle so gentle that even they themselves almost fail to hear it (IC.4.3.2), will begin calling them (the faculties) to their center. But even then the faculties will keep turning aside from their recollection. They must again and again be called back by the one engaged in prayer as a way of assisting the Lord. This prayer is partly active and partly passive (WP.26.7).

Teresa, often bewildered, asked how it was possible that the soul could be occupied and recollected in God while the mind, or thought (*pensamiento*), would be distracted (IC IV.1.8). She used terms the meanings of which were vague for her. She wasn't aware of the distinction that the philosophers made between the imagination and the intellect.

The Experience of Mind and Spirit

Only her experience made her begin to realize that there is a distinction between the imagination and the intellect, and when she had her discovery confirmed, perhaps by St. John of the Cross (IC. 4.1.8), it gave her much relief. Even after this, however, she took few pains to be careful in her use of terms. How she came to learn the difference experientially was through her awareness that "the faculties of her soul [spiritual faculties] were occupied and recollected in God" and her mind, or the sense faculty of imagination, was on the other hand distracted (IC.4.1.8).

The restlessness of this mind of hers in prayer was "a real affliction." No matter how hard she tried to do something about it, she did not succeed. Finally, she concluded that there is nothing one can do about it and so there's no point in being disturbed. In her vivid description she says "you just have to let the millclapper go clacking on" (IC.4.1.13).

Teresa usually describes passive prayer by its affective elements of peace, quiet, and sweetness. These proceed from an inner depth where the will finds profound rest in the Lord. The experience, though, added to her awareness of the clamor of the mind or imagination. Her advice remains the same and the terminology imprecise: Don't pay any attention to the "clamor of the intellect." Getting disturbed only makes matters worse; you end up losing what the will enjoys. One "should let the intellect go and surrender oneself into the arms of love" (IC.4.3.8). Do what stirs you to love, she says. The little fire of God's love can be kept alive with simple words of love (BL.15.6). These words are like straws or small pieces of wood. Much thinking will smother the fire.

The prayer of recollection unfolds into the prayer of quiet. In the prayer of quiet the soul feels that God is very close, the awareness of God's presence being given. Teresa explains that in this prayer, similarly, the soul can be completely joined to God in the dwelling places close to the center, while the mind remains on the outskirts of the castle suffering from a thousand wild and poisonous beasts (IC.4.1.9).

At times in prayer God brings the soul still deeper into recollection, when, to borrow from the Song of Songs, the Beloved brings his lover into the inner wine cellar. Here all the faculties stop, or, as Teresa says, are "truly asleep to the things of the world and ourselves" (IC.4.1.4). What happens here is what she terms the suspension of the faculties. The wine cellar itself is the center of the soul where God dwells, and during this union all the powers of the soul are immersed in God. In this prayer Teresa's troubles with the wandering mind cease, that is, for the time that the prayer lasts. In a period of prayer a person may pass in and out of the various stages outlined by Teresa. She did not think that the suspension of the faculties experienced in union lasted long, at the most twenty minutes, although its good effects did last. In sum, distractions are a part of the fabric of prayer, and even provide an unwelcome accompaniment to the experience of the infused prayer of recollection and quiet.

John of the Cross's Terms and Descriptions

John of the Cross spoke as well of our psychological makeup and experience in terms of the faculties of the soul, but he did so with more precision than Teresa, having been schooled in philosophy. He describes human beings as having bodily and spiritual faculties, with the bodily faculties divided into external and internal. In turning to the inner bodily faculties, he speaks of imagination, phantasy, and sense memory. These powers always deal with particular and specific things, events, and persons.

What John then stresses is that the images, figures, or forms present in these faculties cannot serve as adequate, proximate means to union with God. There comes the moment in prayer when they must be left aside, that is, when the loving knowledge of God, gathered through their assistance, becomes habitual, and the need and desire for thinking and imagining decrease. God begins at this point to change his mode of self-communication and bestow directly on the spirit, without the assistance of the inner senses, a more abundant, general, loving knowledge.

Without going into the question of how this change is discerned through certain signs, which John explains in detail, I want to mention two other aspects of this transition. First, in the beginning the loving knowledge, or contemplation, being received from God is hardly perceptible because of its subtlety and delicacy. It is difficult for people immersed in the outer world of the sense to perceive spiritual experience. Only gradually by learning to be calm and unflustered in the midst of sensory dryness does a person begin to grow accustomed to the loss of satisfaction found in the use of the senses. Second, in the contemplative practice of general, loving awareness, the inner sense faculty, called the imagination, will continue to come and go, John says, and will do so even in deep recollection (A.2.13.3).

At moments, though, for John, as for Teresa, the wisdom or loving knowledge abstracts the soul from all activity surrounding particular objects. In this state a person becomes forgetful of all things, unaware of the passing of time, then only knowing God without knowing how she knows him (A.2.14.11).

John and Teresa Compared

With little difficulty we can recognize the similarity between Teresa's teachings on prayer and contemplation and John's. Both admit to an activity on our own part, especially at the beginning, an activity of reading, thinking, and recollection. Both direct this activity to the loving knowledge of, or presence to, or relationship with Christ. In both, we find descriptions of the prayer of recollection, active and passive, of quiet, and of union. Both admit that the wandering mind or imagination is an accompaniment to prayer and even contemplation.

The Stream of Consciousness

At the turn of the century William James published a two-volume work on psychology, which he treated as the description of states of consciousness as such.[2] He held that what the soul is and whether it exists belong to metaphysics. He wanted to turn his attention, not to the soul itself but to the phenomena of mind found in the stream of thought, to the immediately known thing, not to the faculties. By states of consciousness he meant such things as sensations, desires, emotions, reasoning, decisions, and the like. His work demonstrates that the focus in psychology shifted from the vital faculties of the soul to consciousness. The clamor of the internal sense faculties, that so afflicted Teresa, could be referred to in James's term as *the stream of consciousness*. He, it seems, is the source of the term.

According to James while, for example, we listen to a lecture, or read the pages of a book, each of us has thoughts going on in our head and each thought belongs with other thoughts. Our thoughts are a part of our personal consciousness. We can never look directly at a thought in someone else's personal consciousness. We can also notice that our mind or consciousness is constantly changing.

When I wake up in the morning, I recognize that I have come out of my sleep. I mentally take hold once again of my consciousness. My past is greeted and accepted into my present, owned by it, and accepted as belonging together with it in a common self. With respect to this self, I am very sensitive. I experience a special feeling of warmth toward anything belonging to me, to what is mine. Then my consciousness begins to move into plans and projects about the day to come. I feel surges of joy or aversion about them and have to cope with them. But the point is that the time gap during which I was sleeping did not break the continuity of my present consciousness with my past, and my present consciousness looking to the past also projects a continuity with the future.

Consciousness flows like a stream. At times it rushes by quickly, at other times it trails along sluggishly. But it seems to be always moving toward some other place than where it just was. All the things that float through the mind have their psychic overtones. Though they may not be separately observed, they blend with the fundamental image and feeling, suffuse it, and alter it. And, in its perceptions, consciousness is always interested more in one part of its object than in another. But we do more than focus on some things and keep others apart, James theorizes, we actually ignore most of the things before us. We notice only those sensations that are signs to us of things that happen to interest us, whether practically or aesthetically.

We can observe the unsettled slipping and sliding of one thought into another, and can observe, too, the influence that the rise and fall of our own feelings has on our stream of thought.[3]

The Word "Consciousness"

Phenomenal advances have been made in the mapping of the brain and in the understanding of its functioning since William James wrote his influential and prized volumes in psychology. Neurological and neuropsychological experiments reveal many facts now about how the brain inside the human organism engenders the mental patterns that are called the images of an object.

Antonio Damasio, one of the world's most outstanding neurologists in brain function, has written a major work that has received wide acclaim.[4] In his study Damasio points out that the word *consciousness* did not appear until the first half of the seventeenth century. Not even Shakespeare uses the word, although he understood deeply the nature of consciousness. English and German have one word for conscience (*Gewissen*) and a different one for conscious (*Bewustsein*). When the concept behind the word *consciousness* began to emerge, users of Romance languages opted for the word *conscience* to denote it rather than devise a new word. The awareness and study of conscience, however, began long before that of consciousness.[5]

We must see consciousness, Damasio finds, in terms of the *organism* and the *object* and then in terms of the relationships those two hold. The organism is involved in relating to some object. The object causes a change in the organism. Signals are received from the object through varied sensory conduits, such as vision, hearing, and touch, and these are processed in complex ways. Emotional responses to several aspects of the object occur as well. When we recall an object, we recall not just the sensory characteristics of the object but the emotional responses too.[6]

Core Consciousness and Extended Consciousness

Damasio's research in people with brain damage has led him to the conclusion, which resembles the teachings of James, that there are two kinds of consciousness: core consciousness and extended consciousness. Core consciousness is present in the here and now. Extended consciousness includes the lived past and the anticipated future. Wakefulness and consciousness tend to go together, although in two exceptional circumstances the coupling of the two can be broken. For one thing, we are obviously not awake during dream sleep and yet we have some consciousness of the events taking place in the mind. Or again, we can be awake and yet be deprived of consciousness as in persistent vegetative states.

Core consciousness is always present except in deep dreamless sleep or in coma or other transient losses due to anesthesia, head injury, or fainting. The other kind of consciousness, extended consciousness, goes beyond the here and now of core consciousness, both backward and forward. The here and now is flanked by both the past and future. Core consciousness allows you to know for a transient moment that it is you having a sensation of pain, extended consciousness still hinges on the same core you, but that you is now connected to the lived past and anticipated future that are part of your autobiographical record.[7]

The Autobiographical Self

The autobiographical self stems from the uniform recall of selected sets of autobiographical memories. Core consciousness is created in pulses, each pulse triggered by each object that we interact with or that we recall. In core consciousness, the sense of self arises in the passing feeling of knowing, fashioned anew in each pulse. Instead, in extended consciousness, the sense of self arises in the coherent repeated display of some of our own personal memories, the objects of our personal past, those that can easily substantiate our identity, moment by moment, and our personhood.

The continuity of consciousness is based on the steady generation of consciousness pulses, which correspond to the endless processing of myriad objects, and whose interactions, actual or recalled, constantly modify us.

When we talk about a stream of consciousness, we may surmise that there is a single sequence of thoughts. But the stream is likely to carry consciousness of not just one object but several. It is also probable that several brain levels can be involved.

Damasio's research resolves the apparent paradox identified by William James that the self in our stream of consciousness changes continuously as it moves forward in time, even as we retain a sense that the self stays the same while our existence continues. The ever-changing self identified by James is the sense of the core self. It is not so much that it changes but rather that it is transitory. The sense of the self that appears to remain the same is the autobiographical self, because it is based on a storehouse of memories of fundamental facts in an individual biography. These can be recalled and thus provide continuity and apparent permanence in our lives.[8]

Emotions and Feelings

Another discovery of Damasio's is that consciousness and emotion are not separable. The fabric of our minds and of our behavior is woven around continuous cycles of emotions followed by feelings that become known and beget new emotions. He speaks of a running polyphony that underscores both specific thoughts in our minds and actions in our behavior.

Damasio distinguishes between emotion and feeling. In a typical emotion certain regions of the brain, which are part of a largely preset neural system related to emotions, send commands to other regions of the brain and to most everywhere in the body proper. The commands are sent via two routes. One route is the bloodstream, where the commands are sent in the form of chemical molecules that act on receptors in the cells which constitute body tissues. The other route consists of neuron pathways and the commands along this route take the form of electrochemical signals, which act on other neurons or on muscular fibers or on organs such as the adrenal gland, which in turn can release chemicals of their own into the bloodstream.

Many are the causes of emotion and its many shades, subtle and not so subtle. Their human impact depends on the feelings engendered by these emotions. Feelings, in Damasio's study, are inward and private. Emotions are outward and public. It is through feelings that emotions begin their impact on the mind. But the full and lasting impact of feelings requires consciousness, because only with the advent of a sense of self do feelings become known to the individual having them. I can have the emotion of feeling anxious or relaxed, then the feeling that the emotion leads to, but then only suddenly in a given situation realize that I am anxious or that I am relaxed. It is necessary to add the process of consciousness in the aftermath of emotion and feeling for us to know that we have the feeling.

The Spirit

Beyond the psycho-physical, body and mind, lies spirit, another dimension of the human being. In the minds of many—certainly most in the Judeo-Christian Western world—God is essentially spiritual. As spiritual beings we may enter into a relationship with God basic to our total functioning. There is a core of spirituality common to all people just because they are human.

Human beings, then, have a sense that there is something that goes beyond the material core consciousness and extended consciousness. Damasio highlights two abilities allowed by extended consciousness: the ability to rise above the dictates of advantage and disadvantage and the ability for the critical detection of discords that leads to a search for truth and a desire to build norms and ideals for behavior. "These two abilities are not only my best candidates for the pinnacle of human distinctiveness, but they are also those which permit the truly human function that is so perfectly captured by the single word conscience."[9]

This transcendent dimension to human life we can attribute to spirit. Edith Stein, before her conversion to the Catholic faith, in her thesis on empathy noted that as physical nature is constituted in perceptual acts, so a new object realm is constituted through the world of values. In joy, subjects have something joyous facing them, in fright something frightening, in fear something threatening. In considering feelings and their expressions as proceeding from experiences, we have the spirit simultaneously reaching into the physical world, the spirit becoming visible in the living body. This is revealed still more strikingly in the realm of the will. What is willed not only has an object correlate facing the volition, but, since volition releases action out of itself, it gives what is willed reality; volition becomes creative. Our whole cultural world, all that the "hand of man" has formed, all utilitarian objects, all works of handicraft, applied science, and art are reality correlative to the spirit.[10]

The spirit then in its natural activity is tied to the senses. It takes in what they offer it, preserves what has been perceived, recalls it when there is an occasion for doing so, combines it with other things, transforms it, by means of comparing, generalizing, concluding, and so on. The spirit arrives at its notional knowledge, at judgments and conclusions, the acts proper to understanding. In the same way the will naturally acts on what it is offered by the senses, finds its joy in it, seeks to possess it, feels pain at its loss, hopes for possession and fears loss. But the spirit is not meant only to know and enjoy created things. It is a perversion of its original and true being that it should be ensnared in them. The spirit must be disentangled from them and lifted up to the true being for which it has been created.

Disentangling the Spirit

One cannot break free from the snares set by creatures without entering the interior castle. Prayer is the way to consciousness of the things of the spirit, to the spirit's destiny, which naturally lies outside the perception of the senses. To get beyond the material world into the experience of the divine mysteries, various procedures have been developed in different parts of the globe and down through the ages.

In the cultures of the Middle and Far East, especially in the past, those investigating consciousness have generally entered the relevant disciplines of their society such as Buddhism, Yoga, and Sufism. Out of the vast literature dealing with the different methods used in these disciplines, one can sketch briefly some broad outlines without meaning to minimize the wealth and depth of human insight to be found there or deny a certain complexity in the details.

One kind of meditation seeks to confine awareness to a single object, doing this for a definite period of time. The successful outcome of such meditation has received the name *one-pointedness of mind.* If the exercise involves vision, the meditator gazes at the object of meditation continuously. If the meditation is auditory, the sound, chant, or prayer is repeated again and again. In all cases awareness is concentrated completely on the visual object, or the sound. One consequence of the way our central nervous system is structured seems to be that if awareness is restricted to one unchanging object, consciousness of the external world gets turned off.

A second form of meditation exercise is closely related to daily activity. The exercise tries to use ordinary life processes in the training of consciousness. This exercise is seen as an opening up of consciousness. For example, one Buddhist practice stems from one component of the Buddha's Eightfold Path, and is usually termed *right-mindedness.* It requires that you be conscious of each action, develop a present-centered consciousness, and open up awareness of daily activities while engaged in them.[11]

Many schools within these traditions combine the two major types of awareness exercises, devoting half an hour or so twice a day to the concentrative method, the turning off of consciousness, and as much as possible of the remainder of the day to the method of opening up consciousness.

These meditation exercises are intended to cause a shift in the mode of consciousness of the practitioner. In many traditions, the full emergence of this new mode of consciousness has come to be known as a mystical experience. This is a mode of consciousness in which the ordinary awareness of a multiplicity of people and objects disappears to be replaced by the awareness of unity. In addition the vividness and richness of normal consciousness is greatly enhanced, in which linear time loses its significance.

During these practices there is a continual effort to return to the practice away from the interfering stream of consciousness. Much research needs yet to be done to distinguish, if possible, what changes occur in the brain as a result of these practices.

The Teachings of Teresa and John

You have probably often thought to yourselves that some Christian forms of meditation resemble the above practices. Father Ernest Larkin in this book examines two forms of contemplative prayer that have become popular today in Christian circles and that, while drawing from our Catholic tradition and being compatible with Carmelite teachings, also resemble the practices from the East just discussed. Here I only want to mention that what stands out in the teaching of both Teresa and John is the indwelling presence of God and our presence to God through Christ. The presence is always a loving one, a loving attention.

God is lovable above all things; yet, in the weakness of our human minds we need a guide not only to the knowledge but also to the love of divine things; we need sensible objects. This guide freely given to us by God is Christ in his humanity. People devoted to prayer may begin by meditating with the use of their imaginations on the scenes from the life of Christ as presented in the gospels and become present to him and receive his graces in that way. But means live and die, a time comes, as the Carmelites point out, when the images are no longer necessary. The gaze of the devotee fixes on the person of Christ. And in contemplation Christ makes a person ever more conscious of his deep presence.

In the merging into oneness, the Christian does not lose his or her unique personality, but discovers it profoundly and anew. Christian mysticism is an experience of that hoped-for fullness of being in love. Christian mystics express themselves through the poetry of the Song of Songs. St. Teresa's words always stand firm: "the important thing is not to think much but to love much; and so do that which best stirs you to love" (IV.1.7). In Christian contemplative prayer we are dealing not with a bare bones method of concentration but with a personal relationship of love.

The Ecstatic Nature of the Human Person

The human person is created in the image and likeness of the God who goes out, an ecstatic God in eternal Filiation and Spiration, ecstatic in the missions of the Son and Holy Spirit. The human being in its inmost activity is essentially and passionately other-directed, self-losing.

The ecstatic nature of the human person is ultimately rooted in the mystery of the inwardly self-giving Trinity. As Father and Son are for each other in the unity of the Holy Spirit, the human person is always a being for, not a being established in and unto self.

In Carmelite prayer, then, the loving awareness or presence to Christ in faith, in mystery, whether active or passive, is what one seeks to sustain. This is a relationship of love, of friendship, of being for and toward the other.

116

Contemplation and the Stream of Consciousness

In the stream of consciousness this central awareness is present in differing degrees. Sometimes other thoughts so intrude as to take over completely. Sometimes the loving presence is pronounced, at other times it almost secretly lingers in the background. But the stream of consciousness continues as a part of our ordinary psycho-physical makeup and involves a great deal of complex neurological and neuropsychological patterns of activity, in which one thought or feeling or pattern triggers another. These are beyond our control. Both John and Teresa agree that there is no point in becoming bothered by this natural activity of the brain. When we become conscious in prayer that our central focus is not where we want it to be, we must be at peace and calmly refocus on Christ in the mystery of his human-divine, glorified presence, whether dry and dark or satisfying and luminous. A chosen prayer-word may be the piece of straw best suited to keep the fire burning.

In the experience of union it seems that only core consciousness remains, so it is interesting that Teresa would compare this infused form of prayer to what happens in sleep. "The faculties are asleep to the things of the world and to ourselves" (IC.5.1.4).

What can we do then about the stream of consciousness? In a sense the response "Welcome to planet earth" fits the reality of distractions in prayer. Rather than trying to stop the stream of consciousness during our prayer, we can influence it indirectly through love, detachment, and humility, the Christian virtues stressed by our saints. As the love of God grows, God will enter all the more frequently into the stream of consciousness. John teaches that the soul lives where it loves, lives through love in the object of its love (SC.8.3). Through love the soul spurs itself to seek and find God everywhere, in all the creatures of the summer heat, in the winter snowflakes at our feet, in all things, all events. The impassioned lover will go out from self and become fixed on the loved object. God begins to pervade all the pieces, large and small, of the bride-soul's consciousness. Especially does she discover Christ in her neighbor, which prompts her to the services of love. In going out to the Beloved, then, she goes out in freedom from the many entanglements of her attachments and self-interests. The effect left on her consciousness is humility, "her heart or love will not be set on herself or her own satisfaction and gain, but on pleasing God and giving him honor and glory" (SC.9.5).

In the seventh dwelling places of *The Interior Castle*, Martha and Mary join hands together. Action flows into contemplation and contemplation pours over into action. The two are not at odds, the troublesome disassociation ends, "the cavalry at the sight of the waters descended" (SC.40.5). God is found present, though ever hidden, in all of life's activities and events. And the little streams of memories and plans about our past and future all flow easily into God. The spiritual marriage "is like what we have when a little stream enters the sea, there is no means of separating the two" (IC.7.2.4).

Notes

1. *Four Quartets,* "Burnt Norton," III.
2. *The Principles of Psychology,* 2 vols. (New York: Henry Holt, 1980).
3. See William James, *Psychology: Briefer Course* (New York: Henry Holt, 1892), 151–75.
4. *The Feeling of What Happens: Body and Emotion in the Making of Consciousness* (New York: Harcourt Brace, 1999).
5. Ibid., 230–33.
6. Ibid., 133–49.
7. Ibid., see 169–94 for a discussion of core consciousness and 195–217 for a discussion on extended consciousness.
8. Ibid., 217–28.
9. Ibid., 230.
10. Cf. Edith Stein, *On The Problem of Empathy,* vol.3, *The Collected Works of Edith Stein* (Washington, D.C.: ICS, 1989), 91–93.
11. These two main approaches have been explained in detail by Robert E. Ornstein in his *The Psychology of Consciousness,* 2nd ed. (New York: Harcourt Brace Jovanovich, 1977).

7

The Dark Night and Depression

Kevin Culligan, O.C.D.

What is the difference between the dark night and clinical depression? This is the question I am most frequently asked in workshops and seminars on spiritual guidance. In this chapter I summarize my responses over the last twenty years to that question. I do so, not to propose the definitive answer, but in the hope that this summary will provide useful information for both spiritual seekers and spiritual guides who continue to ask the question.

Because of the specific focus of this volume, I address this question primarily in relation to the development of one's prayer life as understood in the Carmelite tradition. Thus, I am not discussing the dark night as a metaphor applied to God, or to the entire spiritual journey (A.1.2.1), or to other phenomena outside Carmelite prayer (e.g., the democratization of the dark night or the dark night of civilization that some suggest Western society is now passing through). I concentrate on identifiable experiences that persons report from their life of prayer to which St. John of the Cross applies the term *dark night*.[1]

In discussing this question, I draw first upon my own experience in prayer and my observations of both the dark night and clinical depression in the lives of those with whom I have worked in spiritual guidance and psychotherapy. A second resource is John of the Cross's presentation of the cause, the purpose, and the phenomena of the dark night. And, finally, I rely upon the descriptions of clinical depression in current psychological theory and practice, realizing that this understanding of depression—its etiology, classification, and treatment—is continually changing with new discoveries both in clinical practice and in psychological research, especially in psychopathology and psychopharmacology.

Deprivation and Loss

John uses darkness as a metaphor to describe deprivations or losses that occur in the life of prayer (A.1.3.1; 4.3; 15.2; DN.2.3.3; 2.7.7). For example, he speaks of our senses being in darkness when we deprive them of the gratification of their appetites in order "to reach union with God" (A.1.5.1–5). Or he describes persons who feel they are in darkness because they seem to have lost the possession of God (DN.2.7.7).

Similarly, persons today use the metaphor of darkness to describe clinical depression, as in *Darkness Visible*, the novelist William Styron's account of his severe depression, or "Out of the Darkness," the story of television star Marie Osmond's post-partum depression in the February 2000 issue of *McCall's*. Here darkness is also used to describe the losses, real or symbolic, that are experienced in clinical depression and are often considered to be its primary cause. It is, in fact, the experience of loss in both the life of prayer and in depression that prompts the question: What is the relationship of John of the Cross's dark nights to modern forms of clinical depression?

In this chapter, we shall review the signs that accompany losses experienced in the life of prayer and the symptoms that emerge from losses in clinical depression. We shall then consider their similarities and differences, and the implications for persons who pray or guide others in prayer according to the Carmelite tradition.

The Life of Prayer

John of the Cross understands the life of prayer as a journey leading to union with God. Persons ordinarily begin this journey with discursive meditation in which they apply their mind and heart to reflection on the mysteries of God and the life of Jesus in order to grow in the knowledge and love of God and in commitment to following Jesus. Discursive meditation is primarily sensory, involving both the external senses and the imagination and memory. One applies the senses to the object of meditation in order to be moved to an emotional response toward that object.

For example, a leader of a meditation group begins a session inviting the group to imagine that they see Jesus tied to a pillar, accepting the scourging of the Roman soldiers for love of them. Later, after a period of quiet reflection on this scene, the leader then instructs the group: "Now, allow yourselves to be moved in love to embrace Jesus by resolving to serve him more courageously in his people." The purpose of such discursive meditation is to fire the affections with "love's urgent longings" (A.1.14) so that persons might be motivated to seek all their pleasure and delight in God and begin to see all things in relation to God rather than solely as sources of self-gratification. John thus considers discursive meditation as the prayer of beginners on the spiritual journey. It is centered primarily in the sensory or most exterior portion of a person's life. Its purpose is to strengthen the sensory self in the ways of God.

Once the commitment to seeking God in the sensory self is sufficiently strengthened through discursive meditation, God begins to lead the person to divine union through contemplative prayer. In contrast to discursive meditation, a person now quiets rather than exercises the external and internal senses in order to receive God's own self-communication. This now becomes one's principal way of praying. One experiences this communication or "inflow of God" (DN.1.10.6; 12.4; DN.2.5.1; SC.13.10; LF.3.49) in the more interior part of the personality or in the spiritual self. The communication is also experienced as knowledge and love that not only purifies persons of their deep resistances to God, but also unites them with God. John applies the term *proficients* to those who are new to and progressing in contemplative prayer, and the *perfect* to those who have been transformed completely in God through contemplative prayer and whose union with God is as complete as possible in this life.

Thus, John of the Cross's three stages in the journey of Christian prayer are: (1) the stage of beginners, or those who practice discursive meditation and whose prayer life is centered in the activity of the sensory self; (2) the stage of proficients, or those who have progressed beyond discursive meditation into contemplative prayer that is centered in the spiritual self; and (3) the stage of the perfect, those whose contemplative prayer has brought them wholly to union with God in love and has totally transformed them—body and soul, sense and spirit—in Jesus Christ, the Risen Lord. These three stages correspond generally to the stages of Christian prayer traditionally called the purgative way, the illuminative way, and the unitive way (SC.theme.1–2).[2] As we shall see in the following section, the losses experienced in prayer that John describes with the metaphor of darkness are caused by an intensification of contemplation or God's self-communication to the person, which purifies the person, first at the level of the sense, and then at the level of spirit, so that, eventually, the entire person may be one with God, transformed in divine knowledge and love.

Discursive Meditation and the Dark Night of Sense

Not long after one seriously begins the journey of prayer through discursive meditation, one encounters the first period of darkness. Persons lose the sensory satisfaction in prayer that they had become accustomed to. John also calls this often-abrupt loss of sensory pleasure dryness or aridity [*sequedad*] (A.2.12.6–7; 13.2; DN.1.9.1–4; LF.3.32–3).

This period, the dark night of sense, begins when persons simultaneously experience three distinct phenomena. First, there is an inability to continue the practice of discursive meditation. No matter how hard persons try, they discover that they are unable to apply their mind, their external senses, imagination, and memory to point-by-point reflection upon the mysteries of God or the life of Christ.

In addition to not being able to meditate discursively, persons also find that they no longer derive any emotional satisfaction from the spiritual journey. The enthusiasm has gone out of both their prayer and spiritual or religious practices and their other relationships. They begin to question whether the idea of leading a spiritual life is an illusion and think that perhaps they have been mistaken to begin this journey in the first place.

Despite the inability to meditate discursively and the loss of pleasure in prayer and spiritual practices, a person nonetheless feels a deep commitment to seeking union with God and following Christ as the Way to this union. As pained and as confused as persons now are because of their difficulties with discursive meditation and loss of fervor, this third phenomenon is an essential requirement to determine whether one is, in fact, in the dark night of sense. The inability to meditate discursively in itself does not indicate the dark night; the person may simply have given up the spiritual journey and decided against a life of prayer. Nor does the loss of felt satisfaction by itself necessarily suggest the presence of the dark night. This might be attributable simply to physical or mental illness, which diminishes all desire to pray. But the presence of the three phenomena together is a reliable sign that the dryness one now experiences in prayer is symptomatic of the dark night of sense.

In practice it may take some time (weeks, possibly several months) to determine whether all three phenomena are present together. When I am uncertain about the simultaneous presence of these three signs, I might ask a person: "What if you were to give up this whole idea of a prayer life?" When that question is met with indifference or long-winded rationalizations, I suspect the person's difficulties are due to some cause other than the dryness of the dark night of sense. But, if someone responds emotionally, sometimes with tearful eyes or cracking in the voice, saying something like "Oh, I couldn't do that! This is my whole life," then I feel more confident that the person is undergoing the loss or dryness that John of the Cross calls the dark night of sense.

John attributes this dryness or dark night of sense primarily to the deepening of God's self-communication to the person. God is now beginning to communicate more directly to the person's spirit or in the interior of the spiritual self, leaving the senses or the exterior self empty and dry. This dryness results from the loss of sensible delight one previously felt in spiritual practices. In Freudian language, dryness purifies the pleasure principle. The result of this dark night of sense, or first major crisis in the journey of contemplative prayer, is that persons must now decide whether they want to seek the living God in prayer or whether they want simply to continue gratifying their need for sensory pleasure through spiritual practices. When persons decide it is God they desire more than self, the spiritual guide assists them through this critical period by assuring them that their experience is developmental (that is, normal and predictable); that discursive meditation and fervent feelings are no longer necessary for their spiritual journey; that they can trust their deeply felt desire for God, and simply sit quietly in God's presence and allow God to communicate more directly to their spirit.

God and Self: the Dark Night of Spirit

After passing through the dark night of sense, one's prayer life ordinarily becomes increasingly contemplative. Persons now attend lovingly to God present in the depths of their own being and quietly open their interior self to receive the inflow of God. They become aware of a divine loving knowledge present within themselves gradually transforming their whole outlook on life and their entire way of being in the world. After some years, however, this loving knowledge produces a second night that purifies persons in the depths of their spirit and readies their entire being for complete transformation in God through love.

This second night may come upon a person gradually and continue for months or even years depending on how deeply the person must be purified to be transformed in God (DN.2.7.3–4). This night is filled with interior pain. Persons complain that they see the disorder in their own lives as they never have before and yet feel completely helpless to change themselves for the better. They are horrified when they see clearly the self-seeking in even their most altruistic motives and cannot believe that they are so alienated from God, themselves, others, and the universe. They often feel an interior emptiness that no diversion can possibly relieve. At the same time, they believe that they no longer know God, that the God they related to so lovingly at earlier stages of their contemplative journey has vanished, and that, even if there is a God, that God could not possibly accept them because of the depravity they see in themselves (DN.2.10.2).

The cause of this pain, John maintains, is the light of God's self-communication to the person, the contemplative knowledge that allows persons to see both God and themselves as they actually are, not as they had formerly imagined God or themselves to be. These are the losses of the dark night of spirit: persons are forced to let go of cherished self images and long-held God images that are no longer tenable in the contemplative light of what they now see. The loss of these images is for the person an experience of death, with all the consequent feelings of anger, sadness, guilt, and grief. These losses are so profound that, were it not for the periodic insights into God's incomprehensible goodness that are also characteristic of the dark night of spirit, one could not emotionally survive this night.

The dark night of spirit ends when these alternating visions of God's goodness and one's own disorder cease (DN.2.18.4). At that point a person's entire life is centered in God and no longer in self. There is no need for further purification. The person's union with God is complete, filled with inner peace, even though externally one may continue to carry heavy burdens or face apparently insurmountable problems. The painful night of the spirit is necessary for the light of God's self-communication to purify persons from their deep-rooted attachments to false images of God and self that were obstacles to their transformation in God. During this dark night of spirit, a spiritual guide's primary support to persons is to walk with them in this time of purification with caring and empathic understanding until God's purifying work is finished, "for until then no remedy—whatever the soul does, or the confessor says—is adequate" (A.Prol.5; DN.2.7.3).

In summary, the dryness of the dark night of sense and the desolation, anguish, confusion, grief, unworthiness, and other interior pain of the dark night of spirit are the effects of God's increasing self-communication to the person that purifies, first, the disordered attachments of the sensory self and, second, the disordered attachments of the spiritual self, so that the entire person might eventually be free of any obstacle to transformation in God.

Clinical Depression

Now let us look briefly at our current understanding of clinical depression before comparing this psychological condition to John of the Cross's dark nights of sense and spirit. Depression is primarily an affective or mood disorder, a disturbance in the way we feel, rather than, as in schizophrenia, the way we think. Our thought processes may be greatly disturbed, even delusional, in depression, but this results primarily from our disrupted mood. Mood disturbances vary along a wide continuum from, at one end, dysphoria or the unpleasant feeling of simply being down in the dumps to, at the other end of the continuum, a state of severe emotional pain that impairs one's normal functioning and requires some kind of medical or psychological intervention. I use the term clinical depression here to refer to those conditions of depression that are serious enough to require professional treatment.

Clinical depression can take many forms: simple depressive disorders or unipolar depression, where serious depression alone is the major feature; bipolar disorders, where depressive episodes alternate with periods of highly agitated or manic activity; dysthymic disorder or a less severe form of depression but with depressed mood lasting over a period of at least two years; depression related to identifiable causes such as post-partum depression; and depression associated with known medical conditions like Parkinson's disease, Huntington's disease, or AIDS.[3]

In a major depression, whether seen by itself alone or in conjunction with other conditions, the prominent symptoms are the following: a person exhibits a dysphoric mood and looks downcast or worried most of the day, nearly every day, and speaks of feeling sad or empty; there is a diminished interest or pleasure in one's activities, most of the day, every day; the appetite is disturbed, causing either undereating or overeating, which in turn leads to significant change in weight, either weight loss not due to a planned diet, or weight gain up to 5 percent of the normal body weight in a month's time; difficulties with sleep, either not being able to fall asleep, or sleeping too much, nearly every day; psychomotor retardation or agitation observable to others nearly every day; fatigue or loss of energy nearly every day; decreased sexual drive; feelings of worthlessness or excessive and inappropriate guilt; diminished ability to think or concentrate, or indecisiveness nearly every day either by subjective account or as observed by others; inability to take care of oneself; and recurring thoughts of death—not fearing to die but wanting to die—and recurring suicidal ideation, often with a specific plan for taking one's own life, and sometimes actual suicidal attempts.

A person is considered clinically depressed when five or more of the above symptoms have been present during the same two-week period and at least one of the symptoms is either depressed mood or loss of interest or pleasure. Furthermore, a serious depression is present when these symptoms represent a marked change from previous behavior and significantly disturb social, occupational, or other important areas of functioning that cannot be accounted for by a known general medical condition, for example, hypothyroidism; or the direct physiological effect of a substance, for example, prescription medication, illegal drugs, and alcohol; or bereavement.

A dysthymic disorder, although not as acutely painful and serious as major depression, presents many of the same symptoms over a longer period of time. Thus, one might have "a depressed mood for most of the day, for more days than not, as indicated either by subjective account or observation by others, for at least two years."[4] Persons with dysthymia generally manifest two or more of the following symptoms: eating disturbances; sleep disturbances; low energy or fatigue; low self-esteem; poor concentration or difficulty making decisions; feelings of futility and hopelessness. The person is seldom without these symptoms for more than two months at a time; and while they may not greatly disrupt one's daily life as a serious depressive episode does, yet one seldom functions at full steam or feels good about one's life.[5]

Theories abound as to the exact cause of depression. These include genetic, biological, neurochemical, sociocultural, and psychological explanations, each supported by considerable research. Although in specific cases, one or a combination of the above etiological factors may be the identifiable cause of a major depressive episode, the experience of loss, real or symbolic, is a prominent feature in most cases of clinical depression. For example, the loss of a spouse in death is accompanied by grieving that exhibits many of the features of depression, but which are considered normal for several months following the death. But when the symptoms continue to persist for months or there appears marked functional impairment, morbid preoccupation with worthlessness, suicidal talk, or psychomotor retardation, we see that grieving has now become serious depression. Menopause in women or retirement in men, while normal occurrences in adult life, may trigger a major clinical depression because they symbolize a loss of productive womanhood or manhood. Even in cases where the onset of a depressive episode seems clearly due to an inherited genetic constitution or an imbalance of neurochemistry, persons often feel deeply their loss of normal functioning, sometimes with anger turned in on themselves for their weakness of character, which then reinforces the feelings of low self-esteem that usually accompany depression.

If there is little consensus about the exact cause of depression, there is also little agreement as to the ideal treatment for major depressive episodes. "We know everything there is to know about mental illness," I remember one of my psychology professors telling us, "except what causes it and how to cure it." This is true in clinical depression. The most typical approaches to treating depression include: psychopharmacology (antidepressants and other psychoactive drugs), electroconvulsive therapy (shock treatments), alternative therapies (vitamin, minerals, and nutritional therapies; acupuncture; massage; deep breathing exercises, etc.), psychotherapy (cognitive therapy, rational emotive therapy, behavior therapy, feminist therapy, etc.), and hospitalization. Because some therapies prove effective with some persons and not with others, or for some periods in a person's life, but not for later episodes, the therapy must be always fitted to the person with each depressive episode. William Styron, for example, in the major depression he described so movingly in his *Darkness Visible*, found that neither antidepressants nor psychotherapy worked for him. Only with hospitalization was he able to find his way back to sanity.[6] Although depression tends to recur, it is highly amenable to treatment. Even with repeated episodes, one or a combination of therapies will usually restore the depressed person to normal functioning.

The Dark Night and Clinical Depression

Having described the symptoms of both the dark night and clinical depression, I would like now to explain how I distinguish between the two in actual practice. Although loss is common to both, this loss is manifested differently in each case. In the dryness of the dark night of sense, for example, there is a loss of pleasure "in the things of God" and in "creatures" (DN.1.9.1), but there is not the dysphoric mood, the psychomotor retardation, the loss of energy or the loss of interest or pleasure in hobbies and enjoyable activities, including sex, that one typically sees in clinical depression. And, while those in the dryness of the dark night of sense are unable to apply their minds and imagination to discursive meditation, they have little difficulty in concentrating and making decisions in daily life.

In the dark night of spirit, there is a painful awareness of one's own incompleteness and imperfection in relation to God; however, one seldom utters morbid statements of abnormal guilt, self-loathing, worthlessness, and suicidal ideation that accompany serious depressive episodes. Thoughts of death do indeed occur in the dark night of spirit, such as "death alone will free me from the pain of what I now see in myself" or "I long to die and be finished with life in this world so that I can be with God," but there is not the obsession with suicide or the intention to destroy oneself that is typical of depression. As a rule, the dark nights of sense and spirit do not, in themselves, involve eating and sleeping disturbances, weight fluctuations, and other physical symptoms (such as headaches, digestive disorders, and chronic pain).

I can usually tell whether persons are depressed or in the dark night by attending closely to my own interior reactions as these persons describe their inner experience. As a disorder of mood or affect, depression communicates across personal relationships. Depressed persons typically look depressed, sound depressed, and make you depressed.[7] After listening to depressed persons describe their suffering, I myself begin to feel helpless and hopeless, as though the dejected mood of persons with depression is contagious. I also frequently feel deep pity for the "profound rejection and hatred of the self" that characterize persons who are truly depressed.[8] By contrast, I seldom feel down when I listen to persons describe the dryness of the dark night of sense or the painful awareness of God and self that accompany the dark nights of sense and spirit. Instead, I frequently feel compassion for what persons suffer as they are spiritually purified, together with admiration for their commitment to do all that God asks. In fact, at these times I feel my own self being energized. It seems that the strengthening of spirit that God brings to persons through darkness is also communicated to me.

With persons whose symptoms are clearly only those of the dark night of sense or spirit, I assist them in the transition from meditative prayer to contemplative prayer in the case of dryness and by being a faithful and empathic companion as they journey through the ups and downs of the dark night of spirit. In these cases, I assume that, as John of the Cross observes, God's self-communication is deepening in these persons, strengthening their spirit, transforming their customary ways of knowing and loving, and preparing them for divine union.

But we cannot always presuppose that persons are either in a dark night or in a serious depression. They may be experiencing both at the same time. A middle-aged father might concurrently be dry in his prayer and also struggling with feelings of worthlessness, losing sleep, and too preoccupied to enjoy downtime with his children or sexual relations with his wife due to a sudden and unexpected loss of employment that has placed his family's financial security in serious jeopardy. Or a woman in her fifties who feels the deep spiritual pain of not knowing whether God really exists may also discover that she cannot get over the grief—the morbid preoccupation with life having no meaning, psychomotor retardation, and suicidal ideation—she has felt since her husband's death from brain cancer six months earlier. In these cases, I attend closely to the symptoms of the night, but do not discount the seriousness of the depression. As a rule of thumb, if these symptoms continue for up to a month, I always recommend professional treatment for the depression. I point out the seriousness of their condition, the effectiveness of professional treatment with depression, and assure them that I will continue to be their spiritual guide, and in consultation with the other professionals involved in their care if that collaboration seems appropriate.

There are also times when persons do not manifest any of the characteristics of the critical periods of darkness in the journey of prayer, but may be seriously depressed as a result of such natural causes as genetic predisposition, biochemical imbalance, sociocultural influences, or an identifiable serious loss. When symptoms of serious depression emerge in persons I work with as a spiritual guide, I address them directly and, if they are serious enough, recommend professional treatment, often suggesting the family physician as the first resource. Frequently, religious persons initially resist this treatment, regarding their symptoms as a sign of spiritual weakness and preferring to manage them with prayer and spiritual practices. I point out to them that their need for treatment itself may indeed be an occasion for spiritual growth, especially in self-knowledge and self-acceptance, and remind them of the known benefits of treatment, particularly medication, for stabilizing their emotions and allowing them to resume a regular prayer life.

In addition to serious depression, spiritual guides should also be alert to three other conditions that may appear in persons they work with that are related to depression: dysthymic disorder, manic episodes, and risk of suicide. Although not as serious as a major depression, the dysthymic condition leaves a person in a dysphoric mood most of the time for more than two years. Religious and spiritual activity—prayer, spiritual practice, and social involvement—easily mask dysthymic symptoms like low energy or fatigue, low self-esteem, feelings of hopelessness, poor concentration, difficulty making decisions, and not functioning up to par socially, occupationally, or interpersonally. While such symptoms might be interpreted as the cross one carries in the spiritual life, they can also be attributed to unrecognized losses. These might include one's marriage and family life not being quite what one had expected, one's religious community being a disappointment from what one had imagined, or one's occupation, while providing a generous income, not offering the personal challenge or creative outlet that one had hoped. If, over a two-year period, a person has not been without one of the above symptoms for more than two months at a time, a spiritual guide might suspect a dysthymic condition and recommend professional evaluation and, if positive, appropriate treatment.

The spiritual life can also easily mask a bipolar disorder or what has traditionally been called a manic-depressive condition. As a mood disorder, depression has usually been linked in systems of classifications of mental disorders with mania, an agitated mood that is at the other end of the affective continuum opposite a depressed or dysphoric mood. Manic symptoms are many: inappropriate elation, excessive irritability, severe insomnia, grandiose notions, increased talking, disconnected and racing thoughts, heightened sexual desire, markedly increased energy, poor judgment, and disruptive social behavior. These symptoms may suddenly appear in a person committed to the spiritual journey and life of prayer as making dramatic prophetic gestures, for example, standing on the street corner denouncing abortion or announcing the imminent Second Coming, or giving away one's financial savings to charitable causes. Teresa of Avila and John of the Cross both stress that social consciousness and service of others are effects of genuine contemplative prayer. However, the sudden, extreme, and, to one's family and friends, embarrassing character of a manic episode makes it easily distinguishable from the social fruits of contemplative prayer. Two or more of the manic symptoms noted above continuing over a two-month period can be an indicator of a bipolar disorder. As with serious depressive symptoms, evaluation and, if necessary, treatment are recommended. Just as we suspect something wrong when a person is continually down, with low energy, and withdrawn, so we also suspect something amiss when a person is on a continual high, with boundless energy, and talking incessantly. The diagnostic rule of thumb with mood disorders is balance between ups and down. When we observe someone at either end of the mood continuum, higher or lower than we expect in normal everyday life, we may suspect a bipolar condition that is possibly in need of treatment.

Finally, I never discount the possibility of suicide in spiritual guidance. Ordinarily, you do not anticipate self-destruction in those committed to a life of prayer or motivated by religious ideals. However, suicide is always a risk in persons with serious depression. Moreover, given enough pressure, suicide can readily appear as possibly the only solution to an overwhelming personal problem, as we have seen in clergymen accused of sexual misconduct and religious diagnosed with AIDS. I therefore listen attentively when a person speaks about death. Does "I want to die" express a longing for life in this world to end so that one can finally be with God—an expression often seen in Christian mystical literature—or is it a cry for help of one whose life suddenly seems in terrible disarray? Asking persons directly what they mean by wanting to die; what they imagine when they think about death; if they ever think of taking their own life, and if so, how often, for what reason, and by what means generally brings information that helps me determine the degree of suicidal risk. The more serious the risk, the more cautiously I proceed, possibly involving other resources, such as family or physician or concurrent crisis counseling, until the precipitating crisis is past.

As you can readily see, I follow a collaborative approach to assisting others with their spiritual journey. With most persons, this assistance is primarily spiritual and religious. Following the principles of the spiritual masters, I help persons with the dryness, interior pain, and whatever else they encounter in the life of prayer. However, when signs typically associated with clinical depression—major depressive episodes, dysthymic disorders, bipolar reactions, and threat of suicide—also appear, I am prepared to consult with, and possibly make referrals to, medical or mental health professionals. I point out to persons the spiritual benefit of using these resources and assure them that I will continue to walk with them as their spiritual guide.

Following the same collaborative model, I may also point out to other helping professionals, when it seems appropriate to do so, that not all dryness or interior suffering is symptomatic of clinical depression. Medication and psychotherapy are not the best treatments for the losses of the dark nights. Indeed, persons may find that, while Prozac relieves some symptoms of depression, the spiritual dryness and interior pain associated with changing images of God and self remain. Paradoxically, modern psychopharmacology underscores what spiritual seekers have known for centuries—that, in addition to body and mind, there is also a spiritual dimension in human life. The spirit, while interactive with mind and body, has its own rules and laws of development and is often beyond the reach of psychopharmacology and psychotherapy. And it is at this deeper level of human life—sometimes called the substance of the soul or the innermost dwelling places of the soul—that persons of prayer most consistently encounter God.

The Benefits of Loss

To this point I have compared and contrasted the psychological phenomena associated with John of the Cross's dark nights and clinical depression, possibly at the risk of minimizing the unique way God purifies each soul and the suffering that accompanies each condition. I have suggested guidelines that spiritual guides may follow in working with persons struggling through the nights and/or serious depression. I would like to conclude now with some words on the benefits of loss. Identifying loss as common to the life of prayer and to clinical depression suggests that loss is an essential part of human life in this world. Rather than signs of dysfunction to be avoided at all costs, they are, rather, reminders that we do not find our ultimate fulfillment in this world. Paradoxically, we cannot become fully human (physically, emotionally, mentally, socially, spiritually) without relationship to countless material, spiritual, and personal objects; yet, neither can we attain our final goal, transformation in God through love, without eventually letting go of our attachment to these same objects. We are, John of the Cross reminds us, created infinite capacities for God and God alone satisfies the boundless longings of our body, mind, and soul. The losses of life, with all their pain and suffering, are continual reminders of this reality.

For this reason, darkness—a metaphor for human loss—is more often blessing than curse. It teaches us that no spiritual feeling, no self-concept, no image of God, no human relationship, no worldly achievement is worth more than God or can replace the thrill of knowing, loving, and, ultimately, being with God forever. John of the Cross lists some of the spiritual benefits of darkness in his letter to a young woman for whom he was a spiritual guide and who had written to him complaining of her darkness.

> You were never better off than you are now because you were never so humble or so submissive, or considered yourself and all worldly things to be so small; nor did you know that you were so evil or that God was so good, nor did you serve God so purely and so disinterestedly as now, nor do you follow after the imperfections of your own will

and interests as perhaps you were accustomed to do....
...God does one a great favor when he darkens the faculties and impoverishes the soul in such a way that one cannot err with these. And if one does not err in this, what
need is there in order to be right other than to walk along
the level road of the law of God and of the church, and
live only in dark and true faith and certain hope and complete charity, expecting all our blessings from heaven, living here below like pilgrims, the poor, the exiled, orphans,
the thirsty, without a road and without anything, hoping
for everything in heaven? (Letter 19, to Juana de Pedraza,
pp. 754–55)

Embracing darkness is possibly the most important spiritual
practice in the life of prayer. As we work through the inevitable losses
of our life, whatever their cause, and also assist others in doing so, we
praise God's mercy to us and learn to say with St. Paul: "...I regard
everything as loss because of the surpassing value of knowing Christ
Jesus my Lord" (Phil 3:8).

Notes

1. I wrote this chapter during the 1999–2000 academic year when I was
writer-in-residence at Saint Mary's College, Notre Dame, Indiana. I am
deeply grateful to Dr. Marilou Eldred, Saint Mary's president, for inviting me to the college; Prof. Keith J. Egan, then Director of Saint Mary's
Center for Spirituality, for arranging a foundation grant to underwrite
my stay on campus; Sister Bernice Hollenhorst, C.S.C., Director of
Saint Mary's Cushwa-Leighton Library, and her staff, for their unfailing
assistance to all my research needs; and to the entire Saint Mary's community—students, faculty, and staff—for their warm welcome, interest,
and encouragement during my stay on campus.
2. For a description of these stages or ways, see Thomas McGonigle,
"Purgation, Purgative Way," "Illumination, Illuminative Way," "Union,
Unitive Way" in *The New Dictionary of Catholic Spirituality*, ed. Michael

Downey (Collegeville, Minn.: Liturgical Press, 1993), 529–31, 800–802, 987–88.

3. American Psychiatric Association, *Diagnostic and Statistical Manual of Mental Disorders*, 4th ed. (Washington, D.C.: American Psychiatric Association, 1994), 317–91.

4. Ibid., 349.

5. Marilyn Sargent, *Depression: What You Need to Know* (Rockville, Md.: National Institute of Mental Health, n.d.), 3.

6. William Styron, *Darkness Visible: A Memoir of Madness* (New York: Vintage Books, 1992), 51–75.

7. Kenneth Tepe, *Depression and Suicide: Multidisciplinary Assessment and Treatment* [audiocassettes] (Silver Spring, Md.: American Healthcare Institute), tape 1, side 1.

8. Raymond J. McCall, *The Varieties of Abnormality: A Phenomenological Analysis* (Springfield, Ill.: Charles C. Thomas, 1975), 142.

8

Transformation and Divine Union in the Carmelite Tradition

Vilma Seelaus, O.C.D.

The Human Reality: Rooted in God

Carmel's tradition of union with God and divine transformation makes sense only within a biblical anthropology that roots the person in God. God is the partner of the human. In God we live and move and have our being. The prophets reiterate the depths of God's covenant love in passionate language. God delights in us. We are loved with an everlasting love. God's goodness and kindness pursue us everyday of our lives (Isa 62:4; Jer 31:3; Ps 23:6).

God's covenant love with Israel becomes enfleshed in Jesus whose life and teachings unfold the deep mystery of trinitarian communion. In the Gospel of John, Jesus invites his followers into an intimacy of indwelling just as Father and Son indwell each other in the Holy Spirit. Jesus became our access into the deep mystery of the eternal self-giving of the divine persons, one to the other. His journey to a death of total outpoured love captures this mystery in each one of us to the extent that we open ourselves to love. From profound experience, mystics like Teresa and John of the Cross knew with certitude that *God* is personally present where we are most ourselves. In fact, the soul's center is God (BL.40.5,10; LF.1.12). From the dark closet of his imprisonment, John learned that no time or place or circumstance exists in which God is not present. Even in the worst of circumstances, God is always present as abiding offer.

It should be known that God dwells secretly in all souls and is hidden in their substance, for otherwise they would not last. Yet there is a difference, a great difference, in his dwelling in them. In some souls he dwells alone, and in others he does not dwell alone. Abiding in some he is pleased; and in others, he is displeased. He lives in some as though in his own house, commanding and ruling everything; and in others as though a stranger in a strange house, where he is not permitted to give orders or do anything (LF.4.14).

In *The Spiritual Canticle*, John describes the modes of God's presence. God's essential presence gives us life and being. God also abides in the soul through grace, and finally God engages the soul through what John calls spiritual affection. Through spiritual affection God refreshes, delights, and gladdens the soul (SC.11.3). The essential union of the soul with God, through which God holds us in being, is like a tiny spark of divine love that God, throughout life, coaxes into a living flame. Both Teresa and John encourage readers to fix their eyes on Jesus, who is the symbol of God's passionate love for each person individually.

God Opens the Door to Our Deepest Self

Teresa maintains that God's presence is so vital to human life that God alone can give access into the deepest dimension of the self, which, for Teresa, is like an inner wine cellar where love freely flows. As Charles Vergé names this impermeable aspect of our being,[1] this inner depth of the divine self is not accessible to us through human effort. Teresa affirms this reality in the fifth dwelling places. God, says

Teresa, brings us into the inner wine cellar and puts charity in order within her (IC.5.2.12). Think for a moment what this means. The wine cellar is the deepest dimension of the self; yet, we cannot approach this inner space until and unless God places us there. To enter the inner wine cellar is the fruit of mystical union with God, however transitory. Teresa writes:

> I understand this union to be the wine cellar where the Lord wishes to place us when He desires and, as he desires. But, however the great effort we make to do so, we cannot enter. His majesty must place us there and enter Himself into the center of our soul. (IC.5.1.12)

Only through union with God can we access our deepest self (see LF.9–13). No amount of inner work on our part brings us there. The deepest part of us is accessible only through a relationship of faith with God. It is God who leads us into the deeper reaches of the human. Using Teresa's imagery, we dispose ourselves by becoming like soft wax ready for the divine imprint (IC.5.2.12). Teresa's experience suggests that mysticism, an ever-deepening faith relationship with God, is essential to full human development. Here, within the inner wine cellar of the divine self, God, through touches of divine union, transforms the waters of our prayer-relationship with God into inebriating wine. Such experiences, however brief, are but a foretaste of the nuptial espousal and union of the soul with its God in the sixth and seventh dwelling places.

The Lover and the Beloved

In accord with biblical imagery, mystics through the ages have used the symbol of the love relationship between man and woman as most expressive of the soul's relationship with God. Images of spiritual espousal and mystical marriage serve as icons into deep truths.

Although these icons are stammering attempts to articulate the inexpressible, in the end they remain the best symbolic language for understanding the reality of the soul united with God. To the extent that faith is alive, God's self-communicating love calls forth our human transcendent potential. The activation of faith, hope, and love creates spiritual energy that propels the soul's relationship with God toward its consummation in divine union. In this context, faith is not to be understood simply as belief in the dogmas of the church, but principally in the person of Jesus Christ as God's abiding invitation to loving intimacy. Faith in Christ initiates an exchange of love with God, who already embraces the soul in its center. As Schneiders points out:

> Jesus' witness is an invitation to accept this unreserved divine love, to response in love, and thus to create a shared life with God....The "place" of that relationship is Jesus himself, in whom God is present and available. The disciple is invited to a mutual indwelling with Jesus as Jesus and the One who sent him indwell each other, as a branch inheres in a vine. And out of this mutual indwelling love will come the works of the disciple, the lasting fruit that the disciple in union with Jesus will bear to the glory of God.[2]

Just as we have many languages for human communication, so too we have a language of the soul. Faith, hope, and love are the language of prayer and of communion with God. This language is God's gift and God's Spirit guides us to fluency. As God's indwelling spirit activates faith, hope, and love, these become dynamic energy that increasingly opens us to God. The soul of our believing, hoping, and loving is in fact the Spirit of Jesus breathing love through us. Day by day the Spirit of Jesus forms and transforms all that is human into divine likeness until we are ready to live within the habitual embrace of God in spiritual marriage (SC.20/21:14).

Prayer: The Channel for
God's Self-Communicating Love

God ever addresses and discloses God's self to us with a desire for loving intimacy. We may remain indifferent to God's self-disclosure. But if we respond, which is what prayer is about, we are along the continuum that leads to union with God. Prayer draws us into the life of God, who indwells the soul. Like the life-giving sap that filters through and permeates the entire tree, God increasingly flows through our prayer, which is what contemplation is about. John of the Cross writes:

> Contemplation is nothing else than a secret, peaceful and loving inflow of God, which, if not hampered fires the soul in the spirit of love.... (DN.1.10.6)

Contemplation gradually thins the veil that hides not only God but the reality that life is all of a piece. For our Carmelite mystics, human life and divine life, our earthly life and life after death are a continuum, a single flow of life empowered by God. Teresa and John would have us realize that not only prayer, but also all the events of each day provide the stuff for divine transformation, so that the soul's essential union with God can come to fruition in spiritual marriage. Purified and transformed in this life, the soul reaches its ultimate fulfillment in the eternal embrace of God in life after death. Everything that happens to us in our life on planet earth is toward this end. Union with God is a now, day-by-day, ever-present reality; mystical union is the culmination, the flowering of what constitutes our essential being. It is the fruit of a life lived in communion with the divine presence, whose name is Love and who, like a divine alchemist, turns all of life into love.

The events of life with their joys and sorrows are like the soil wherein the buried seeds of faith, hope, and love, stirred by grace, sprout and begin to have a life of their own.[3] When faith, hope, and love are activated, we are on the road that leads us to divine union. The believing, hoping, and loving dynamic that characterizes the movements of the divine self is in fact God acting through the human. Every time we bring a faith perspective to a human event or situation our human way of knowing and understanding is being transformed. A divine way of seeing and understanding unveils itself within. We begin to see things and persons as God sees them. John summarizes this reality for us in *The Living Flame of Love* (2:32–36) and in *The Spiritual Canticle* (38.3). Further, in *The Dark Night* (2.19–20), using biblical imagery, John shows the progression of the soul as ten steps on the mystical ladder of divine love until "all it is will become like God." He summarizes his reflections on the transformed soul with the daring assertion: "Thus it will be called, and shall be, God through participation" (DN.2.20.5). "He (Christ) gives His voice to her that so united with him she may give it together with him to God (SC.39.9). The first thing the bride "...desires on coming to the vision of God is to know and enjoy the deep secrets and mysteries of the Incarnation..." (SC.37.1).

For both Teresa and John of the Cross, the image of Christ Crucified best expresses both the process and the finality of the soul's transformation in God. John of the Cross insists that trials condition the soul for God because these in particular call forth the activity of faith, hope, and love so that our purely human way of knowing, understanding, and loving can be purified and transformed. Gradually, as we abandon our limited way of seeing things, especially in regard to life's trials, our inner being is opened to further realize its infinite capacity for God. Relationship to the Crucified One is a recurring theme in all of John's writings but is found most succinctly in *The Sayings of Light and Love*: "Crucified inwardly and outwardly with Christ, you will live in this life with fulness and satisfaction of soul..." (87). "Let Christ crucified be enough for you..." (92). The image of the crucified captures the repeated phrase in John that we are in the totality of Christ's surrender to his Father through our total self-surrender.

Teresa concurs with John. In the seventh dwelling places the soul becomes a slave of the Crucified (IC.7.4.8), and has an intense desire that through its own sufferings, now one with those of Christ, others could actualize their life in God (IC.7.3.6). The depth of believing, hoping, and loving that such surrender elicits becomes an ever deeper access to God within the mystery of Christ Crucified. Life's inevitable struggles challenge us to an ever-deepening surrender if one is not to be undone by them. Loving others with the fullness of self-giving trinitarian love inevitably leaves one close to the Crucified with the heart opened to wounding like his.

Finding the Self in God

Characteristic of inner transformation is a striking shift in consciousness found in the writings of both Teresa and John. In the first five dwelling places of *The Interior Castle*, the castle is an image of the soul with the divine king residing in the center room. The journey is inward. In the sixth dwelling places, Teresa describes something quite remarkable. As she tells us the manifold ways in which God delights in communicating with the soul, a unique experience leaves Teresa insisting that she be heard correctly. She writes:

> It will happen, when the Lord is pleased, that while the soul is in prayer and very much in its senses a suspension will suddenly be experienced in which the Lord will reveal deep secrets. It seems the soul sees these secrets in God

Himself....In this vision it is revealed how all things are seen in God and how He has them all in Himself.

Teresa continues: "Let's suppose that God is like an immense and beautiful dwelling or palace and that this palace, as I say, is God Himself." In this vision, Teresa sees "...the abominations, indecent actions and evil deeds committed by us sinners take place" within this palace itself, that is, within God Himself (IC.6.10.2–3). Teresa is astonished at the mercy and compassion of God and left with a desire to endure everything and to love those who offend her because God "...has not ceased to love us even though we have offended Him very much" (IC. 6.10.4).

John of the Cross has a similar focus. Throughout his writings, he emphasizes the reality of the soul as being transformed in God. He writes that "the soul will be clothed in a new understanding of God in God..." (A.1.5.7), and that the memory is absorbed in God (A.3.2.8–9).[4] In *The Spiritual Canticle* (32.6), John says the following:

> It should be noted for an understanding of this that just as God loves nothing outside himself, he bears no love for anything lower than the love he has for himself. He loves all things for himself; thus love becomes the purpose for which he loves. He therefore does not love things because of what they are in themselves. With God, to love the soul is to put her somehow in himself and make her his equal....This is why the soul merits the love of God in all her works insofar as she does them in God.

Stanza 36 of *The Spiritual Canticle* continues the theme: "Let us rejoice, beloved, and let us go forth to behold ourselves in your beauty." Number 5 of this stanza, like a mantra, echoes being transformed *in your beauty*, beholding ourselves *in your beauty*. "...I shall see you in your beauty, and you will see me in your beauty, and I shall see myself in you in your beauty."[5] Finally, John says: "The ninth step of love causes the soul to burn gently. It is the step of the perfect who burn gently in God" (DN.2.20.4).

A Nature Analogy

Teresa begins *The Interior Castle* comparing the soul to the biblical tree "planted in the very living waters of life…that is, in God…" (IC.1.2.1). The symbol of the tree, used by both Teresa and John, gives us a way, however inadequate, of visualizing the contemplative prayer process that leads to union with God.[6] A tree draws life through its outer leaves from the sun; the roots absorb moisture from the rain that waters the earth. All the elements of nature interact with the tree to strengthen it, beautify or distort its shape, or in a storm, to completely uproot it. The sap, the life force of the tree, flows through the trunk and the branches. The tree is rooted in soil, from which the roots draw both moisture and nutrients. The fine, invisible hair roots deep in the soil are most important to the life of the tree, drawing up needed trace elements from deep down. In winter the tree can look dead, bare of leaves with the sap drawn into the trunk. In spring, with the sun's warmth, the sap again flows through the branches and tight buds expand and break out of their protective covering to release tiny leaves for another cycle of growth.

In our prayer journey, as we consciously open ourselves to God's self-communication, two realities are at work: God's activity and our faith response. Vocal prayer, reading, meditation, and all the many other ways we use our sense life to foster a relationship with God are like the outer dimensions of the tree. Such activity is essential to us as human beings and through it we grow in our life with God. We come to a deeper knowledge of God and of God's love for us. In this process, inevitably as the soul increasingly opens itself to God, we reach a place in prayer where God's presence evades us. Our senses can no longer absorb God's self-communicating love.[7] We reach, as it were, the threshold of human ability to know and love the God of incomprehensible mystery. Conversion of heart here means surrender to a deeper faith that postures us into a whole new reality, into a profound realization that only God can unite us with God. The poignant "where have you hidden, Beloved" of *The Spiritual Canticle* expresses the depth of God inaccessible to human effort.

From the fourth to the seventh dwelling places Teresa struggles to describe the reality of God as hidden and yet who desires to communicate with us.[8] God's very nature is self-communicating, self-giving love. For union with God to be realized, we enter into the very life of God through a mutuality of self-giving love. Herein is the meaning of the dark night: we enter into a process in which God divests us of all that impedes total self-giving so that God's life and ours might become one reality. Only God can accomplish this in us.

Here the image of the tree can again be useful. God is the soil in which the tree of our life is planted. What John of the Cross refers to as the substance of the soul, or in Teresa's symbol, the center room of the castle, is where the life force of our being is grounded. While the tree interacts with its environment, it depends essentially on the soil for moisture and sustenance so that each spring the sap can again flow upward into the branches and cause the tree to sprout new leaves for another season of growth. In our life with God the process is somewhat similar. As God's self-communication from the depths of our inner self meets our human efforts to communicate with God, the inadequacy of human effort is starkly realized. The structures of the psyche, the faculties of the soul, become paralyzed before this divine self-communication. God seems increasingly hidden only because God is drawing us closer to God.

The difficulty is that our faculties are unconditioned for God. The believing, hoping, loving dynamic which is the work of God's transforming Spirit, has yet to transform our human way of knowing, understanding, and loving. We are still all too much within the human mode of operating. The depth of faith by which we totally surrender to God's way of knowing and loving is the work of the dark nights. Dark nights condition the soul to receive the increasing inflow of God; God makes room for God by either easing out or transforming what is less than God. In the process, the soul becomes increasingly fluent in faith, hope, and love. In contemplative prayer, God's self-communication in the depths of the soul begins to penetrate human consciousness. Faith, hope, and love still into silence as eternal Wisdom speaks love to the heart. This is not a silence of emptiness, for within the silence resounds quietly the music of trinitarian communion.

Everything in Life Becomes an Access to God

As we become detached from that which limits us in our relationship with God, the contextual, conditioned, transitional aspects of the self, and as we surrender to the inflow of divine love, everything in life becomes as access to God and acclimates us for God. Our human failings, psychological limitations, physical infirmities, and other imperfections may continue to be a part of life, but these serve only to deepen humility. As Teresa writes in the seventh dwelling places:

> Nor should it pass through your minds that, since these souls have such determination and strong desires not to commit any imperfection for anything on earth, they fail to commit many imperfections, and even sins. Advertently, no; for the Lord must give souls such as these very particular help against such a thing. For [as she says] sometimes our Lord leaves these individuals in their natural state, and then it seems all the poisonous creatures from the outskirts and other dwelling places of the castle band together to take revenge for the time they were unable to have these souls under their control. (IC.7.4.3 and 1)

Teresa understands why this is so. She continues this line of thought:

> As I say this disturbance is rare, but our Lord does not want the soul to forget its being, so that, for one thing, it might always be humble; for another, that it might better understand the tremendous favor it receives, what it owes His Majesty, and that it might praise Him. (IC.7.4.2)

Humility: Centered in Truth

Humility characterizes the person transformed in God. In the sixth dwelling places (IC.6.10.7–8), Teresa describes in detail the moment when the depth of humility's meaning opens itself up to her.

> Once I was pondering why our Lord was so fond of this virtue of humility, and this thought came to me—in my opinion not as a result of reflection but suddenly: It is because God is supreme Truth; and to be humble is to walk in truth, for it is a very deep truth that of ourselves we have nothing good but only misery and nothingness. Whoever does not understand this walks in falsehood.

The self-knowledge that humility invites is a profound realization "that of ourselves we have nothing good but only misery and nothingness. Whoever does not understand this walks in falsehood." Our truth is that we receive our being from God. Divine transformation is God's doing. God is supreme truth and God's truth is that God desires to communicate with us as Teresa demonstrates throughout *The Interior Castle*. The freedom of humility is that it grounds us in the truth both of our finitude—that we are fragile creatures of God, dependent on God for life's breath, and at the same time this humility awakens us to our transcendent calling, that we are infinitely loved by God and God desires to communicate with us.[9]

Thérèse of Lisieux is a fine example of a saint who understood humility's true meaning within the context of herself as infinitely loved by God. She knew well that as long as her heart was intent on loving, her failures were not an issue with God. On the contrary, at the heart of Thérèse's well known little way is an ability to feel secure within weakness. With disarming simplicity, Thérèse writes:

> If you can bear in peace the trial of being displeasing to yourself, you offer a sweet shelter to Jesus. It is true that it hurts you to find yourself thrust outside the door of your own self, so to speak, but fear not; the poorer you become the more Jesus will love you.[10]

To a novice who expressed desire for more strength and energy for the practice of virtue, Thérèse countered:

> And suppose God wishes to have you as feeble and powerless as a child? Do you think that would be less worthy in God's eyes? Consent to stumble, or even to fall at every step, to bear your cross feebly; love your weakness. Your soul will draw more profit from that than if, sustained by grace, you vigorously performed heroic deeds which would fill your soul with self-satisfaction and pride.[11]

Humility enabled Thérèse to surrender to the wedding of seeming opposites: perfection and imperfection. Through a profound union with God, although shrouded in darkness, she views all of life through the eyes of God and, therefore, also through the lens of what was yet to come. She already understood that knowing God and living according to Christ meant entering a new order of existence in which God is center and light. As this reality increasingly penetrates her soul, she begins to live all of life as an anticipation of the glory to come. This glory is hers now in the life of Christ that she already possesses through faith.[12]

A Dilemma: Transformation in John vis-à-vis Teresa and Thérèse

Both Teresa and Thérèse allow for human imperfection within the state of spiritual marriage, through which the person is habitually united with God in the substance of the soul.[13] However, in reading John of the Cross one might be led to think otherwise. In *The Spiritual Canticle* the voice of the Beloved "...provides melody for the ear and refreshment for the spirit" to the extent that "...she is freed from and protected against all temporal disturbances and changes, and divested and purged of imperfections, penalties and clouds in the senses and the spirit, she feels a new spring in spiritual freedom and breadth and gladness" (SC.39.8).

John goes on to say that God desires to have the soul sing to him with this voice of perfect jubilation (39.9). Some passages nuance John's description of perfect union (SC.22.4), where he gives the difference between spiritual betrothal and spiritual marriage with the remarks that in this life the union cannot be perfect. At the same time, in describing the effects of the soul's transformation in Wisdom, John writes that

> she is so innocent that she does not understand evil, nor does she judge anything in a bad light. And she will hear very evil things and see them with her own eyes and be unable to understand that they are so, since she does not have within herself the habit of evil by which to judge them; for God, by means of the perfect habit of true wisdom, has destroyed her habitual imperfections and ignorances that include the evil of sin. (SC.26.14)

In this state neither the devil, the flesh, the world, nor the appetites molest her (SC 22.7). John's understanding of the transformed soul includes peace and tranquility, the conforming of the "lower part to the higher part" cleansing the soul of all its imperfections and a quieting of the appetites (SC.20/21). She can enjoy the gentle sleep of love at will (SC.20/21.19). The properties of perfect love are that the soul does not attribute anything to itself but all to the Beloved. God loves the soul with the very love with which he loves himself. He loves the soul within himself (SC.32.6). The soul performs no works without God (SC.37.6). God transforms her into his love; he gives her his own strength by which she can love him. As if he were to put an instrument in her hands and show her how it works by operating it jointly with her, he shows her how to love and gives her the ability to do so (SC.38.4).

This does indeed sound like a state of perfection and John seems to be living more in heaven than on earth. But, in the context of John's actual life, we get a different picture. In a letter to Ana de San Alberto in 1586, John writes: "The Lord gives us so much to do these days that we can hardly keep up with it all" (Letter 5). Three years later the story is the same. To María de Jesús he writes: "Now I want to answer all of your questions briefly because I have a little time" (Letter 14). These are words of someone very involved in life.

As one reads the concluding pages of Teresa's *Book of Her Life*, one is left with the same impression. She too is living more in heaven than on earth. In Teresa's case the scene quickly changes. A year after completing her final version of her autobiography, at the request of the nuns of her newly founded reformed monastery of St. Joseph in Avila, Teresa begins to compose *The Way of Perfection*. Here a different Teresa emerges. The opening chapters show her extremely troubled by the events of the Protestant Reformation and passionate in her desire to do something in the service of the Lord. She is also immersed in the problem of her new foundation of nuns as well as in the challenge of convincing her nuns, contrary to the opinion of the day, that mental prayer and contemplation will not be harmful to them. Gone are the days when Teresa seems to live more in heaven than on earth.

However, as Teresa's relationship with Christ intensifies, the opposites in her life come together. Not only can she befriend her imperfections, the seeming dichotomy between prayer and activity find a coordinating center in Christ. After eleven years on the rough roads of Spain founding monasteries, dealing with lawsuits, coping with difficult benefactors and with the interpersonal problems of the nuns, and as her own prayer deepens into spiritual marriage with Christ her Beloved, a remarkable conviction shapes itself in Teresa. She now knows by experience that prayer and works for God are not in conflict with each other. In the seventh dwelling places, Martha and Mary are not in opposition to each other, instead, they join together in serving the Lord. Teresa can now say with conviction, "This is the reason for prayer, my daughters, the purpose of this spiritual marriage: the birth always of good works, good works" (IC.7.4.6).

Here again John of the Cross might seem to take a different position as he seems to do in regard to imperfections and a state of union with God. He reminds us that the Lord reproves Martha when she tried to call Mary away from her place at his feet in order to busy herself with active things in his service. Here are his words:

> It should be noted that until the soul reaches this state of union of love she should practice love in both the active and contemplative life. Yet once she arrives she should not become involved in other works and exterior exercises that might be of the slightest hindrance to the attentiveness of love toward God, even though the work be of great service to God. For a little of this pure love is more precious to God and the soul and more beneficial to the Church, even though it seems one is doing nothing, than all these other works put together. (SC.29.2)

John died at age forty-nine whereas Teresa was sixty-seven when she died. Is it possible that Teresa reached a degree of spiritual maturity in the coming together of Martha and Mary that was not part of John's experience? Does difference in temperament, John being more introverted than Teresa, account for the seeming divergence? Or is it really a divergence? John of the Cross died in 1591, but two years before his death, John is both prior of his monastery and also first councilor in provincial government. Only a year before his death, he makes important improvements on the property at Granada, he undertakes building the new monastery, and does some of the work himself. He continues to be attentive to the sick; he writes at times lengthy letters of advice; and he continues to guide many persons in their spiritual journey. John's advice about Martha and Mary directs us away from frenetic, compulsive, self-serving activity to loving service of others that flows from a heart centered in God.

Transformation Today: Beyond Teresa and John?

We can only intuit what the passion of his poetry meant to John of the Cross. The full meaning of Teresian symbol and metaphor remain within the heart of Teresa. Mystics through the ages have struggled to find words to express what in the end defies adequate expression.[14] Ultimately, any attempt to articulate the experience of union with God and the transformation it effects in a person takes one into the realm of mystery. The writings of Teresa and John take us to the threshold of that mystery, which is the mystery of the Trinity itself. For both Teresa and John, the transformed person enters into a profound union with the Most Blessed Trinity.

> When the soul is brought into that dwelling place, the Most Blessed Trinity, all three Persons, through an intellectual vision, is revealed to it through a certain representation

of the truth. First there comes an enkindling in the spirit in the manner of a cloud of magnificent splendor; and these Persons are distinct, and through an admirable knowledge the soul understands as a most profound truth that all three Persons are one substance and one power and one knowledge and one God alone. It knows in such a way that what we hold by faith, it understands, we can say, through sight—although the sight is not with the bodily eyes nor with the eyes of the soul, because we are not dealing with an imaginative vision. (IC.7.1.6)

There are over one hundred references in John of the Cross to the place of wisdom in the soul's transformation; repeatedly he writes of transformation in wisdom. Like Teresa, John's final description is in trinitarian language: "There would not be a true and total transformation if the soul were not transformed in the three Persons of the Most Holy Trinity in an open and manifest degree" (SC.39.3; see LF.2.1).

Along with transformation in the Trinity, Teresa and John agree that when the person has attained union with God in a state of transformation, theirs is a condition of profound peace, because the soul is now habitually centered in God. They both describe a state of transformed consciousness in which the sensory and the spiritual are in harmony. The soul is now as it were conditioned for God insofar as is possible in this life.[15] Consciousness of God and consciousness of the self become one consciousness. Not only does the soul see itself in God as in a mirror (IC.7.2.8), it also sees all things in God.

Our Carmelite mystics recognize love's transformative power, but of necessity they experience and express it within the limits of their own world view. Developments in science, technology, philosophy, and psychology, as well as advances in biblical studies and theological understandings influence our experience of God. It is within the context of this changed world view that we now read and internalize the texts that shape the Carmelite tradition. As our experience of God and that of Teresa and John meet, something new inevitably comes to birth. To facilitate such a birthing is what the Carmelite Forum is about in this book and elsewhere.

The divine invitation to love stirring within the depth of persons today resonates with what Carmelite saints, in symbolic language, unfold for us. As their experience of God connects with ours, so different from theirs, as these two experiences meet each other, a creative process begins. From this should develop a contemporary symbolic language that includes cosmic images. The traditional symbols of bride and bridegroom, of lover and beloved find a more expansive meaning within today's challenge toward global spirituality that is at the same time historically grounded. Union of lover with the beloved opens one to embrace the many faces of God reflected in ethnic and racial differences, which are now a part of everyday experience. As the theologian Van Beeck points out, the accepting and forgiving appropriation of every human concern by Christ means that every human concern is capable of becoming a name of Jesus.[16]

In the attempt to integrate spirituality with human concerns, spirituality today has multiple names such as biblical, contemplative, liberation, ecological, feminist, ecumenical, and others. These are based on a new understanding of our role in relation to planet earth, to the oppressed, and to issues of gender. The feminine reality suggests other namings for God to complement traditional masculine imagery. Furthermore, today's scientific enterprise offers humanity a deeper realization of integral human bondedness, of a profound communion not only within our species, but also throughout the living and non-living universe. Images of interconnectedness, of holographic paradigms, of a universe genetically related inevitably find their way into the religious experience of persons today.[17]

Contemporary Christian spiritual writers struggle to articulate what union with God and divine transformation means in this third millennium that unfolds around us. The influential American philosopher, Ken Wilber, in the eight volumes of his collected works, deals with the many faces of the contemporary search for transcendence. Volume four deals particularly with transformations of consciousness as found within world religions and other systems of thought such as transpersonal psychology and the diversity of postmodern beliefs. The complexity of contemporary human understandings is beyond the wildest imaginings of a Teresa or John of the Cross. According to Wilber,

> every time we move beyond a narrow concern to broader perspectives, we feel we have risen above the situation. There is a sense of being free, a sense of release, an increase of spaciousness, a transcendence. To move from egocentric to ethnocentric to world centric to theocentric is to ascend into greater and wider and higher spheres of release and embrace, transcendence and inclusion, freedom and compassion.[18]

Is it possible that the divine energies of Holy Wisdom, who interpenetrates our world today with all its advances and all its darkness, desire to draw us even deeper into the mystery of divine union and inner transformation even beyond the experience of a Teresa or a John of the Cross? God is ever present as abiding offer. Like Teresa and John, we desire inner peace, and many authors, from many perspectives, tell us how to achieve it.[19] The internet overflows with sites dedicated to the achievement of inner peace and transformation of consciousness. The techniques and attitudinal changes they offer can be helpful provided we bear in mind that the transformation Teresa and John write about is not the work of human effort. Instead, peace comes from a heart free for God since "cares do not molest the detached..." (A.3.20.3). As John of the Cross puts it: "Liberality is one of God's principal attributes and can in no way coexist with covetousness. Moreover, they acquire liberty of spirit, clarity of reason, rest, tranquility, peaceful confidence in God, and in their will, the true cult and homage of God" (A.3.20.2). Union with God, which centers the person in truth, in humility, leads to a life consciously lived in God and so within the mystery of God's trinitarian life. "…when the spiritual marriage between the soul and God is consummated, there are two natures in one spirit and love…" (SC.22.3). Here, the mystery of the Trinity finds human expression in the transformed person. As Catherine LaCugna insisted, the Trinity is not an abstract idea, nor a theological principle but the life of God and the creature existing together as one. Her understanding of God's trinitarian life could well describe transformation today.

> …the perfection of God is the perfection of love, of communion, of personhood. Divine perfection is the antithesis of self-sufficiency; rather it is the absolute capacity to be who and what one is by being for and from another. The living God is the God who is alive in relationship, alive in communion with the creature, alive with desire for union with every creature. God is so thoroughly involved in every last detail of creation that if we could truly grasp this it would altogether change how we approach each moment of our lives. For everything that exists—insect, agate, galaxy—manifests the mystery of the living God.[20]

"When glory does not glorify," writes John of the Cross, "it weighs heavily on the one who beholds it" (LF.4.11).[21] Is this the burden of our postmodern world that it beholds the glory but does not allow glory to transform it? Our trinitarian God is truly *for us*. We are called to be truly for one another, to stretch beyond racial, cultural, and ethnic differences. In the end, it means to become divine, to become God through participation, insofar as is possible in this life (SC.22.3). We bear the challenge to manifest the mystery of the living God in our postmodern world, as did Teresa and John in theirs.

Notes

1. Charles Vergé, "Foundations for Spiritually Based Psychotherapy," Laurel A. Burton, *Religion and the Family When God Helps* (New York: Haworth Pastoral Press, 1992), 41–59.
2. Sandra M. Schneiders, *Written that You May Believe: Encountering Jesus in the Fourth Gospel* (New York: Crossroad, 1999), 51.
3. The expansiveness of the souls is such, as John of the Cross points out in LF.2:10 where he writes of the wounding of the soul by God with a fiery dart, that: "the soul feels that the point is like a tiny mustard seed, very much alive and enkindled, sending into its surroundings a living and enkindled fire of love....It seems to it [the soul] that the entire universe is a sea of love in which it is engulfed, for conscious of the living point or center within itself, it is unable to catch sight of the boundaries of this love."
4. To cite but a few passages see SC.26.14; 27.6; 28.5; 36.7.
5. See John 14:19–20.
6. John of the Cross also uses the tree as a symbol of human/divine realities. In A.1.10.1–4 he says that the appetites weaken a person's virtue because they are like shoots burgeoning around a tree, sapping its strength and causing it to be fruitless. The purification of the nights is the soul's pruning.
7. See SC.19.4–7.
8. For a lucid understanding of God as both separate and distant yet with whom the most intimate communion can happen, see Mark McIntosh, *Mystical Theology* (Oxford: Blackwell, 1998), 110.
9. See Vilma Seelaus, "Teresa Revisions Humility: A Matter of Justice," *The Land of Carmel*; eds. Paul Chandler and Keith J. Egan (Rome: Institutum Carmelitanum, 1991), 337–46.
10. This delightful translation is found in Ida Friederike Görres, *The Hidden Face* (New York: Pantheon, 1959), 330.
11. Ibid., 331. Thérèse gives a good picture of the application of her little way to her everyday life experience in SS.238–44.
12. See Vilma Seelaus, "Spirituality of Imperfection," *Spiritual Life* 44 (1998), 199–212.
13. Edith Stein, in a quote often found on cards writes: "God is there in these moments of rest and can give us in a single instant exactly what we need. Then the rest of the day can take its course under the same effort and strain perhaps—but in peace. When night comes and you look back over the day and see how fragmentary everything has been—how much you planned that has gone undone—all the reasons you have

to be embarrassed and ashamed. Just take everything exactly as it is, put it in God's hands and leave it with him. Then you will be able to rest in him—really rest—and start the next day as a new life."

14. See DN.2.17.3: "The language of God has this trait: Since it is very spiritual and intimate to the soul, transcending everything sensory, it immediately silences the entire ability and harmonious composite of the exterior and interior senses."

15. See LF.4.11–12 where John of the Cross gives reasons why a person is now able to absorb the divine communication.

16. Frans Jozef van Beeck, *Christ Proclaimed: Christology as Rhetoric* (New York: Paulist Press, 1979). See chapter 4, "The Human Concerns: Included and Made Obedient," especially 154–55. Although this is one of van Beeck's earlier works, it offers profound insights into Jesus' relational identity and how this was lived particularly in his passion. See 418ff.

17. A fine example of contemporary challenge to traditional spiritual understandings is Sallie McFague, *The Body of God: An Ecological Theology* (Minneapolis: Fortress Press, 1993). See also Susan J. White, *Christian Worship and Technological Change* (Nashville, Tenn.: Abingdon Press, 1994) for startling insights into the relation between Christian prayer and technological dehumanization. See also *Liberating Life: Contemporary Approaches to Ecological Theology;* eds. Charles Birch, William Eakin, Jay B. McDaniel (Maryknoll, N.Y.: Orbis Books, 1994); *Divine Representations: Postmodernism and Spirituality;* ed. Ann Astell (New York/Mahwah: Paulist Press, 1994) and see the writings of Diarmuid O' Murchu.

18. *The Collected Works of Ken Wilber,* Vol. 4: (Boston: Shambhala, 1999), 543.

19. See books like Peter Russell, *Waking Up in Time: Finding Inner Peace in Times of Accelerating Change* (Novato, Calif.: Origin Press, 1998), author of the bestseller, *The Global Brain.*

20. Catherine Mowry LaCugna, *God for Us: The Trinity and Christian Life* (San Francisco: HarperSanFrancisco, 1991), 304.

21. *The Complete Works of Saint John of the Cross;* trans. E. Allison Peers, Vol. 3 (London: Burns Oates & Washbourne, 1953), 191: translates this sentence: "For glory *oppresses* him that looks upon it if it glorifies him not." [Emphasis mine.] Are some of today's violence and oppression a projection of inner feelings of oppression due to lack of response to the soul's cry for transcendence and divine transformation?

9

Thérèse and the Eternal Shore

John Welch, O. Carm.

Thérèse of Lisieux frequently uses the image of sailing to express her religious experience. This latest doctor of the church contrasts sharply with her parental figures in Carmel, Teresa of Avila and John of the Cross. Thérèse's testimony to the mercy of God is as heartfelt as that of Teresa and John, but the imagery she uses to chart those mercies is quite different.

Both Teresa of Avila and John of the Cross used imagery that could be called developmental. Their relationship with God moved through a series of phases and their prayer at each stage changed accordingly. In particular, Teresa's use of a journey through a castle and its seven suites of rooms or dwelling places gave image to movements she experienced in prayer. And John of the Cross offers a map to guide one through the phases of a night, from twilight, through midnight, to dawn.

People who read the castle and the night journeys of Teresa and John usually ask if life is really that direct in its movement. Does the prayerful person progress through seven stages of prayer in sequence? Are the nights experienced pretty much on time and in order? Is there any possibility for deviation? The temptation is to take the chartings of these saints and put them over our lives, much like a template, to find out where we are in our own lives, as prescribed by Teresa and John. Just how normative are their descriptions?

Most people suspect, intuitively, that life does not proceed in such a measured way. But these saints seem convinced that life does unfold in predictable patterns. Actually, developmental theorists also make the same observation. Details in lives differ greatly, but that there are predictable passages and describable seasons appears to be a conviction.

Perhaps, many of us are more comfortable with Thérèse of Lisieux because she seems much simpler. She does not seem to have produced a chart against which a Christian can measure his or her progress. Thérèse does not describe her relationship with God as taking place in stages, nor does she assign certain ways of praying to particular stages on life's journey. True to her own way, she is simpler, at least on the surface.

Sailing Toward the Eternal Shore

However, there is one image Thérèse frequently uses to convey her changing experience of God. She often compares her life's journey to a sailboat on a sea. It was, while on vacation at Trouville as a young girl, that Thérèse had this inspiration as she watched the rays of the setting sun shine on the sea. Her description allows a reader to see what she saw:

In the evening at that moment when the sun seems to bathe itself in the immensity of the waves, leaving a *luminous trail* behind, I went and sat down on a huge rock with *Pauline*....I contemplated this luminous trail for a long time. It was to me the image of God's grace shedding its light across the path the little white-sailed vessel had to travel. And near Pauline, I made the resolution never to

wander far away from the glance of Jesus in order to travel
peacefully towards the eternal shore! (SS.48–49)

Here is a basic motif for Thérèse. She is in a sailboat traveling
a sunlit path over the sea to an eternal shore. Is it her equivalent of
the castle and night journeys of Teresa and John? Just how prevalent
is this sailing image in her writing? And how does she use it? I would
specifically like to examine her use of water, boat, and shore, the
basic elements of her epiphany at Trouville. Is there a consistency
and perhaps an unfolding of this imagery as Thérèse grows in age
and wisdom?

Fascination with Water

Thérèse greatly enjoyed landscapes which had immensity,
breadth, height, and depth. And, usually, water was an element in
these scenes. They spoke to her soul. Such vistas inspired her to rise
to lyrical descriptions in her autobiography. Here is what she saw in
Switzerland on her way to Rome:

> At times, we were climbing a mountain peak, and at our
> feet were ravines the depths of which our glance could not
> possibly fathom. They seemed about to engulf us. A little
> later, we were passing through a ravishing little village
> with its graceful cottages and its belfry over which floated
> immaculately white clouds. There was, farther on, a huge
> lake gilded by the sun's last rays, its calm waters blending
> their azure tints with the fires of the setting sun. All this
> presented to our enraptured gaze the most poetic and
> enchanting spectacle one could possibly imagine. And at
> the end of the vast horizon, we perceived mountains
> whose indistinct contours would have escaped us had not
> their snowy summits made visible by the sun not come to

add one more charm to the beautiful lake which thrilled us so. (SS.125)

Thérèse was not just admiring beauty in its many forms. These scenes evoked realities deep in her soul and gave expression to the immensity of her desires. We are this mixture of spirit and psyche. Our spirit stretches us forth ceaselessly to an ever-receding horizon. Our psyche conjures imagery to capture the yearnings of spirit. Thérèse's Swiss images were freighted with her spirit's yearning. The mountains and lakes of Switzerland provided a landscape for her soul.

What did such scenes do to her? They did to her what they do to us. They gave her perspective. They freed her from the constrictions of her mind and worries, and let her spirit soar and grow. She could realize the larger realities at play within which our small lives have their part. "When I saw all these beauties very profound thoughts came to life in my soul. I seemed to understand already the grandeur of God and the marvels of heaven" (SS.125). She said that such vistas took her away from her self-preoccupation. "...I understood how easy it is to become all wrapped up in self..." (SS.125).

Paradoxically, she saw her soul mirrored not only in the immensity of an ocean or the grandeur of a mountain lake, but also in places of confinement and constriction. Her desires were inflamed on the hot, dusty floor of the Colosseum, where Christian martyrs witnessed to their faith; she found inspiration in the underground, dark passages of the catacombs; and later she would delight in the hiddenness of Carmel, which was her desert, her prison, her catacomb, her Colosseum floor. She remembers her thoughts in Switzerland: "When I am a prisoner in Carmel and trials come my way and I have only a tiny bit of the starry heavens to contemplate, I shall remember what my eyes have seen today. This thought will encourage me and I shall easily forget my own little interests..." (SS.125).

Heights and depths, wide vistas and constricted spaces, became the geography of her soul. It became for her part of the land of

Carmel, a metaphorical region of soul where God wooed her into a lifelong love. And usually, somewhere near, was water.

Life as a Boat

Thérèse likens her life to a boat sailing on the water. For most people, a boat is not a home. Thérèse comforted herself with the thought, "Life is your barque, not your home" (SS.87, see note). She remembers the book of Wisdom: "Life is like a ship that plows the restless waves and leaves after it no trace of its rapid passage (5:10)" (SS.87, underscored in the text).

Thérèse particularly identifies with gospel scenes involving boats. Specifically, after her Christmas conversion, when ten years of hypersensitivity and self-absorption were taken away seemingly in an instant, she spoke of her own ineffective efforts in the words of the apostles: "Master, I fished all night and caught nothing" (Luke 5:5) (SS. 98–99). And, typically, she refashions the story by having the Lord himself take the net, throw it into the sea, and haul in the fish.

The experience she is reporting is one that has been verified over and over by people caught in addictions. They "fish all night" but catch nothing; nothing takes away the addiction; nothing has control over the addictive behavior. Only grace, God's healing presence, can do what all our efforts alone cannot do. The Lord has to take the net, and do it.

Times of trial find Thérèse comparing her life to a storm-tossed boat. When her uncle was hesitating in giving her permission to enter Carmel, she likened it to wind and waves pounding her little vessel. She says she had no pilot to guide her passage. But the Lord was present, asleep in her boat. She just knew he was there, although it was too dark to see him.

This image reminds us that suffering was a major part of Thérèse's life. She had her own neuroticisms; her father became mentally unbalanced; and from the time she entered Carmel the normal consolations in prayer were absent. Carmel was truly a dry experience on one level. But the absence of a tangible experience of God deepened her conviction in the presence of God. She was positive he was with her, in her boat, although it was too dark to see him. This trial eventually passed, but it was not the last. She wrote: "Awakening, Jesus brought back joy, the noise of the waves was abated, and in place of the wind of trial, a light breeze expanded my sail and I believed I'd reach the blessed *shore*, now seemingly so close! It was really very close to my boat, but *more than one storm* was still to arise. Hiding from me the view of the luminous beacon, these storms caused me to fear lest I should be driven far from the shore so ardently desired without any hope of return" (SS.111).

As Thérèse's dream of entering Carmel came closer to becoming a reality, she made this observation of Céline who remained at home: "Céline was watching my little boat approach Carmel's shore, and she was resigned to remain on the stormy sea of the world as long as God willed it. She was sure that she too would approach the same shore which was the object of her desires" (SS.133).

Mixing her imagery, Carmel was, at the same time, the shore toward which Thérèse was traveling, and also the boat or ark within which she was making the journey. When she was finally accepted but was asked to wait three more months before entering Carmel, she complained: "...this time it was the holy ark itself which refused entrance to the poor little dove" (SS.143).

She returns to this image for Carmel when she is finally received at the age of fifteen. Her father takes her to Carmel, kneels down and blesses her, tears flowing down his cheeks. And then, Thérèse writes, "A few moments later, the doors of the holy ark closed upon me, and there I was received by the *dear* Sisters who embraced me" (SS.148). It was a thrilling time for her, and she quickly returns to her original sailing image: "...the joy I was experiencing was *calm*, the lightest breeze did not undulate the quiet waters upon which my little boat was floating and no cloud darkened my blue heaven" (SS.148).

Thérèse finally entered Carmel, but the retreat before her profession did not bring Thérèse any consolation. She described experiencing "...the most absolute aridity and almost total abandonment..." (SS.165). Once again, she said that Jesus was sleeping as usual in her boat. She finds a unique way to express her faith. She understands Jesus' fatigue and his need to sleep. Others make demands on Jesus, and he has to take the initiative over and over again with them. Thérèse refuses to attempt to wake him up, and she allows him to sleep peacefully in her boat. Rather than be troubled about it, Jesus' sleeping gives her extreme pleasure. He may be asleep during this profession retreat, she says, but "He will undoubtedly awaken before my great eternal retreat..." (SS.165).

On the evening before taking her vows Thérèse reports that another storm arose, "...the like of which I'd never seen before" (SS.166). For a desperate moment she doubted her vocation to Carmel. Perhaps it would be better to leave and go home to try to find God's will, rather than remain in Carmel doing her own will. What made her think she might simply be doing her own will was the fact that living in Carmel was a beautiful experience for her. A quick discussion with the Novice Mistress and the storm abated.

Then, staying with her nautical theme, Thérèse reports that during a retreat months after her profession, the retreat director assured her that her faults caused God no pain; on the contrary, God was pleased with her. This assurance, she said, "...launched me full sail upon the waves of *confidence and love...*" (SS.174).

When her father finally dies, and Céline enters Carmel, a sign to Thérèse that her father is in heaven, Thérèse reports a change in navigation. Previously, her desire for suffering and death had been strong. She wrote, "...I possessed suffering and believed I had touched the shores of heaven...." But now she had learned to give up even those desires. "Now, abandonment alone guides me. I have no other compass!" (SS.178). She identified with John of the Cross in his *Spiritual Canticle*, "…nor have I any other work / now that my every act is love" (SC.28).

Eternal Shore

And what is this eternal shore toward which Thérèse was sailing? An easy answer is "heaven." Even as a little child Thérèse saw, as the goal of her life, heaven. The stars in this heaven formed a "T" for Thérèse. Heaven was the never-ending Sunday, the eternal retreat, the eternal shore. The eternal shore is an expression holding her deepest desires. Remember, she chose all in life, and this image for her is an expression of all that she desires. But her concepts do not satisfy her. "I feel how powerless I am to express in human language the secrets of heaven, and after writing page upon page I find that I have not yet begun. There are so many different horizons, so many nuances of infinite variety…" (SS.189).

We are here touching a fundamental fact about the human condition. Our hearts desire all. They want a fulfillment that is ever elusive. We reach out to this and that, lured by a promise of fulfillment, only to be disappointed time and time again. Using Thérèse's image, we arrive at many shores, but each time we realize it is not the eternal shore. We remain restless. Thérèse herself said the key to her life was, "I choose all!"

We cannot really conclude that Thérèse's imagery is developmental. Her image of sailing on a luminous path to the eternal shore does not actually show movement the way the castle and night journeys do. The boat does not go from place to place so that one can look backward and forward and see overall development or movement.

Rather than moving *through* an image such as castle or night, Thérèse's entire image changes. There are scenes of sailing on a calm sea toward the setting sun and the distant horizon. There are scenes of recurrent storms where the wind and waves record the battering of her soul. There are moments of believing the shore has been reached. But then the observation that the more one advances the farther away the goal appears. She speaks of multiple horizons with nuances of infinite variety, and "only the palette of a Celestial Painter" (SS.189) can capture them. Thérèse's sailing image is not sequential but more multifaceted.

Thérèse's image has its evocative strengths, and also its obvious limitations. It does not provide a consistent framework on which she can attempt to hang the story of her experience of God, as does the castle for Teresa of Avila or the night for John of the Cross.

The Basic Story?

But is there a more fundamental pattern underneath, or perhaps within, these images? Is there a basic story, a metanarrative these saints are trying to express, each with her or his own imagery?

Certainly, one possibility for a fundamental pattern taking shape in all lives is the Paschal Mystery, the pattern seen in the dying and rising of Christ. Theologian James Empereur makes this observation:

> The basic pattern of Christian living is Paschal. That means that Christian life is happening in terms of a transition. It is the movement from dark to light, from captivity to freedom, from dryness to growth, and from alienation to union. This passover, this exodus, responds to the deep human need to be saved from death.[1]

The Paschal Mystery permeates all of Christian spirituality.

Do we not, time after time, learn to let go, to admit being powerless, and turn our lives over to God? Is there any other way? Is not John's description of the night his own version of the cross, an account of a dying process in his life, which presumably will be replicated in other lives? Again, Empereur: "It is in the human experiences of suffering, pain, and fear of death that this Paschal mystery becomes a reality for most people. Death and resurrection are part of a human passage through life."[2] Are the saints of Carmel, in their own imagery, charting the Paschal Mystery, a fundamental pattern of dying and rising?

It is true that Carmel's saints often emphasize suffering, and Carmel has a popular image of an ascetical group. Mottos such as "Either to suffer or to die" and "Not to die but to suffer" give evidence of an apparent preoccupation with suffering. Is that really Carmel's message, Carmel's understanding of its reality? For Carmelites, is the basic pattern or story death and resurrection, or is there another story they prefer?

The Lover and the Beloved

Along with the image of traveling through a night, John of the Cross uses the image of journeying to God who is at the center of one's life. But, he writes, with one degree of love we are in the center. In other words, the center is not a distant goal to be reached after a lengthy process. We are *already in the center*. John explains that the journey, now, is to go deeper into the center, to go deeper in God. The center has come to us. Teresa rejected the idea that we first have to laboriously change ourselves before meeting God. God meets us where we are in our lives. Our challenge is to accept the fact that we are already accepted by God. Contemplation is an openness to that transforming love.

Is it possible to say the basic story these Carmelites tell is *being found by love*? Is the real metanarrative they return to again and again the story in the Song of Songs in the Old Testament, the story of a passionate love between the lover and the beloved? "The voice of my beloved! / Look, he comes, / leaping upon the mountains, / bounding over the hills" (Song 2:8).

Thérèse was convinced this love affair was the basic story or pattern taking place in our lives. In her own backhanded way she draws on this narrative when she says that, unlike the bride in the Song of Songs, she always found the Beloved in her bed (SS.71). She anticipated a renewal of the theology of grace in her understanding of grace as primarily relational, a freely given, loving Presence. Thérèse wanted to be one in whom God's love would find a willing partner. This immense love needed a vessel into which it could be poured. "He finds few hearts who surrender to Him without reservations, who understand the real tenderness of His infinite Love" (SS.189).

Thinking they were looking for an absent God, these Carmelites returned convinced that God had been looking for them all along, pursuing them in love. Thérèse identified with the bride, John drew on the Song of Songs for his "Spiritual Canticle," and Teresa wrote a commentary on this classic from the Hebrew Scriptures. They understood their lives as a story of God's mercies, of having been found by love. On more than one occasion John rehearses Hosea's lines, "…I will now allure her, and bring her into the wilderness, and speak tenderly to her" (2:14).

Fog-Bound

In her short life, Thérèse had to let go of the story of her sailboat traveling a luminous, golden trail of sunlight to an eternal shore. The golden trail evaporated, the beacon disappeared, and the mists settled in around her. She admits, much like Columbus, she had dreamed of being in another place: "…I felt that another land would one day serve me as a permanent dwelling place." But then she reports the journey not only became confused but even the goal was called into question: "Then suddenly the fog which surrounds me becomes more dense; it penetrates my soul and envelops it in such a way that

it is impossible to discover within it the sweet image of my Fatherland; everything has disappeared!" (SS.213).

Céline had anticipated the needs of her little sister even earlier when Thérèse was impatiently awaiting permission to enter Carmel. Thérèse felt as though she were a ball Jesus had stopped playing with while he slept. Christmas arrived, and after the midnight Mass she returned home to a gift Céline had prepared: "I found in my room, in the center of a charming basin, a *little* boat carrying the *Little* Jesus asleep with a *little* ball at His side, and Céline had written these words on the white sail: 'I sleep but my heart watches,' and on the boat itself this one word: 'Abandonment!'" (SS.142–43).

At the end she had no sense of journey or direction, only hope. And, as John of the Cross reminded us, hope is in what we do not possess. Thérèse sailed on, in faith, plunging into "the shoreless ocean of Your Love" (SS.254). And she wrote to her missionary brother, Father Bellière, these faith-filled words: "When I shall have arrived at port, I will teach you how to travel, dear little brother of my soul, on the stormy sea of the world: with the surrender and love of a child who knows his Father loves him and cannot leave him alone in the hour of danger....The way of simple love and confidence is really made for you" (SS.266–67).[3]

Notes

1. James Empereur, "Paschal Mystery," *The New Dictionary of Theology*; eds. Joseph Komanchak, Mary Collins, Dermot Lane (Wilmington, Del.: Michael Glazier, 1987), 747.
2. Ibid., 746.
3. In the *Story of a Soul* this entire quotation is underscored.

10

Passion in the Carmelite Tradition: Edith Stein

Constance FitzGerald, O.C.D.

Introduction

The Carmelite tradition transmits a legacy of profound passion. While the Carmelite Rule (1206–1214) cautions moderation in everything, in all the major texts and personalities of the tradition, beginning with its Elian myth in the *Institution of the First Monks* and moving through the life and writings of Teresa of Avila, John of the Cross, Thérèse of Lisieux, Edith Stein, and others, one encounters magnificent passion bordering on excess.[1] The way the Carmelite prayer tradition helps and educates is by showing us how passion for God matures, that is, how desire grows in ardor, how communion and being God's partner in love comes about in our lives.

In *Webster's Dictionary* passion is defined, first of all, as suffering or agony (from the Latin *to suffer*) and secondarily, as compelling emotion, specifically enthusiasm, strong love, and desire. Taken together these meanings show the complexity and richness of my understanding of the word *passion* as I use it in this essay.[2]

The ardor of their desire to love and be transformed in love, and the intensity of their experience of, reflection on, and appropriation of human suffering, is precisely what characterizes those marked by the Carmelite ethos. In fact, nothing is so expressive of the passion we find in the Carmelite prayer tradition as this simultaneous inter-twining emphasis on love and suffering, which we see elegantly por-trayed, for example, in the poetry of John of the Cross and more simply demonstrated in the writings of Thérèse of Lisieux. John sings:

> O living flame of love
> that tenderly wounds my soul
> in its deepest center! Since
> now you are not oppressive,
> now consummate! if it be your will:
> tear through the veil of this sweet encounter.
>   (LF. Stanza 1)

When Thérèse, in her turn, writes that "she had but one desire, that of being taken to the summit of the mountain of love,"[3] she is echo-ing the aspiration of Carmel through eight hundred years. "Love, how well our heart is made for that!...Sometimes, I seek for another word to express love, but on this earth of exile words are powerless to express all the soul's vibrations, so we have to keep to this one word: (love!)...."[4]

If we study *The Story of a Soul*, we are not only awed by the mag-nitude of Thérèse's love, but also perplexed by the way she seems actively to pursue suffering, unable to learn the borderline between acceptance of the human condition and actually precipitating suffer-ing. This is a danger she poses to those who do not read her work critically, who do not interpret her text. In this she is probably as "dangerous" as her Carmelite mentor, John of the Cross. John says that "love consists not in feeling great things but in having great detachment and in suffering for the Beloved." He *seems* to counsel us to deny all human desires and choose what is most difficult, that is, make ourselves suffer (SL.115, 93).

Edith Stein, the focus of this study, in her turn attempts to fathom the significance of this attitude toward suffering in John and in her own

Carmelite life in an essay written around 1934 in which she explores "the burden of the cross."[5] I suspect that this is so important to her that in her last written and unfinished work, *The Science of the Cross*, composed during the year before her death in the gas chambers of Auschwitz in August, 1942, she uses her own philosophical theory of empathy, initially developed in her doctoral dissertation, as a hermeneutic to trace the inner experience and processes of prayer that John goes through in his life and writing to reach his convictions about love and suffering. By means of this profound, original analysis she, herself, connects with and lays claim to his meanings, which empower and energize her life, motivation, and ultimately her death. One conclusion stands out: the more important loving becomes for John, Thérèse, and finally also Edith, the more significant or desirous suffering is. It is an expression of their passion; it becomes a proof of love, a medium of solidarity, and a threshold to depth and transformation.

We, on the other hand, in the repudiation of a spirituality that seemed to stress an excessive and sometimes unhealthy self-sacrifice and love of suffering, have perhaps lost passion as evidenced by a certain spiritual fatigue, softness, and malaise. Modernity, with its often one-sided emphasis on the development and realization of the autonomous self without adequate concern for the common good or multipersonal community, has left us bereft of passion, and herein, I suggest, lies a radical call to self-transcendence.[6] Our passionless, "so-what" society needs a new language of selflessness or of the cross that describes and supports the loss of possessive selfhood. Such a forfeiture is indispensable in the contemporary quest for the transforming love, universal communion, and cosmic consciousness that seem today beyond the achievement of human ability.

This is why I want to concentrate on Edith Stein, a victim of the Holocaust who literally disappeared with six million other people into the hell "where God died." I intend, first, to follow in some measure the mysterious faith/prayer process whereby the rejections, exclusions, and marginalization she experienced were transmuted into the

Way of the Cross. Second, I hope to discover how her understanding of atonement and expiation together with her convictions about community shaped this entrance into and appropriation of the mystery of the cross. Third, I desire thereby to see how the energy of her powerful love and singular perception of suffering, particularly as this was mediated to her through her mentor, John of the Cross, seeps into and enlarges or distinctly marks the passion of the Carmelite tradition, and in so doing possibly points to a meaningful spirituality of selflessness, solidarity, and communion that pierces through the limitation of accustomed boundaries.

Edith Stein—Passion for Greatness

In sharp contrast to the obvious revelatory character of both Thérèse of Lisieux's and Teresa of Avila's writing, Edith Stein did not leave us a personal journal or autobiographical account of her prayer or spiritual experience. While her letters and autobiography certainly provide insight into her inner life, she bore witness to her desire for anonymity by keeping secret the depth of her soul life. We are left to discover the footprints of her soul from her more objective writings, her intellectual passion, and her life. Her message, however, is not less powerful for this reason, since in studying her spiritual writings one cannot doubt that she *knew* whereof she spoke.

From her youth, long before Edith became a Catholic, we see in her a raw passion for greatness that could only be assuaged by the absorption of self into an overwhelming plan beyond her own personal life.[7] She could not really know what a step-by-step immersion in anonymity and sacrifice would ultimately cost her nor imagine where the final focus of her love and devotion would be directed. Nevertheless, her employment of a phenomenological methodology to observe her own passionate behavior, emotion, and absolute convictions concerning "German-ness" provides us with an entry point for tracking, in depth, a movement of displacement that began in a total, extreme, chilling dedication to the German State and evolved into complete, unconditional commitment to God and the cross in radical solidarity with her own Jewish people.

In 1917, when she was twenty-five years old, Edith looked back on her experience of her country's mobilization day for World War I. At that time it became crystal clear to her that her individual life with its private affairs and concerns had ceased and that, by her own free desire, all that she had and was belonged to the state, to be used up completely in the service of the fatherland. She agonized continually because she could not find "the right place in which [she] could live up to this conviction."[8]

This woman, who struggled in young adulthood to give her life in passionate self-forgetfulness to an ultimate cause in the German state, who could not bear being at *any one* person's disposition, even the great Edmund Husserl's,[9] would by 1935 write that the real content of her life, of the Carmelite vocation, was "to stand before the face of God...looking up [in prayer] into the face of the Eternal," believing that a fountain of grace would bubble up over everything, without her knowing precisely where it would go and without those whom it would reach ever knowing from whence it came.[10] By 1938, on the eve of her departure from her cherished fatherland to escape the extreme exclusionary policies of Nazi Germany and guarantee the safety of her community in Cologne, in a poem entitled "I Will Remain With You," Edith wrote with simple poignancy: "Heaven is my glorious homeland [now]."[11] She revealed, moreover, the completeness of the displacement of her extravagant desire and capacity for dedication by the very manner in which she explains "the highest stage of personal life" in *The Science of the Cross*:

> When [the soul] has reached [this inmost sphere] God will
> work everything in the soul, itself will have to do no more
> than to receive. Yet its share of freedom is expressed in just
> this receiving. Beyond this, however, freedom is involved

even far more decisively, for in this state [mystical mar-
riage] God works everything only because the soul surren-
ders itself to God perfectly. This surrender is itself the
highest achievement of its freedom. St. John [of the Cross]
describes the mystical marriage as the voluntary mutual
surrender of God and the soul [in love] and attributes to
the soul at this stage of perfection so great a power that it
can dispose not only of itself, but even of God.[12]

Marginalization, Anonymity

Her passion notwithstanding, mutual surrender did not come
easily to Edith Stein. She learned slowly in her experience, undoubtedly by the revisioning of her own life, that this union with God is
"bought by the Cross, accomplished on the Cross, and sealed with
the Cross for all eternity."[13] Little of what this truly brilliant Jewish
woman philosopher aspired to or was capable of reached fulfillment.
Caught in the confluence of personalities, an inflexible German,
male, academic structure and pervasive anti-Semitism, she was effectively marginalized as an intellectual not only because she was a
woman, but specifically because she was a single woman. Although
she attempted several times over a period of years to follow her
summa cum laude doctorate in philosophy with a normal university
appointment, no one, not even her mentor Husserl, would put his life
on the line to sponsor her second thesis to obtain habilitation, that is,
the license to lecture necessary for a university position.[14] Limited,
therefore, in what she was allowed to do as a woman and a Jew, she
spent her professional career, following her conversion to
Catholicism, at a Dominican teachers' college for women and as a
well-known and much sought after lecturer, principally in Germany,
Austria, and Switzerland. Her competency included theory of pedagogy, women's education, equality of sexes' abilities for professions
and scholarship, and broad work with Thomistic themes.

179

Edith's recurring doubts about her ability as a scholar must undoubtedly be traced in large part to her cumulative experience in the academic arena. In 1932 she wrote to Sr. Adelgundis Jaegerschmid expressing the inadequacy she felt as a scholar created by her ten-year exclusion from the continuity of academic work and her isolation from the contemporary intellectual scene.[15] Her very next extant letter, written to a Thomist scholar who had found fault with her translation of Thomas Aquinas, again cited her deficiency and lack of resources.[16] Even more poignant is the correspondence with Hedwig Conrad-Martius, in which Edith admitted to her own limitations in philosophizing and to the fear she had lost connection with technical thoroughness and was generally incompetent to function in the world of academia, that is, in the classroom, the lecture hall, or as a philosopher.[17] She asked, nevertheless, for a radical critique of her writings in the hope that Hedwig might mediate for Edith the meaning of her life's task and assure her that she was not overreaching her own capabilities in the philosophical work she had undertaken.[18] But running through all her doubts was the realization that anything she could now accomplish would be far more fragmentary than she had dreamed.[19] Her losses were irreversible and would never be recouped. What remains significant in terms of her spiritual evolution is the fact that throughout this especially ambiguous, bleak time she delivered some of her most effective lectures verifying the presence of a hidden power not her own.

With her conversion to Catholicism in 1922, Edith was isolated on another level by the serious separation it created, first of all, between her and some of her close friends with whom she had felt there existed an unshakable bond.[20] Even more distressing was the deep misunderstanding between her and her family, particularly her dearly loved and greatly admired mother whose youngest child she was. Seen by her family initially as a rejection of her Jewishness and later as an effort to save herself from the fate of the Jews in Nazi Germany by entering Carmel, Edith's conversion and vocation effected further alienation in her life. With the rise to power of Hitler's National Socialism in 1933, her marginalization became even more acute. The fatherland pronounced her an outcast, specifically because she was a Jew—something unimaginable to Edith at the time of World War I, when she had described what being German meant to her.[21]

It is ironic that her very German-ness and Jewishness, along with her intellectual life, the once thought solid parts of her identity, would be so challenged and so thoroughly stretched. A displacement and even forfeiture of identity, which she was helpless to protest effectively, was forced upon her. One supposes she was attempting to deal with all these various facets of exclusion, personal and social, when, prior to her entering Carmel, she gathered together the memories of her family experience, intellectual life, and cultural milieu in *Life In a Jewish Family*. Not only was she attempting, as a phenomenologist, to educate German youth to see the similarities between the lives of assimilated, German Jews and their own, thereby making hatred of Jews (other I's) impossible, she was also, in accordance with her own philosophical convictions about human solidarity, freely taking her stand with her own persecuted people and publicly recognizing herself as one of them, an outcast. This autobiographical self re-creation as a Jew was, as Rachel Felday Brenner rightly suggests, absolutely essential to Edith's evolving self-understanding prior to entering Carmel.[22] It was the expression of a solidarity that drew meaning from her phenomenological understanding of the devoted individual who is a "carrier" of the communal life, insofar as her personal being is faithful to a particular community and remains steadfastly planted within it even if she's been excluded from or, in fact, excludes herself from the communal life.[23] Whereas Edith's family and friends believed she was distancing herself from the Jewish community, and the state was attempting to ostracize her from her Germanness, she was, in fact, more deeply associating herself with both. In her Carmelite life of prayer this perception would expand into a desire to bear the burden of the cross in communion and expiation and would reach its logical consummation in her final words as she left Carmel for the extermination camp: "Rosa, come, let us go for our people."[24]

Prayer Development and the Mystery of the Cross

But how did the path of the outcast become the Way of the Cross? If we try to follow the intimate trail of her spirit, the pathway of her prayer, it leads to the cross so that no one can doubt that the passion and death of Jesus became her inner mystery, and the suffering and destruction of her people the preoccupation of her Carmelite life. Her spiritual writings provide ample evidence that she understood clearly by experience and education how growth in prayer works. She had learned well the tradition of contemplation from her Carmelite teachers, John of the Cross and Teresa of Avila, but she also comprehended the process as a phenomenologist, as a scholar. In *The Science of the Cross*, after describing faith and meditation with amazing clarity, she explained:

> St. John [of the Cross] also knows a higher form of meditation: a naturally lively and highly gifted mind may deeply penetrate into the truths of faith, consider them in all their aspects, converse about them with itself, develop them to their intellectual conclusions and discover their inner connexions. This activity will become even more lively, easy and fruitful if the Holy Spirit inspires the human mind and raises it above itself. Then it will feel to be in the hands of a higher power enlightening it, so that it seems no longer to be active itself, but to be instructed by divine revelation.
>
> Anything the spirit has acquired by meditation in one of these forms becomes its permanent possession....

Through its constant occupation with God, the spirit—
and this means here not only the understanding but also
the heart—becomes familiar with him [sic], it knows and
loves him. This knowledge and love have become part of
its being; the relation between God and man [sic] at this
stage may be compared with that between two people
who have lived together for a long time and are on most
intimate terms.[25]

I believe Edith learned to pray in Speyer. Following her conversion to Catholicism she resided there with the Dominican Sisters who
ran St. Magdalena's training institute for women teachers. During the
eight years she taught there she lived like an enclosed nun dedicating
herself to prayer and rarely going out except to lecture. She immersed
herself totally in Christ through daily Eucharist, the Liturgy of the
Hours, theological study, and the intimacy of silent prayer, thereby
learning "how to go about living at the Lord's hand."[26] Meditating on
the gospels, she grew to know Jesus and discovered what God wanted
of her by "learn[ing] from him [sic] eye to eye."[27] At the end of this
period she wrote to a friend: "God leads each of us on an individual
way.... We can do very little ourselves, compared to what is done to
us. But that little bit we must do. Primarily this consists before all else
of persevering in prayer to find the right way."[28]

In the same year, 1931, in an essay on St. Elizabeth of Hungary,
Edith painted what was likely a mirror image of her own soul:

Mighty was the tug of war in the soul of the child
Elizabeth. It set her on fire, and the flame of the love of
God flared up, breaking through every cloak and barrier.
Then this human child placed herself in the hands of the
divine Creator. Her will became pliant material for the
divine will, and, guided by this will, it could set about tam-
ing and curtailing her nature to channel the inner form.

Her will could also find an outer form suitable to its inner one and a form into which she could grow without losing her natural direction. And so she rose to that perfected humanity, the pure consequence of a nature freed and clarified by the power of grace.[29]

During these years, her spiritual guide described her as "...filled with grace, rich in the love of God and men [sic], filled with the spirit of the scriptures and the liturgy, from which she draws, in which she prays and meditates, and by which she lives."[30]

Later Edith, anonymously bearing witness to her own growth, would acknowledge that "no human eye can see what God does in the soul during hours of inner prayer. It is grace upon grace."[31]

Inasmuch as consulting human experience is an identifying mark of phenomenology, we must assume Edith consciously brought into her prayer all her physical, emotional, and intellectual experiences of exclusion along with the increasing suffering of her people. Then her own precise, internalized understanding of the science of empathy, so fundamental to her own identity, had to lead her so to follow in her meditation the suffering (emotional and mental) of Jesus that her spirit quite literally connected or "ported" to a transcendent source of energy, of "motivation," beyond herself in the passion and death of Jesus.[32] "Before you hangs the Savior on the Cross....The arms of the Crucified are spread out to draw you to his heart. He wants your life in order to give you his...Look at the Cross...Look at the Crucified," she wrote.[33] Edith's commentary on John of the Cross's dark night communicates the power of the energy she received:

> Faith offers [the soul] Christ, poor, humble, crucified, forsaken on the Cross even by his divine Father. In his poverty and desolation the soul recognizes its own. Aridity, distaste and pain are the "purely spiritual Cross" presented to it. If it accepts this, the soul will find that the

yoke is sweet and the burden light; the Cross will become its staff by which it quickly mounts upward. For Christ accomplished his greatest work, the reconciliation and union of mankind [sic] with God, in the utmost humiliation and annihilation on the Cross. When the soul realizes this it will begin to understand that it, too, must be led to union with God through annihilation, a "living crucifixion...." As, in the desolation of his death, Jesus surrendered himself into the hands of the invisible and incomprehensible God, so the soul must enter the midnight darkness of faith, which is the only way to God.[34]

For the realist phenomenologist there was no way to experience as her own Jesus' physical death, the material body broken, the blood poured out—this would come for her. But from the quality of Jesus' attitudes of loving surrender for others, of giving up his life freely in complete selflessness, of loving his friends, his people, even to death, of prizing truth and fidelity to his mission to the end above his own safety, of absorbing violence and evil while refusing to hate, of forgiving his killers and sending back love, she assimilated an intrinsic infinity of meaning. From his suffering her spirit accessed a profound explosion of energy in the realm of significance that could never be spent down. When Edith encountered such meaning in prayer, as a phenomenologist she "owed" it reception. Her attitude toward such value became nonoptional. It tugged at her and demanded to be let in. She willingly, therefore, opened the gates of her inner spirit, the vestibule to the spiritual realm—like letting down the drawbridge into a castle—to soak up suffering from the Jewish Jesus by connecting or "porting" to his feelings and attitudes which empowered her toward love and impelled her "to take up the burden of the Cross," in what she called "expiation."[35] This is how Edith Stein, the philosopher, the Carmelite, became a passionate "lover of the Cross."

Community

To comprehend better, however, both the complexity and con-
gruence of her passion for the cross and the resulting inner movement
toward expiation, we need to stress how integrally they grew out of
the soil of an already existing sensibility that pervades her philosophical work and can be traced back to her early schooling at the
University of Breslau (1911–1913). At that time she admitted to a
feeling for the solidarity not only of all humankind but also of smaller
social groupings.[36] The singular attention Edith gave to the study of
the essence of community and mutual communication between
human beings in her doctoral dissertation, *On the Problem of Empathy*
(1916), and in *Individual and Community* (1920) was an expression of
and enlargement upon this initial intuition. But community solidarity
was far more than just a major theoretical concern for her, as her
friend, Roman Ingarden, points out. Belonging to a community was a
personal necessity; solidarity a requisite for her life.[37]

But precisely what convictions about community were so foundational in Edith's thought that they remained a bedrock influencing
her spiritual experience and development as a Carmelite? First, she
believed that the very essence of community is the union of free persons who are connected on the deep level of their innermost personal
lives and, therefore, have a vital influence on each other. Each one
feels responsible for herself and for the community. Second, a community like a person can be said to have a spirit, a character, a soul.
Third, some community members are carriers of the communal life.
Their personal being is so totally given to the community that they
are its core, from which its spirit or character or soul is shaped and
which guarantees its enduring reality. The further their devotion
extends the more secure are the values and outward face of the community. Fourth, some individuals with higher sensitivity—often these
are the carriers of community—function as the open eyes with which
their community (or communities) look at the world.[38]

Grasping Edith's prophetic perception concerning the truly faithful person who is a carrier of the communal life and a shaper of its spirit, and realizing the different communities to which she passionately belonged, we are in a better position to understand the manner in which four particular experiences were unfolding simultaneously in her prayer life: first, a typically Carmelite intimacy with the Crucified was constantly maturing; second, as their oppression mounted, a more profound identification with the Jewish people was developing that paralleled her growing communion with Christ; third, some kind of responsibility for the violence of the German Nazi state pressed in upon her; fourth, she was integrating her long-held philosophical convictions about human community with both a theological understanding and experience of the Body of Christ and the prayer of the church. As these four realities coalesced in her life, a deep unitive experience of solidarity took hold of her.[39]

Expiation

From the perspective of Carmelite growth in prayer, this development was to be expected. In her specific time and place in history, however, she named it the desire for "voluntary expiatory suffering" or the willingness to commit herself to "the works of expiation" which, she observed, only served to bind her even more closely in love to Christ in a powerful exchange of energy, meaning, and direction.[40] Some of Edith's most passionate spiritual writing is expressed in the language of expiation.

What many find difficult to interpret today is not that Edith voluntarily desired to share the suffering of her people in intimate union with the Crucified—Oscar Romero, for example, and numerous others have done that in our own time—but that she did so depending on the theological categories of sacrifice, satisfaction, substitution, and expiation. These classical salvation theories have a long history in theology.[41] Particularly since the early Middle Ages, it has been said that Christ, the God-man, offered through the sacrifice of his death infinite satisfaction and expiation to his Father and that in our place he atoned for the limitless offense inflicted on God through human sin. Even if Augustine's hypothesis on sacrifice, satisfaction, and substitution, and Anselm's lucid interpretation of salvation in terms of satisfaction and substitution, especially in their vulgarized forms, which penetrated the public consciousness of the church, appear extravagant to us inasmuch as they seem to contradict New Testament statements and no longer fit with the way we postmoderns think about God and Christ, in the 1930s and 1940s before and after Edith entered Carmel, substitution and satisfaction were operative, viable theological constructs in soteriology and expiation profoundly influential and inspiring in the spiritual life of Carmelites.

Clearly, however, Edith's evident appropriation of an attitude of expiation or atonement—she differentiated between the two—was not only a function of Carmelite devotion nor simply a consequence of a Christian theological theory of salvation. It was also rooted in her Jewish origins and her scholarly work. Pivotal for Edith's self-understanding as a Carmelite nun was her birth on the Day of Atonement, the highest of the Jewish festivals "when the High Priest used to enter the Holy of Holies to offer the sacrifice of atonement for his own sins and the sins of all the people," after which the scape-goat was driven out into the desert with the sins of all upon his head.[42] Not through mere nostalgia, but with passionate purpose and identi-fication did Edith repeatedly refer in her spiritual writings to the sig-nificance of this scapegoat ritual and the offering of expiation for sin.[43] Furthermore, as long as she lived she celebrated Yom Kippur each year by fasting throughout the entire day. Thus she could not fail to see the scapegoat mechanism in operation as the violence and hatred within the Nazi soul was projected upon her people. Such sin demanded an offering of expiation!

Even as an academic, as far back as 1921, prior to her conversion, Edith pursued the topic of expiation in a very technical essay, "On the

State," in which she analyzed the distinction between legal guilt or crime, which demands punishment, and moral guilt or sin, which requires atonement or expiation. Expiation, she explained, is born of contrition, which has its effects "in the soul." Expiation is, accordingly, carried out interiorly, as is atonement, but expiation is characterized by the free taking upon oneself of a quite definite suffering or punishment to offset or balance a concrete sin *(peccatum actuale)*. Atonement, on the other hand, is directed against the sinful state of the soul and not a specific sin.[44]

Edith's powerful reflections on suffering and the cross written during the last years of her life are clearly marked by the distinctions in this very early study. For her, therefore, it was logical that the extreme violence of Hitler's Germany had to be balanced or blotted out by a greater measure of suffering freely borne in expiation. This is apparent in a meditation inspired by John of the Cross's love of suffering. He was the guide of Edith's desire, the person whose life and teaching undoubtedly had the most profound influence of all on her desire for voluntary expiatory suffering.[45] Edith's words bear the mark of John's passion for the way of the cross:

> The entire sum of human failures...must be blotted out by a corresponding measure of expiation. The way of the cross is this expiation....Typical of those who submit to the suffering inflicted on them and experience his blessing by bearing it is Simon of Cyrene....Christ the head effects expiation in these members of his Mystical Body who put themselves, body and soul, at his disposal for carrying out his work of salvation....[46] The meaning of the way of the cross is to carry this burden [of sin] out of the world [like the scapegoat and like Jesus].[47]

Edith Stein was concerned about the Body of Christ, her own people, the human community, and as an authentic carrier of the communal life she was squarely, and some would say audaciously, placing herself in the battle going on between good and evil in that community, striving to shape its spirit. Is it blasphemous to suggest that, in a prophetic critique of the idolatrous and barbarous plans of her own German people, she, like Jesus in his death, wanted to absorb the evil energy of hate and violence of the Nazi regime, throw down the drawbridge to receive the evil abroad in the world, and carry it out into the desert to its death in her own body, like Jesus, on the shoulders of a love that could not be spent down? Even though she knew it would kill her? Like a scapegoat, in a collective transfer of energy to a victim, she desired to soak up the violence of the German state, ultimately of humankind, and thereby be a cause of harmony and peace, to surrender herself like Jesus so that men and women could be freed from their hate by unloading their wickedness on her.[48] Only love could bear the freight of such suffering, and yet she yearned to give back in love more than was being taken away in hate.[49]

I believe Edith knew God needs no human expiation or atonement, but rather human persons must be extricated from their own prison if they are to be capable of opening their hearts to God's freely-offered love and thereby be liberated from their resentment. Her theology, on some issues, manifests such a surprisingly close affinity with the thought of German theologian Raymund Schwager that his theology actually throws light on hers. Writing some thirty-seven years after Edith's death, Schwager insists, in his analysis of violence and redemption in the Bible, that it is not God who must be appeased, but humans who must be delivered from their hatred, resentment, and will to kill.[50]

We must remember that Edith's personalist phenomenology was built upon the certainty that no human being is a mere individual; we all tap into a kind of energy from other persons and especially from the common reservoir of the community.[51] Because we are all connected in a vast network, whether we send love or hate along the energy currents is critical for the healing and evolution of human consciousness.[52] If we take into account Edith's strong assertion of woman's superior destiny to be educator and empathic redeemer of humanity, that is, to bring true humanity in herself and then in others to more mature development,[53] her words in 1939 for the feast of the Exaltation of the Cross, the day vows are renewed in Carmel, pierce our hearts in all their poignant passion and strong critique of immediate consciousness:

> Will you remain faithful to the Crucified?...The world is in flames, the battle between Christ and the Antichrist has broken into the open. If you decide for Christ, it could cost you your life....Before you hangs the Savior on the cross...*obedient* unto death on the cross....The Savior hangs naked and destitute before you....Do not be concerned with your own body....The Savior hangs before you with a pierced heart....It is the loving heart of your Savior that invites you to follow....From the open heart gushes the blood of the Savior. This extinguishes the flames of hell. Make your heart free...then the flood of divine love will be poured [concretely ported, hardwired] into your heart until it overflows and becomes fruitful to all the ends of the earth....If you are nuptially bound to him...your *being* is precious blood. Bound to him, you are omnipresent as he is....You can be at all fronts, wherever there is grief, in the power of the cross. Your compassionate love takes you everywhere, this love from the divine heart. Its precious blood is poured everywhere—soothing, healing, saving.[54]

"Your *being* is precious blood." We are stunned by such a forfeiture of selfhood, such a transparent premonition of her physical death and so profound a consciousness of her vocation to carry compassionate love, the fruit of mature contemplative prayer, out of the very circumscribed space of the cloister into the depths of the abyss, "to walk on the dirty and rough paths of this earth...and [to] cry with the children of this world,"[55] to be, in fact, a carrier of helpless compassionate divinity into the bowels of hell and to answer the conspiracy of hatred with an outpouring of love. The cross revealed to her that God is to be found in the midst of pain and violence, with Christ and with crucified people; so would she be and thus could she write:

> The more powerfully God woos the soul and the more completely it surrenders to him [sic], the darker will be the night and the more painful the death.[56]

Solidarity

Edith Stein could not intellectually unravel the scandal of suffering and human violence, the mystery of the cross, any more than we can. As her union with God deepened, she could only enter more and more radically, and even joyfully, into solidarity with the Crucified Christ and those who suffer after the pattern confirmed by John of the Cross toward the end of *The Spiritual Canticle*.

> It will be a singular comfort and happiness for her [the one united to God] to enter all the afflictions and trials of the world, and everything that might be a means to this, however difficult and painful, even the anguish and agony of death, all in order to see herself further within her God. (SC.36.11–13)[57]

During the nine years Edith lived in Carmel, what carrying the cross really meant for her evolved in tandem with Germany's escalating hatred of the Jews. Even before she entered Carmel, however, she sensed their fate would also be hers. This premonition is not altogether surprising, but what is profoundly disturbing, at first read-ing, is her interpretation of the Jewish oppression.[58]

> I talked with the Savior [she remembers] and told him I
> knew that it was His Cross that was now being placed
> upon the Jewish people; that most of them did not under-
> stand this, but that those who did, would have to take it up
> willingly in the name of all. I would do that. He should
> only show me how. At the end of the service I was certain
> that I had been heard. But what this carrying of the cross
> would consist in, that I did not yet know.[59]

What reading do we give to Edith's experience? As early as
1933, she seemed to grasp by a kind of prophetic intuition that both
in Jesus' death on the cross and in the Nazis' torturous, evil repression
of the Jews we see the same unmitigated violence and hatred of the
other, the same sin. We see the same projection of violence onto a
scapegoat, the same sins of the many placed upon the innocent. The
Jews were not sinless as Jesus was. They were human; they were not
flawless but in their innocence as a collective racial scapegoat, they
were like Jesus in bearing the sins of the many. Edith may have been
suggesting that, like Jesus, they were dying for all because all had
already turned against them, rejected them, concretely transferring to
them their resentment against God and their will to kill.[60] In this
sense, the gas chamber was like the cross in that the same burden of
hatred and exclusion was placed upon the Jews as had been placed
upon Jesus. What had killed Jesus, Marianne Sawicki suggests, also
killed the Jews: hatred of humanity.[61] In both cases, in fact, we detect
the rejection of the full, overflowing humanity of the Jew Jesus and
by implication the presence of the divine in every human person.
Manifested in the extermination of the Jews and all Jewishness from
the human gene pool was, therefore, the real hatred and ultimate
rejection of God. Edith apparently recognized this deep-seated

human resentment against God that showed itself in the repudiation of the reality of Incarnation and God-likeness in which every kind of degradation becomes possible.

In the last analysis, what the systematic dehumanization and death of the Jews signified for Edith was the abhorrence and denial of humanity's fundamental, intrinsic, unbreakable interconnectedness, solidarity, and communion in God beneath all socially constructed differences. This amounted to a radical rejection of the lifelong pillars of her intellectual and spiritual life. I am convinced that the pronounced orientation of her spirituality toward voluntary expiation in identification with Jesus Crucified must be interpreted in terms of solidarity, and its central significance as a value coming out of her particular work as a phenomenologist and her prayer development as a Carmelite. Here, I believe, we find the contemporary key for accessing her passionate language of expiation and intentional suffering.

Conclusion: Contemplative Conviction and Prophetic Vision

Edith was one of those persons, as she herself described in 1920, who with special sensitivity serves as the open eyes with which the community looks at the world. She knew even then that when the failure of the masses stands in the way of the receptivity of a true vision of values, it is crucial for those who possess eyes open to the world of spiritual values not to be closed in on or concerned about themselves, but rather turned outward to permit the wealth of their inner life to become visible in the community—even if the community at large is not receptive or succumbs to collective delusion.[62]

Twenty years later, having been educated by Carmelite tradition, life, and prayer, her early insight matured into a prophetic, contemplative conviction. Thus she explained only a year and a half before her death:

The deeper a soul is bound to God…[The silent working of the Holy Spirit made them into friends of God], the stronger will be its influence on the form of the church. Conversely, the more an era is engulfed in sin and estrangement from God the more it needs souls united to God….The greatest figures of prophecy and sanctity step forth out of the darkest night. But for the most part the formative stream of the mystical life remains invisible. Certainly the decisive turning points in world history are substantially co-determined by souls whom no history ever mentions….Because hidden souls do not live in isolation, but are a part of the living nexus and have a position in a great divine order, we speak of an invisible church. Their impact and affinity can remain hidden from themselves and others for their entire earthly lives. But it is also possible for some of this to become visible in the external world…[e.g., Mary, Joseph, Anna, Zechariah, Elizabeth, etc.] all of these had behind them a solitary life with God and were prepared for their special tasks before they found themselves together in those awesome encounters and events and, in retrospect, could understand how the paths left behind led to this climax.[63]

Edith was a carrier of the communal life and consciousness of Carmel, of the Jews, of the church, of the Germans, of humanity, into the belly of hell. Her voluntary going, "Rosa, come, let us go for our people," signaled her deliberate desire to stand in the face of communal blindness for an unbreakable love and solidarity, for a defiance of the conspiracy of hatred, of exclusion, and marginalization, of reprisal, of evil for evil. Ultimately, she witnessed like Jesus to God's salvation to humanity in overflowing love. She took the mystical stream of the church, its deepest life, beyond the confinement of cloister and the boundaries of Carmel into the horror of Auschwitz.

Words from her last letter on the way to the gas chamber, "So far I have been able to pray gloriously,"[64] epitomize with peaceful simplicity an earlier expression of her belief:

> When this mystical stream breaks through traditional forms, it does so because the Spirit that blows where it will is living in it, this Spirit that has created all traditional forms and must ever create new ones....[Then the carriers of the mystical stream] can do nothing but radiate to other hearts the divine love that fills them and so participate in the perfection of all into unity in God which was and is Jesus' great desire.[65]

I sense that in her life as an intellectual, in her death in the Holocaust as a voluntary scapegoat, Edith broke though the traditional form of the Carmelite nun, a stone rejected and yet destined to become, in the twenty-first century, a cornerstone in Carmel. This is why we dare not minimize the extent of the influence of her passionate intellectual life upon her equally passionate contemplative prayer, nor the radicality of her total involvement in the social situation. Neither may we spiritualize the brutality and anonymity of her death: one among six million, stripped naked, violated at the very least by the eyes of the guards, herded into the gas chamber, murdered, reduced to smoke billowing into Polish skies, with only vague memories of her peace and care of the women and children remaining. With an unspeakable, fathomless forfeiture of possessive selfhood, she took the life of Carmel, of the Carmelite nun, to a new frontier far beyond the familiar.

If, as many pray, our civilization with its dying totalitarian systems, its holocausts, its destruction of life, its mass tortures, rapes, and murders, its rampant ethnic hatred, its oppression of the poor and marginal, even its struggle over the death penalty, is the last long gasp of a vengeful society, it will be because people like Edith have dismantled hatred by refusing to imitate evil with corresponding vengeance, and have injected love into the energy current connecting humankind and everything living in the universe in a vast network of interdependence. Edith Stein offers a key to the passion of the Carmelite prayer tradition today. She is an inspiration and teacher in fashioning a healthy, though demanding, contemporary Carmelite spirituality of selflessness and cosmic communion that makes a place for a very real, inescapable dispossession of selfhood in the service of love and solidarity.

The way Edith described John of the Cross at the end of *The Science of the Cross*, after following him through his life and writings, I want to apply to her because it summarizes and completes this study:

> [Her] soul had, indeed, attained to perfect detachment, to simplicity and silence in union with God. But this was the fruit of an interior purification in which a richly gifted nature burdened itself with the Cross and surrendered itself to God to be crucified, a most powerful and lively spirit made [herself] a prisoner, an impassioned fiery heart found peace in radical resignation. The accounts of the witnesses confirm this result.[66]

Notes

1. For the author, three questions form a background for this essay. First, where do we really find passion or excess in the Carmelite tradition? Second, how does the passion of the Carmelite tradition meet the hunger of our own time for spirituality and even mystical experience, the thirst for the divine and for community? Third, how does the Carmelite tradition move out from the familiar, from an enclosure of language and esotericism into new social and cultural situations? I am deeply indebted to Leah Hargis, O.C.D., for formatting the endnotes and helping me with the Edith Stein sources which she knows extremely well. My discussions with her were invaluable.
2. *Webster's Twentieth Century Unabridged Dictionary*, 2d ed., s.v. "passion." It is instructive to note synonyms for passion such as: ardor, rapture, vehemence, zeal, devotion, pathos, and attachment.

3. Thérèse to Sr. Agnes of Jesus, August 30-31, 1890, *Saint Thérèse of Lisieux: General Correspondence,* Vol. 1; trans. John Clarke (Washington, D.C.: ICS, 1982), no. 110.

4. Ibid. Thérèse to Marie Guerin, July 27–29, 1890, no. 109.

5. Edith Stein, "Love of the Cross: Some Thoughts for the Feast of St. John of the Cross," *The Hidden Life: Hagiographic Essays, Meditations, Spiritual Texts,* trans. Waltraut Stein (Washington, D.C.: ICS, 1992), 91. This is vol. 4, *The Collected Works of Edith Stein.*

6. I am aware that some have difficulty with a call to self-transcendence. They see it as a denial of the human, of the need for a strong, well-developed sense of self. This is especially threatening and even unfair for women, many of whom have come so belatedly into full selfhood. Nevertheless, the summons to a cosmic consciousness is so urgent and the spiritual experience of some women so compelling that I think we must speak of self-transcendence until we have another word that expresses the true radicality of the challenge today.

7. See Patricia Hampl, I *Could Tell You Stories: Sojourns in the Land of Memory* (New York: W.W. Norton, 1999), 104–5.

8. Edith Stein to Roman Ingarden, February 3 and 9,1917, *Self-Portrait in Letters: 1916–1942,* trans. Josephine Koeppel (Washington, D.C.: ICS, 1993), nos. 6 and 7.

9. Ibid. Edith to Roman Ingarden, February 19,1918, no. 19.

10. Stein," On the History and Spirit of Carmel," *The Hidden Life,* 1–6.

11. Stein, "I Will Remain With You…" *The Hidden Life,* 135.

12. Edith Stein, *The Science of the Cross: A Study of St. John of the Cross,* trans. Hilda Graef (Chicago: Henry Regnery, 1960), 122.

13. Ibid., 207.

14. Edith Stein, *Life in a Jewish Family,* trans. Josephine Koeppel (Washington, D.C.: ICS, 1986), 185, n. 86. And Edith to Fritz Kaufmann, November 8, 1919, *Self-Portrait in Letters,* no. 31.

15. Edith to Sr. Adelgundis Jaegerschmid, June 9, 1932, *Self-Portrait in Letters,* no. 116.

16. Ibid., Edith to P. Petrus Wintrath, June 12, 1932, no. 117.

17. Ibid., Edith to Hedwig Conrad-Martius, November 13, 1932, no. 126.

18. Ibid., Edith to Hedwig, February 24, 1933, no. 135.

19. Ibid., Edith to Hedwig, April 5, 1933, no. 139.

20. Ibid., Edith to Fritz Kaufmann, September 13, 1925, no. 38a.

21. Ibid., Edith to Roman Ingarden, February 9, 1917, no. 7.

22. Rachel Felday Brenner, *Writing as Resistance: Four Women Confronting the Holocaust* (University Park, Pa.: Pennsylvania State University, 1996), 80–84.

23. Edith Stein, *Philosophy of Psychology and the Humanities*, ed. and trans., Marianne Sawicki (Washington, D.C.: ICS, 2000), vol. 7, *The Collected Works of Edith Stein*, 273–83.

24. This statement was the last one made by Edith Stein to her sister Rosa upon their arrest and departure from the Carmel at Echt in the Netherlands and is widely quoted in numerous biographical works.

25. Stein, *Science of the Cross*, 85, see also 137.

26. Edith to Sr. Adelgundis Jaegerschmid, April 28, 1931, *Self-Portrait in Letters*, no. 89.

27. Ibid., Edith to Rose Magold, August 20, 1931, no. 103.

28. Ibid., Edith to Anneliese Lichtenberger, August 17 ,1931, no. 102.

29. Stein, "The Spirit of St. Elizabeth as It Informed Her Life," *The Hidden Life*, 28.

30. Hilda C. Graef, *The Scholar and the Cross: The Life and Writings of Edith Stein* (London: Longmans, Green, 1955), 100.

31. Stein, "On the History and Spirit of Carmel," *The Hidden Life*, 6.

32. I was greatly assisted toward a more thorough comprehension of phenomenology as Edith understood it by a lengthy conversation with Dr. Marianne Sawicki in the spring of 2000. She introduced the notion of "porting" and defined "motivation," "demand," and "value" as Edith would have understood them. This paragraph and the one that follows have been influenced by Dr. Sawicki's explanations.

33. Stein, "Elevation of the Cross, September 14, 1939: Ave Crux, Spes Unica!" *The Hidden Life*, 94–96. Edith Stein would have understood contemporary Christologies which see the suffering Christ as "the paradigmatic locus of divine involvement in the pain of the world." See Elizabeth A. Johnson, *She Who Is* (New York: Crossroad, 1992), 263.

34. Stein, *Science of the Cross*, 89.

35. Stein, "Love of the Cross," *The Hidden Life*, 92.

36. Stein, *Life in a Jewish Family*, 190.

37. Mary Catherine Baseheart, *Person in the World: Introduction to the Philosophy of Edith Stein* (Dordrecht, The Netherlands: Kluwer Academic Publishers, 1997), vol. 27, *Contributions to Phenomenology*, 69.

38. Ibid., 62–66. See also Stein, *Philosophy of Psychology and the Humanities*, 278–79.

39. Stein, "Love of the Cross," *The Hidden Life*, 93.

40. Ibid., 92.

41. I have drawn in this paragraph from the excellent synthesis of Roger Haight, *Jesus: Symbol of God* (Maryknoll, N.Y.: Orbis, 1999), 223-43 and also Raymund Schwager, *Must There Be Scapegoats?: Violence and Redemption in the Bible* (New York: Crossroad, 2000), 206.

42. Stein, *Life in a Jewish Family*, 71.
43. See, for example, Stein, "The Prayer of the Church," and "The Marriage of the Lamb," *The Hidden Life*, 12 and 97–98.
44. Edith Stein, "Eine Untersuchung über den Staat," *Jahrbuch fur Philosophie und phanomenologische Forschung* 7 (1925): 103-8, footnote. (Reprinted Tubingen: Niemeyer, 1970).
45. Edith spent her retreat for her "clothing" in the Carmelite habit with *The Ascent of Mount Carmel*, her retreat for first profession with *The Dark Night*. *The Science of the Cross* is her study of John's complete works. She referred several times in her letters to her ongoing reading of and meditation on the writings of John of the Cross.
46. Stein, "Love of the Cross," *The Hidden Life*, 91–92.
47. Ibid., 91.
48. Note that Roger Haight points to Raymund Schwager's soteriology as one theological view of "how Jesus saves." Schwager employs the anthropological theory of René Girard regarding violence as a hermeneutical framework for interpreting the manner in which the death of Jesus mediates God's salvation. Haight, *Jesus: Symbol of God*, 349; see also Schwager, *Must There Be Scapegoats?* 212, and 190–214.
49. See Roger Haight's explanation of Anselm's theory of satisfaction in *Jesus: Symbol of God*, 229: "Satisfaction presupposes injury done. It consists not in rendering to God what is owed God...but in making up to God for an injury done and repairing damage....This means going beyond restitution.....It entails that one 'give back more than one takes away.'" Edith uses Anselm's exact words from *Cur Deus Homo*.
50. Schwager, *Must There Be Scapegoats?* 209.
51. Marianne Sawicki, "Edith Stein and the Prospects for Jewish-Catholic Dialogue" (Comments prepared for the panel discussion at Holy Cross College, October 20, 1999), 3.
52. Edith to Erna Stein, July 6, 1918, *Self-Portrait in Letters*, no. 24.
53. See Brenner, *Writing As Resistance*, 164–73. In words closer to Augustine we could say the real sacrifice of her life, in an inner act of total devotion, was motivated by an overwhelming desire to make visible or bring closer to fulfillment humankind's unity through Christ in God. See Haight, *Jesus: Symbol of God*, 224–25.
54. Stein, "Elevation of the Cross, September 14, 1939: Ave Crux, Spes Unica!" *The Hidden Life*, 94–96.
55. Stein, "Love of the Cross," *The Hidden Life*, 93.
56. Stein, *Science of the Cross*, 207.
57. I have described this kind of spiritual maturity in my essay, "Transformation in Wisdom: The Subversive Character and Educative

Power of Sophia in Contemplation," *Carmel and Contemplation* (Washington, D.C.: ICS, 2000), 334–35.

58. Sawicki, "Edith Stein and the Prospects for Jewish-Catholic Dialogue," 4.

59. Stein, "How I Came to the Cologne Carmel," December 18,1938, *Edith Stein: Selected Writings with Comments, Reminiscences and Translations of Her Prayers and Poems by Her Niece,* trans. Susanne M. Batzdorff (Springfield, Ill.: Templegate, 1990), 17.

60. Although the application to the Jews is mine, I am clearly indebted to Schwager's interpretation of Jesus' suffering and death in *Must There Be Scapegoats?* 205–14.

61. Sawicki, "Edith Stein and the Prospects for Jewish-Catholic Dialogue," 4.

62. Baseheart, *Person in the World,* 62.

63. Stein, "The Hidden Life and Epiphany," *The Hidden Life,* 110–11.

64. Edith to Mother Ambrosia Antonia Engelmann of Echt Carmel, August 6, 1942, *Self-Portrait in Letters,* no. 342.

65. Stein, "The Prayer of the Church," *The Hidden Life,* 15–16.

66. Stein, *Science of the Cross,* 223.

11

The Carmelite Tradition and Centering Prayer/ Christian Meditation

Ernest E. Larkin, O. Carm.

In this chapter I propose to interface the Carmelite tradition on contemplative prayer and two popular forms of contemplative practice called Centering Prayer and Christian Meditation. We are asking how these widely used, current practices fit into that tradition. Do the new forms agree or disagree with past thinking? What does the Carmelite tradition have to say about them, for and against?

These forms are new, though their proponents maintain that they are simply the contemplative tradition of the church in contemporary dress. How should the Carmelite tradition regard them? Are they in continuity with the past and to what extent do they represent something new? These are the questions of this essay.

An Historical Vignette

Let me begin with a little history that sets the stage for our inquiry. One of the first generation of Discalced Carmelite writers, José de J.-M. Quiroga (1562–1628) set down the method of mental prayer taught by St. John of the Cross. It consisted of three steps:

(1) the representation of some mysteries; (2) pondering them; and (3) experiencing the fruit of the process in "an attentive and loving quietude toward God," "a peaceful, loving and calm quiet of faith," and a "simple attention to God."¹ The method was contemplative, because it led into passing moments of contemplation; these moments became longer and longer and soon dominated the prayer. The pondering too was likely more a prayer of the heart than heavy-handed reasoning, weighing the truth rather than analyzing it. The contemplative moments coalesced into the habit or state of contemplation, as taught by St. John of the Cross in *The Ascent of Mount Carmel* (2.14.2). Thus the habit of contemplation was built up, according to the adage: sow an act and you reap a habit. This result was called acquired contemplation, a contemplative experience of God that by definition could be achieved by ordinary grace and human industry.

Contemplation was thus deemed accessible to any sincere seeker. According to Quiroga, John of the Cross expected his novices to reach at least this state of initial contemplation by the end of the one-year novitiate, an opinion shared by Thomas of Jesus (1564–1627) and others.²

This thumbnail history recalls a time very much like our own, a time of great enthusiasm and optimism about reaching contemplation. The concept of an acquired contemplation democratized contemplation and made it available to all. John himself spoke explicitly only about special, infused contemplation, a mystical gift which presumably was not available to everybody. This transitional, acquired contemplation was there for the taking according to the early Discalced teachers, who claimed John of the Cross as warranty for this opinion.

In this essay we accept both kinds of contemplation as valid outcomes of contemplative practice.³ We believe that acquired contemplation is the same reality as initial infused contemplation; only the naming and theological explanation are different. The legitimacy of

acquired contemplation was defended as recently as the 1940s by the
eminent Discalced Carmelite, Gabriel of St. Mary Magdalen.[4]

Contemplative Prayer Today

We cite this history as a backdrop for the topic of this chapter.
Today thousands of devout Christians are pondering the mystery of
God's presence in daily contemplative prayer. They sit silently before
an ikon or the tabernacle and, if asked, they would describe their
prayer as simple, loving attention beyond words or images. "I look at
him and he looks at me." They ponder in very simple attention as John
of the Cross's second step directs, and they experience a sense of loving presence as in the third step of John of the Cross's method of meditation. The third step, in fact, is the point of the prayer, its beginning
of attention to God and end. The ability to stay in this posture of
attention to God is assumed, and no clear distinction is drawn between
the discrete acts and the state of contemplation that is developed.

The ancients postulated a long and consistent effort at daily
meditation to reach the state of acquired contemplation—one year
was thought sufficient but likely necessary among the Carmelites
cited above. More recently, say in the fifties or sixties, this view was
considered optimistic because contemplation was seen as a far-off
goal. Now we are being taught to practice directly and immediately
a quiet, gentle resting in God that is considered to be contemplation
and to lead to ever higher degrees of contemplation.

The contemporary methods consist in the very acts that were
the fruit of the representation and the pondering in John of the
Cross's meditation. The contemplation in these contemplative acts is
left generic in nature, having lost its specificity. In modern writing
contemplation describes almost any mental prayer that is silent and
wordless, from quiet resting in the divine presence to infused contemplation. Infused contemplation remains a special mystical gift,

admittedly rare and extraordinary in the spiritual life. But contemplation is for everyone to practice in these new methods.

What are these methods? We single out Centering Prayer,
taught by Contemplative Outreach under the leadership of Thomas
Keating, and Christian Meditation, as developed by John Main and
promoted by the World Community for Christian Meditation under
the leadership of Laurence Freeman. These two methods of simple,
non-discursive, loving attention to God are chosen for study out of a
plethora of nondiscursive ways of praying because they are widely
known and practiced in North America today. They are lumped
together, because they are similar in approach. They have the same
roots in the Western mystical tradition, and while they have significant differences, they are more alike than different and they offer
name recognition for each other.

Lectio Divina

Let me introduce these prayers in the context of *lectio divina*.
Lectio divina is the ancient, monastic formula for appropriating the biblical text and for leading the practitioner into the experience of contemplation. A biblical text is read, pondered, prayed over, and finally
experienced. The first three acts of *lectio divina*—reading, meditating,
praying—culminate in the fourth act of tasting or touching the reality in the text. The fourth act is called *contemplation*. It is more receptive than the first three, though the whole *lectio divina* in the monastic
tradition is a contemplative exercise.

Thomas Keating often presents Centering Prayer as a way to
restore this contemplative dimension of *lectio divina*. For too long the
prayer has been too heady and rationalistic; the first three discursive
acts have received almost exclusive attention and the final act is neglected. He would correct that imbalance by promoting the fourth act
on its own as the way to renew the contemplative character of *lectio
divina*. The Trappists designed a prayer form that begins and ends

with the fourth act. This Centering Prayer is to be practiced method-ically and regularly twice a day as the keystone of one's prayer life. Centering Prayer does not replace *lectio*, nor is it a new form of *lectio divina*. It is an exercise to sharpen one's contemplative awareness, a way to renew all four acts by raising the contemplative character of a person's life. Christian Meditation has a similar purpose.

John Main considers his discipline of meditating to be the tra-ditional Christian meditation of the past. He is simply renewing the meditative or contemplative practice of the past, and for him medita-tion and contemplation are the same. He calls his prayer "contempla-tion, contemplative prayer, and meditative practice," all three terms being synonyms with meditation.[5] Main's meditation, in his view, is mainline Christian practice from the past, and it is practiced in the rosary or litanies, in the Jesus prayer, and in the short ejaculatory phrases as taught by John Cassian and *The Cloud of Unknowing*. Christian Meditation for him stands on its own as the meditation of the Christian tradition over against rational, discursive methods; it is receptive and nondiscursive by definition.

These two methods of prayer represent one answer to the yearning for the experience of God in our time. Centering Prayer came out of the sixties and seventies, when many people, youth espe-cially, were turning to Eastern religions and transcendental medita-tion for spiritual experience and enlightenment. Older spiritually awakened Christians were likewise experiencing a hunger for God and for a deeper prayer life. Both young and old were concerned with the practical question of how to pray contemplatively. They were looking for methods like those available in the Eastern religions.

The architects of these new prayer forms learned from the East, but they based their teaching on the ancient, Western mystical tradi-tion. The Trappists at Spencer, Massachusetts developed Centering Prayer largely from *The Cloud of Unknowing*. John Main discovered Christian Meditation in John Cassian. As a layman Main had learned the original lines of his approach from an Eastern swami, but he found his way of meditating in John Cassian and the *Cloud*. John Main made the teaching of contemplative prayer to lay people the life-work of his later years.

The new styles of contemplative prayer go right to the heart of prayer, seeking experience and contact with the living God in loving faith and quiet presence. They are a discipline that is anchored in the two periods of prayer each day, each for twenty minutes to a half hour. The two periods represent a conversion, a new commitment that is to be the heart and soul of a new prayer life. The two periods are to be faithfully carried out as the first order of one's prayer life each day. The rest of one's spiritual life is energized from here. The contemplative union fostered in Centering Prayer or Christian Meditation brings a contemplative dimension to the celebration of liturgy, to Bible reading, and the practice of *lectio divina*, as well as to vocal prayer, to community life, and ministry.

The new methods are not magic. They are providential discoveries of our time, gifts of God that are there for the taking, and they promise intimacy with God. They are active prayer, but the activity is simple and receptive. One sits before the Lord, and the hoped-for outcome is the inbreaking of God from the other side, the divine touch that is God's response to the human efforts, which themselves are antecedently inspired by God. The contemplation or experience of God is not necessarily verifiable psychologically. The divine visit is validated by the fruits of the Spirit. The person strives to be open and welcoming, to be empty and poor in spirit, and these attitudes are invitations to a deeper divine presence. Whatever the empirical experience in the human consciousness, the contemplative activity is bringing about transformation in the depths of the person and this conversion will show itself in the person's life.

The whole person—body, soul, and spirit—is engaged in the prayer. The body is brought into the process via posture, breathing, relaxation, and the use of a holy word or mantra. The psychological functions of thinking, feeling, willing, and loving are definitely in play in muted, simple ways. The main task of the one praying is nondiscursive attention by use of the mantra throughout the prayer in Christian Meditation, or attending and consenting to the presence of God within and using the sacred word as needed in Centering Prayer. The one praying is knocking ever so gently at the door of the Spirit deep within, awaiting further action from the indwelling God.

The Carmelite Tradition

We are now ready to look at the Carmelite tradition for its evaluation of these two new methods of prayer. The sources we shall examine are *The Rule of St. Albert, The Institution of the First Monks*, the writings of Teresa of Avila and John of the Cross, and of the Touraine Reform. I shall identify each of the less known sources as we address them.

We begin our inquiry with the earliest document of the Carmelite Order, *The Rule of St. Albert*, composed between 1206 and 1214. It was originally a letter from the patriarch of Jerusalem that presented a *formula vitae* or life pattern for the hermits; it was revised into a full-fledged rule by Innocent IV in 1247. This latter is the primitive rule in Teresa of Avila's understanding and the ideal to which she recalled the Order.

The Rule describes a life rather than particular practices of prayer. This is brought out by the Dutch artist Arie Trum in the beautiful symbol designed to express the rule entitled "No Image Satisfies." The entire text of the Rule is written out in cruciform with a golden circle in the center. The Rule leads one into the circle. The circle is empty and it is the place of encounter with God. This empty space represents "purity of heart," which is the condition for full "allegiance to Jesus Christ" (Rule, prologue). Emptiness and fullness are the core of the Carmelite Rule.

The Rule itself is eminently scriptural, being a collage of explicit and implicit citations. The Word of God forms the Carmelite and it is mediated through the liturgy (daily Mass); the psalms, originally read privately, later recited in the Divine Office; public Bible reading at meetings and in the refectory; and above all *lectio divina*, prescribed in the famous chapter seven: "Let all remain in their cells, or near them, meditating day and night on the law of the Lord and keeping vigil in prayer, unless occupied with other lawful duties." This is the defining chapter of the Rule, though the communal aspects emphasized in studies today are likewise foundational. The community is the place where personal transformation takes place and ministry originates.

What is the meaning of "meditating" and "keeping vigil in prayer" in this primary text of the Rule? The answer will be found in the monastic practice of the time, which came from the Desert Fathers and Mothers through John Cassian and the ancient rules of Basil and Benedict; it was the monastic form of *lectio divina*. There were other forms of praying as well, such as the Our Father, the psalms, and the Jesus prayer. But one special way of meditating or pondering the Word of God was repeating phrases of Scripture, often aloud, after the teaching of Cassian, who suggested the words, "God, come to my assistance; Lord, make haste to help me."[6] This use of a mantra fits the prayer of the heart, which Thomas Merton characterizes as meditation in the Desert tradition.[7] This prayer was not intellectual analysis or active use of the imagination. Prayer of the heart consisted in entering deeply into one's self to seek purity of heart, that is, utter detachment and surrender to the indwelling God. The way to the heart was the Word of God. Biblical phrases were repeated and pondered as in the Jesus prayer, which is a perfect example of the method followed. The goal was both transformation and continuous, loving conversation with God according to the exhortation of chapter fourteen, which says: "May you possess abundantly in your mouth and hearts the sword of the spirit, which is God's Word. Just so whatever you do, let it be done in the Lord's Word." This way of meditation was the *hagah* tradition of the Old

Testament, which consisted in reciting passages from sacred Scripture aloud from memory and repeating short phrases of the psalms to root the thought in the mind and heart.[8] The continuous repetition was called murmuring. Kees Waaijman describes the practice in an Old Testament context:

> One "murmured" the Torah, "ruminating" it until the text had completely become one's own, and began to "sigh from within" as the cooing of a dove. One made the Torah one's own bodily, emotionally, cognitively, memorizing it so that he ultimately became one with Torah.[9]

The whole person was involved—the voice, the imagination, the feelings, the mind, and heart—and the whole person was to be "clothed" with the Word of God. A new person emerged.

The method of meditating, therefore, was not objectified thinking, but pondering the Word of God in one's heart, with one's whole interior being in nondiscursive attention. Even the mouth and the tongue participated, so that the pondering was physical as well as interior. This was one reason for placing the solitary cells at a distance from each other in order not to disturb the neighbors by noisy prayer.[10] The end in view, however, was both public praise and the transformation of the person, letting the word of God penetrate one's very being for a new, personal identity after the scriptural model.

How close all this is to the mantra of John Main, and to a lesser extent to the sacred word of Thomas Keating. The Carmelite is called to the prayer of the heart, a prayer thoroughly contemplative in method and goal. The prayer is holistic as well, involving body and soul. John Main's selfless attention and Thomas Keating's consent to the divine presence are expressed in the ancient practice. All these forms are ways into the golden circle of Arie Trum, where self-emptying makes room for the living God.

The Institution of the First Monks

The same perspectives of the Rule are found in the second document under inquiry, *The Institution of the First Monks*, a treatise on Carmelite life written by Felip Ribot, a Catalonian, about A.D. 1370 The work is a symbolic history of Elijah that was to function as a spiritual directory for the Carmelites who were living in new circumstances in Europe away from Mount Carmel. Originally the book purported to be history; then it was interpreted to be a record of myths and legends. Today it is regarded as symbolic history, a serious effort to interpret Carmelite life through the life of Elijah. The mystical character of the Order is affirmed in the strongest terms with the same perspectives on emptiness and fullness found in the golden circle of Arie Trum.

The key passage is a commentary on the command to Elijah to "go eastward and hide in the brook Carith," where he would "drink of the torrent" (cf. 1 Kings 17:2–4). The spiritual or mystical interpretation of these words is as follows:

> These words to Elijah...reveal the twofold aim of religious life and the path God wants us to follow to perfection: 1) "To offer to God a heart holy and pure from all stain of sin," [and] 2) "To taste in our hearts and experience in our minds, not only after death but even in this life, something of the power of the divine presence and the bliss of eternal glory..."[11]

In an unpublished paper delivered at a study week at the Washington Theological Union in September, 1996, Hein Blommestijn used John Cassian to analyze this passage and to show that the twofold purpose is one movement of the Spirit with a proximate objective *(skopos)* and an ultimate goal *(telos)*. The *skopos* is to present to God a pure heart; the *telos* to experience God. Like the farmer's planting and cultivating his field with a view to the harvest, the work of purification is done in view of the experience of God. The first step occurs when one leaves one's own center and enters the empty circle; there God meets the person in a mystical encounter. The work is all God's. I enter the center and I become a new person, the result of what God is doing in me. The self-emptying and the encounter continue progressively throughout life. They are one movement with two stages, not first a life of asceticism and then another of mysticism. "Before Elijah could take a single step," the *Institution* says, "God had already set him in motion."[12]

The theology of Christian Meditation parallels this perspective of Felip Ribot. The mantra is an exercise in self-emptying. The mantra is the prayer, as Main repeats, and it is an exercise in selfless attention, the experience of poverty before God. At the same time it is an invitation for God to come, and this is the contemplation hoped for in the practice. John Cassian extends the role of the mantra beyond formal prayer into continuous prayer. It will effect purification and union, he says:

> Never cease to recite it in whatever task or service or journey you find yourself....This heartfelt thought will prove to be a formula of salvation for you. Not only will it protect you against all devilish attack, but it will purify you from the stain of all earthly sin and will lead you on to the contemplation of the unseen and the heavenly and to that fiery urgency of prayer which is indescribable and which is experienced by very few.[13]

Centering Prayer too has the same tasks of purification and union. Early on its practice reveals and confronts the false self, the wounded believer who is the victim of false emotional patterns of happiness that stand in opposition to the call of grace. These false systems are largely unconscious; Centering Prayer uncovers them, helps one recognize them as one's own, then effects their release, much as in the teaching of St. John of the Cross about the dark night of the senses. The emphasis on receptive consent in Centering Prayer hastens the unloading of the unconscious, to use Keating's phrase, and addresses the work of purification with more intensity.[14] In both Christian Meditation and Centering Prayer the organic connection between self-emptying and fullness, *kenosis* and *pleroma*, is basic to the practice.

St. Teresa of Avila

While Teresa had a prayer life before and after she entered Carmel in 1535, she confesses that she did not know how to go about praying until 1538, when she discovered Francis of Osuna's *Third Spiritual Alphabet* (BL.4.7). There she learned in a new way the fact of the divine indwelling and prayer as contact with the living God. "We need no wings to go in search of him," she wrote, "but have only to find a place where we can be alone and look upon him present within us" (WP.28.2).

Temperamentally Teresa could not search in discursive prayer, nor could she control her restless imagination and memory. Methodical meditation was an impossibility for her. She writes for people like herself, "for souls and minds so scattered that they are like wild horses no one can stop" (WP.19.2). Prayer for her was presence, loving presence, a fact she learned from Osuna as the heart of recollection. Recollection was gathering up one's soul, "collecting all one's faculties together and entering within itself to be with its God" (WP.28.4). Thus one moves within beyond the confining world of creatures into the sacred space of God.

Active recollection is the person's own doing. Once recollected one fruitfully practices vocal prayer like the Our Father. Recollection and vocal prayer were Teresa's mainstay. With gaze fixed on Christ she prayed the Our Father; this double practice was her recommendation for everyone and an easy way to the prayer of quiet (WP.28.4).[15]

Teresa also practiced and taught a silent prayer of recollection that is remarkably like Centering Prayer.[16] In this prayer the recall of an image from the Passion functioned in the same way as the sacred word. First, Teresa strove to be present to Christ. She used many stratagems to help her find this recollection, such as a book at hand, like a "Linus blanket," to be utilized as needed; inviting favorite saints like Mary Magdalen and the Samaritan woman to accompany her; holy cards; and nature scenes. But her main strategy and the very goal of the prayer was "representing Christ interiorly" (BL.4.7; WP.28.4).

This phrase is peculiarly Teresian. It does not mean imagining Christ—Teresa had little skill in this area. It means realizing that Christ is present now in her soul. This is a real presence of the living Christ. He is there: "your Spouse never takes his eyes off you" (WP.26.3). She does not see him; but he is there as if in the darkness, and he can be apprehended the way a blind person recognizes another person in the room. Representing Christ for Teresa means tuning into that real presence.

But, you say, does not Teresa counsel imagining Christ in some mystery of the Passion? Yes, she recommends recalling Christ suffering in Gethsemane or at the pillar when awareness and attention are fading. These recalls are accessories, images to reinvigorate a fading loving attention. They are means to heighten the sense of presence. They are images to be superimposed on the reality of the Christ within, to put a face on the faceless Christ. This recall of a gospel scene is like the sacred word in Centering Prayer. It is used as needed to refocus. The essence of the prayer is attending to the real Christ within; the imaging is totally secondary.

This method soon brought Teresa into mystical experiences of quiet and union. Notice how she connects these graces with the practice of "representing Christ":

> It used to happen, when I represented Christ within me in order to place myself in His presence, or even while reading, that a feeling of the presence of God would come over me unexpectedly, so that I could in no way doubt He was in me or I totally immersed in Him. This did not occur after the manner of a vision. I believe they call the experience "mystical theology." (BL.10.1)

Her full entry into the mystical state came after the long struggle of eighteen to twenty years. It took that long to integrate her whole being in God. Throughout this period as well as afterwards her basic strategy at prayer was the prayer of active recollection twice daily for an hour each time. This was a foundation stone of her reform. Today in the contemplative movements there are two briefer periods of similar prayer with the same goal of personal reform and renewal. The different specifications address different life situations and cultural conditions and are tailored accordingly.

St. John of the Cross

John of the Cross has no equivalent of active recollection in his synthesis. He has only two large categories of ways of relating to God, which he calls meditation and contemplation. These two forms describe self-directed activity (meditation), or pure receptivity before God (contemplation). They are adequately distinct from one another. Meditation uses our faculties and human potential always under grace to come to know and love God, and contemplation is infused light and love that are pure gifts of God. Contemplation in both Teresa of Avila and John of the Cross is always infused contemplation. John calls meditation a natural operation, contemplation a supernatural one, a terminology peculiar to Teresa, John, and others of the time.

We saw in the first part of this chapter that early followers of John developed a theory of acquired contemplation and appealed to his authority for the teaching. For some interpreters acquired contemplation is an oxymoron, a contradiction in terms. For others the self-directed achievement of a quiet, loving, restful presence to God beyond words and images is a real possibility. Acquired contemplation does not go beyond beginning contemplation, the experience described by John as "loving awareness of God, without particular considerations, in interior peace and quiet and repose, and without the acts and exercises (at least discursive, those in which one progresses from point to point)..." (A.2.13.4). This general loving awareness lacks the specific difference that defines classical or extraordinary infused contemplation, namely, the mystical union of the felt experience of God. Acquired contemplation is ordinary contemplation, in contrast to the extraordinary contemplation of the higher states. It is one possible outcome of active contemplative practice.

Centering Prayer and Christian Meditation are definitely active contemplative practice. The loving attention which they espouse comes from one's own initiative and deliberate choice and is different from the passive loving attention in the presence of infused contemplation, which John describes as the awareness of "a person who opens his eyes with loving attention" (LF.3.33). This latter use is pure receptivity, "doing nothing" in the strongest definition of that phrase. Active contemplative practice is doing something and this is why this practice belongs to meditation in John's schema.

John of the Cross may not speak as directly and volubly to budding contemplatives as does Teresa, but his teaching goes to the essentials. He knows exactly what practitioners of Centering Prayer and Christian Meditation must do to reach the transforming union. He spells out in detail what the Carmelite Rule and *The Institution of the First Monks* laid out in global terms about self-emptying and encountering God. The basis for this common understanding about growth in prayer is the Paschal Mystery, the life principle of the followers of Jesus Christ.

Death and resurrection are achieved in the contemplative through the practice of faith. Faith is the only proximate means of union with God, says John of the Cross, and this principle applies to the whole journey. Why is this so? Because faith screens out all that is not of God in our lives and welcomes God in all God's truth and beauty. Our Blessed Lady is the perfect example of this principle. She is the woman of faith, who listens and carries out the Word of God. She is like a window without spot, so that the sunlight totally dominates it; it is impossible to tell where the sunlight ends and the window begins. In Mary's case all her choices come from faith; she waits on the Word of God and follows it completely. There are no other choices in her life. Thus God dominates her life; God and her soul (herself) are "one in participant transformation, and the soul appears to be God more than a soul" (A.2.5.7). This is the ultimate goal of all contemplative prayer and the way to the deepening and expansion of the life of faith.

The Touraine Reform

The Touraine Reform is the glory of the Ancient Observance of the Carmelite Order. The reform began in the French province of Touraine in 1608 under the leadership of Philip Thibault (1572–1638); it spread through the lowlands and eventually affected the whole Order. The most famous spiritual leader in the reform was the blind brother, John of St. Samson, who has been called the French John of the Cross. The old Order lives by the spirit of Touraine more than any other influence.

Like the Teresian Reform, Touraine was not just aggiornamento or upgrading monastic discipline. It was a return to the primitive spirit of the Order, which Kilian Healy describes as "a life that was primarily (but not exclusively) contemplative wherein the spirit of solitude, silence and prayer reign supreme."[17] To this end the reform produced a significant body of spiritual literature, one element of which were four volumes of directories for novices. The fourth volume, whose Latin short title is *Methodus orandi* (Way of Praying), treats discursive meditation, affective prayer, and the prayer of simple regard (equated with acquired contemplation) as forms of active prayer that dispose the subject for infused contemplation. This is traditional teaching. What is a special contribution is the practice of aspirative prayer, or aspirations. This topic receives extended consideration because it is seen as the way to fulfill Chapter Seven of the Rule and to carry out the very purpose of the Order, which is actual, continuous, loving conversation with God.

Aspirative prayer is a step beyond ejaculations; it is more unctious, more affective, and more mystical insofar as it is connected with the breathing of the Holy Spirit within the person. Aspirations are not thoughts or phrases, but "darts out of the flaming fire of love," so that "the most simple affection is worth more than all the thoughts that are written in books."[18] Aspiratory prayer uses the word as the carrier of tremendous love: "all the affections of the heart are in the one word."[19] This practice is an expression of the deep conviction of Touraine that contemplative is synonymous with loving, and that the contemplative life is simply a life of deep love of God.

The *Methodus* considers aspiratory prayer an advanced way of praying that builds on previous meditation and affective prayer and looks toward divine union; it is part of the illuminative way. While the practice is not original with the Carmelites, since it comes out of the spirituality of introversion found in Augustine and popular in the lowlands and France at the time, it was adopted by Touraine as germane to the Order's spirit. John of St. Samson became its outstanding proponent.

What does aspiratory prayer have to say to Centering Prayer and Christian Meditation? It signals the primordial role of love in all contemplative prayer. This devotion can enrich the two contemplative forms of prayer by reminding them of this quality.

Like everything associated with contemplation in the seventeenth century, aspiratory prayer was presented as a higher form of prayer. Were Centering Prayer or Christian Meditation to have existed at that time, they would have been restricted to advanced souls. In our day there is no restriction. The two forms are available to all. We are less regimented in relating forms to stages of prayer. In Touraine, as in the rest of the Catholic world at the time, the four acts of *lectio divina* had become stages of prayer rather than parts of an organic whole. There were three degrees of mental prayer—meditation, affective prayer, and contemplation—corresponding with the three stages of the purgative, illuminative, and unitive ways. Practitioners were locked into the prayer form that belonged to their state. The words of one great master of the period, Louis Lallemant, were typical: "Everyone should remain faithful to the prayer proper to the degree or state of his [sic] spiritual life."[20]

Contemporary thinking breaks out of these hard and fast categories. No doubt some knowledge and love of God are necessary presuppositions, but no particular experience of mental prayer is demanded for Centering Prayer and Christian Meditation This indicates that these ways are basic Christian practice; they are not tied into advanced states. In the monastic form of *lectio divina* the four acts are like moments or points on a circle; they are iterrelated and inclusive of each other.[21] Thus one can enter the prayer at any one of the points. This is not to deny their internal relationships to each other. Even the first theorist on *lectio divina*, Guiges II, taught that "it would be a rare exception or a miracle to gain contemplation without prayer."[22] Both forms of contemplative prayer under discussion have a good deal of prayer built into them.

Conclusion

We come now to the end of our inquiry and draw the following conclusions:

1. The new forms of Centering Prayer and Christian Meditation relate positively to the Carmelite tradition. Christian Meditation is like

a mirror of Chapter Seven of the Rule and an application of the perspectives of *The Institution of the First Monks*. Centering Prayer is like a variant of the active recollection of St. Teresa of Avila. The Carmelite tradition has great affinity with these new forms of contemplative prayer.

2. Carmelite prayer is contemplative through and through. Even the method of mental prayer attributed to John of the Cross by Quiroga is probably closer to the new forms than to the highly rational discursive meditation or even the active imagination of our times, since the pondering (step two) was ordered to the quiet resting in God (step three).

3. The basic assumption of all Carmelite prayer is found in the twofold goal of the Order set down by Felip Ribot, namely, purity of heart and experience of the divine presence. The monastic prayer of the heart was designed to achieve this double goal; it is the prayer of Chapter Seven of the Rule. Centering Prayer and Christian Meditation are forms of that prayer of the heart.

4. The Carmelite tradition emphasizes the fact that the Word of God is the way to God. A recent document from the two Fathers General of the Carmelite Order puts it well: "The Word of God in Scripture becomes the Word of God in us to be joined to the Word of God in life."[23] Both contemporary methods engage the Word of God truly, not in discursive fashion, but in concentrated single words or phrases.

5. The teaching of Touraine on aspirative prayer deserves further study in order to align it with the two forms, either as another contemplative form for everyone or a quality of all these methods. Aspirative prayer has special affinity with Centering Prayer.

In summary our investigation indicates that Centering Prayer and Christian Meditation are friendly developments, not only in the monastic but also in the Carmelite tradition. They are new things and old, drawn out of the storehouse of the riches of the Western mystical tradition (Matt 13:52).

Notes

1. The phrases in quotation marks are taken from Quiroga as quoted from James Arraj, *From John of the Cross to Us* (Chiloquin, Ore.: Inner Growth Books, 1999), 103–4. This book reopens the inquiry into acquired contemplation from the viewpoint of St. John of the Cross and the Carmelites. He believes that the concept is a misinterpretation of John of the Cross (e.g., in regard to Thomas of Jesus see pp. 78–79). The error is a serious one in his opinion, because it caused the Quietist errors of the seventeenth century and the low esteem and malaise about mysticism in the eighteenth and nineteenth centuries.

2. Arraj, 64–65.

3. The tangled controversy about acquired contemplation is largely laid to rest today in favor of a broad description of the experience of contemplation. This irenic interpretation is offered in my recent essay "Contemporary Prayer Forms—Are They Contemplation?" *Review for Religious* 57 (1998), 77–87.

4. *St. John of the Cross, Doctor of Divine Love and Contemplation*, published with *Acquired Contemplation*, 100–202. The latter is a translation of a 1938 Latin text (Westminster, Md.: Newman, 1946).

5. *Talks on Meditation* (Montreal, 1979), 10.

6. *Conferences of John Cassian*, trans. Colum Luibheid (New York: Paulist Press, 1985) 10.19, pp. 185–86. Simon Tugwell points out that Guigo II, one of the earliest architects of *lectio divina*, equated meditating with repeating the word. See Tugwell, *Ways of Imperfection* (Springfield, 1985), 94–95. Later he points out that the word *meditate* actually means repeat, p. 105.

7. See William Shannon, *Thomas Merton's Paradise Journey* (Cincinnati: St. Anthony, 2000), 188–205. Merton's meditation is the contemplative prayer described in these pages.

8. Keith J. Egan, "Contemplative Meditation: A Challenge from the Tradition," *Handbook of Spirituality for Ministers*, vol. 2, ed. Robert Wicks (New York/Mahwah: Paulist Press, 2000), 445–46.

9. *Albert's Way*, ed. Michael Mulhall (Rome: Institutum Carmelitanum, 1989), 93.

10. Kees Waaijman, *The Mystical Space of Carmel*, trans. John Vriend (Leuven: Peeters, 1999), 93.

11. Felip Ribot, *The Institution of the First Monks*, 1.2, as quoted by Paul Chandler, O. Carm., in "Workbook" on this document (Rome: Institutum Carmelitanum, 1992), 7.

12. Ribot/Chandler, 5.

13. Cassian, *Conferences*, 10.14.
14. Cynthia Bourgeault, "From Woundedness to Union," *Review for Religious* 58 (1999), 158–67.
15. Kieran Kavanaugh, "Introduction," *The Interior Castle* (New York: Paulist Press, 1979), 12–15.
16. Teresa describes active recollection in WP.28–29; IC.4.3 and 6.7. I have analyzed Teresa's personal experience of this prayer in BL: "Teresa of Avila and Centering Prayer," *Carmelite Studies* 3 (Washington, D.C.: ICS, 1984), 203–9. This description parallels Thomas Alvarez in his beautiful exposition in *Living with God, St. Teresa's Concept of Prayer* (Dublin: Carmelite Centre of Spirituality, n.d.), 12–18.
17. *Methods of Prayer in the Directory of the Carmelite Reform of Touraine* (Rome: Institutum Carmelitanum, 1956), 16.
18. Ibid., 63.
19. John Brenninger, *The Carmelite Directory of the Spiritual Life*, trans. Leo J. Walter (Chicago: Carmelite Press, 1951), 471. This manual has an excellent treatment of aspirative prayer, as does Vernard Poslusney, *Prayer, Aspiration, and Contemplation* (Asbury, N.J., 1994).
20. Cited in Paul Philippe, "Mental Prayer in the Catholic Tradition," *Mental Prayer and Modern Life, A Symposium*, trans. Francis C. Lehner (New York: Kennedy, 1950), 3.
21. Thomas Keating, "The Classical Monastic Practice of *Lectio Divina*," *Contemplative Outreach News* 12 (1998), n.2.
22. *Scala claustralium* cited in ibid., 23.
23. "Passing Through the Holy Door," Circular Letter of O.C.D/O. Carm. Superiors General at the Beginning of the Third Millennium (Rome, 1999), 12.

12

A Modern Pioneer
of Carmelite Spirituality:
Ernest E. Larkin

Keith J. Egan

The twentieth century had many memorable moments. Some of them were all too violent and destructive. Yet, there were times and events to savor. For Christianity, there was no more important, influential, and energizing event than the Second Vatican Council (1962–1965). This gathering of Catholic bishops in Rome brought the Catholic Church and much of Christianity into dialogue with the modern world. The council's deliberations were shaped by the Word of God and by classical Christian resources. The council was an effort to achieve a genuine pastoral renewal of Catholic life and even to seek the realization of the prayer of Jesus that "they may all be one" (John 17:21). As a result Catholics began to dialogue with other Christians and to some extent with adherents of world religions. Leaving behind Catholic insularity, the council declared that "humanity forms but one community" and that "the Catholic Church rejects nothing of what is true and holy in these religions."[1] Moreover, the council affirmed "...that the human person has a right to religious freedom."[2] These electrifying conciliar convictions were the fruition of Pope John XXIII's desire that the council be a New Pentecost, an aggiornamento, an updating, a time for opening the windows of the church.

The council's proceedings pointed to new horizons for the church and Christianity. Perhaps as far-reaching as any of the council's progressive declarations was its affirmation of a "Universal Call to Holiness": "The Lord Jesus, divine teacher and model of all perfection, preached holiness of life...to each and every one of his disciples no matter what their condition of life...."[3] To affirm that holiness belongs to all shattered not a few myths about who was called to be holy and what holiness is. The Universal Call to Holiness was a mandate for a retrieval of an expansive spirituality rooted in sound tradition but understood within the context of what Pope John referred to as "the signs of the times." Modern pioneer of Carmelite spirituality that he is, much of Father Ernest Larkin's adult life has been a living commentary on Vatican II's new horizons, and he has taken up the council's challenges with a discerning eye on the signs of the times. Moreover, the story of the contemporary retrieval of Carmelite spirituality and contemplative prayer can be traced in the contours of his life. As a Carmelite priest who embraced the spirit of Vatican II, Father Ernest brought unique gifts and special training to the recovery of an authentic Carmelite spirituality in North America.

Vatican II and the Recovery of Christian Spirituality

Toward the end of the social and cultural upheavals of the 1960s there occurred a turn *within*, a search for a deeper life that thrived in the religious climate that had been created by Vatican II. The birth of a widespread interest in spirituality emerged from the council's renewed spiritual environment. Moreover, there was a realization that the secular city, on its own, could not bring about a lasting transformation of the modern world as a just and peaceful society. In this atmosphere women and men could now get in touch with the transcendent yearnings of the human heart. They could bring gospel values to traditions that had often been overlaid with stultifying accretions.

Religious orders and congregations began to ask what they might do to renew their own spirit and how they might contribute to the challenges opened up by the initiatives of Vatican II. The Jesuits with their historical studies already in place were first in North America to offer major guidance to those touched by this new interest in spirituality. The Jesuits shared with countless spiritual searchers a renewed understanding of the Spiritual Exercises of St. Ignatius. These Exercises retrieved for the modern world a healthy awareness that a prayerful life could attune one to God's loving presence and to a judicious discernment of God's will. The Jesuit renewal of Ignatian discernment had a crucial impact on the development of a contemporary spirituality that needed to pay more than lip service to the universal call to holiness and to the spiritual practices involved in a life open to God's designs. The recovery of the contemplative and mystical grounding of the Ignatian Exercises laid the foundations for an appreciation of contemplative prayer.

With the classical writings of Teresa of Avila and John of the Cross available in many modern translations, the Carmelite tradition has been a natural supplement to Jesuit discernment. Signs of renewal among Carmelites were in place before the council and would blossom in the new atmosphere created by the council. In the first half of the twentieth century the Discalced Carmelites near Paris had explored important spiritual issues and published their explorations in a series of lively monographs known as *Études Carmélitaines*. Some volumes in this series were translated into English.[4] Later the Teresianum in Rome became the international center of Discalced Carmelite studies in theology and spirituality.[5] Discalced Carmelites have subsequently opened national centers where the spirituality of Teresa and John have been disseminated.

In 1951 the Carmelites of the Ancient Observance (O.Carm.), under the leadership of the then prior general Father Kilian Lynch, inaugurated in Rome the Institutum Carmelitanum with its three branches devoted to Carmelite history, mariology, and spirituality. The institute began publication of its scholarly journal *Carmelus* in 1954.[6] This international Institute heralded a new day in the retrieval of the Carmelite charism and its tradition. Various O. Carm. provinces around the world have since that time inaugurated programs and publications for the study and practice of Carmelite spirituality.

In North America the journal *Spiritual Life* and the publications of the Institute of Carmelite Studies, both Discalced undertakings, were evidence of a desire to share the Carmelite spirituality with a wider audience. The establishment of the Carmelite Forum in the early 1980s was an expression of not only the renewed interest in Carmelite spirituality but has been an example of the many collaborative efforts that the two branches of the Carmelite Order have undertaken in recent decades. In a day when a consumer and a self-absorbed culture seems ever present there is a remarkable interest in the Carmelite contemplative tradition.

The Making of a Carmelite Theologian

After the Second World War, the Chicago province of the American Carmelites (Ancient Observance) made a prophetic and decisive contribution to the life of the mind and the spirit of the Order. The Chicago province sent young Carmelite priests to pursue advanced studies. Among these candidates for higher degrees was Ernest E. Larkin. From 1948 to 1950 Father Ernest undertook doctoral studies in theology at the University of Saint Thomas Aquinas in Rome (then referred to as the Angelicum). Father Larkin wrote his dissertation on *The Ecstasies of 'The Forty Days' of St. Mary Magdalen de' Pazzi*.[7] Studies at the Angelicum including courses with Reginald Garrigou-Lagrange, O.P., and direction of his dissertation by Paul Philippe, O.P., prepared Father Larkin to become a studious and articulate theologian with a profound interest in spirituality. His dissertation and various courses at the Angelicum set him on his way as a theologian who would make significant contributions to the retrieval of an authentic Vatican II spirituality. In addition, Larkin's theological training and Carmelite vocation made it possible for him to be a leader in the recovery of Carmelite spirituality in North America. As a theologian deeply interested in Christian spirituality, Father Larkin has been an active agent in the healing in our time of the longstanding and unfortunate divorce between theology and spirituality.[8]

A Carmelite Vocation

On August 19, 1922, Eldon Larkin (Ernest is a religious name) was born into a Catholic family on the south side of Chicago. After a Catholic grade school education in Chicago, he entered the Carmelite high-school seminary at Niagara Falls, Ontario, in 1935. He became a Carmelite novice at New Baltimore, Pennsylvania, where he made his first profession of vows on the feast of Our Lady's Assumption in 1940. Larkin received his bachelor in philosophy degree from Mount Carmel College, Niagara Falls, Ontario, in June 1943. His theological studies were undertaken from 1943 to 1947 at Whitefriars Hall, the Carmelite major seminary in Washington, D.C. He also attended the Catholic University of America for graduate studies in English at this time. Father Ernest was ordained to the priesthood on June 8, 1946. For a year following his ordination he continued his theological studies at Whitefriars Hall.

Father Larkin spent the academic year of 1947–1948 teaching young men at Mount Carmel High School on the south side of Chicago. As mentioned above, Ernest Larkin was chosen at this time by his province to pursue doctoral studies in theology at the Angelicum in Rome. Upon completion of his studies at the Angelicum, he taught high school once again during the academic year 1950–1951 at Joliet Catholic High School, Joliet, Illinois. Ernest

Larkin thus by study and teaching prepared for a lifetime of ministry as a professor, writer, preacher, spiritual director and retreat master. Over more than fifty-five years as a priest, Ernest Larkin has been an avid student who has maintained throughout his life a hearty appetite for reading broadly and for studying incisively. Whatever he has done as scholar, professor, and priest has been done out of a profound dedication to his vocation as a Carmelite. This Carmelite commitment has earned Father Ernest the very evident affection and admiration of his Carmelite brothers and sisters.

Theological and Spiritual Educator

From 1951 to 1959 Father Larkin taught theology and acted as a spiritual director for Carmelite seminarians studying theology at Whitefriars Hall, Washington, D.C. He served from 1956 to 1959, at a time when vocations were still numerous, as master of students in charge of their formation. As an innovation to the theological curriculum at Whitefriars Hall, Father Ernest designed and taught courses on Teresa of Avila and John of the Cross. He had been introduced to the study of the writings of these two Carmelite mystics during his doctoral studies in Rome. Ever since those Roman days, he has been a keen student of the teachings of Teresa and John, and he has done much to disseminate an accessible, contemporary understanding of their doctrines. During this period Father Ernest was also director of a vigorous Lay Carmelite program that was affiliated with Whitefriars Hall. In the summers of 1955, 1956, and 1957 he began another of his lifelong commitments by offering summer courses in scripture and theology for religious and laity at various sites around the country. At this time he also acted as retreat master at places like Carmel Retreat in Mahwah, New Jersey. His colleague, Ronald Gray, O. Carm., inaugurated a program called the Conference-a-Month Club for which Father Larkin recorded lectures intended for religious.

The 1950s were very productive and happy years for Ernest Larkin. He much enjoyed his assignment at Whitefriars Hall where he was part of a team of studious and productive theologians. The 1950s laid the groundwork for Father Larkin's new ministries in the 1960s and for his role as a leader in the church's new directions during the Vatican II era.

Professor at the Catholic University of America

From 1959 until 1971 Ernest Larkin was a professor of spiritual theology at the Catholic University of America in Washington, D.C. In his teaching and direction of dissertations, he exercised a far-reaching influence on those who would teach theology and spirituality during the post-Vatican II era in North American seminaries and institutions of higher learning. It is not uncommon to meet priests and others who attribute their grasp of contemporary theology and spirituality to their teacher and mentor, Ernest Larkin. This was another busy and productive decade for Father Larkin. In 1962 he delivered his first scholarly address at the annual convention of the Catholic Theological Society of America. Father Larkin also acted as a consulting editor for the *New Catholic Encyclopedia* (1967), and he composed various entries for this vast undertaking in Catholic scholarship.[9] During the time that Larkin was at the Catholic University of America he lectured nationally and in Canada on a number of important topics: "Liturgy and Contemplation," "Action and Contemplation," "John of the Cross," "The Scriptural Theological Aspects of Religious Life," and "The Religious Woman, God and the World." From 1966 until 1972 Father Larkin served on the provincial council of his order during a critical time for American religious orders. This was an era when departures from religious life and the priesthood began, and it was a time when seminary education was being reevaluated. An indication of the esteem in which Father Ernest was held by his Carmelite confreres was his repeated election as a delegate to the Carmelite Order's general chapters that were convened at Rome in 1965, 1968, 1971, and 1983. He brought a level-headed but progressive and engaged theology to these chapters.

New Ventures in the Southwest

Many friends and colleagues at the Catholic University of America and at Whitefriars Hall were deeply disappointed when ill health precipitated Father Larkin's resignation from the university's theology department in 1971. Yet, the move to Phoenix, Arizona, created new ventures that benefited from Father Larkin's congeniality and his gifts as priest and theologian. Bishop Edward A. McCarthy, who had become Bishop of Phoenix when the diocese was created in 1969, invited Father Larkin to become the diocese's theologian-in-residence in 1971. That assignment, meant to be for one year during a leave of absence from Catholic University, lasted for eleven years.

In September of 1972 Father Larkin cofounded Kino Institute, the diocese of Phoenix's school of adult religious education that was placed under the care of the Carmelites. This Institute has been crucial to the theological, ministerial, and spiritual formation of those engaged in ministry in a state where there is no Catholic institution of higher learning. Father Larkin was Kino Institute's first president, an office he held until 1977. He has continued teaching at Kino Institute during all the years that he has been resident in Phoenix. Since he arrived there in 1971 until today, Ernest Larkin has been a telling influence on the spiritual lives of the clergy, religious, and laity in the diocese of Phoenix.

In his first years in Phoenix, Father Larkin was a member of a national team of priests who conducted priests' retreats around the country. This ministry entailed the responsibility for articulating a contemporary spirituality for priests. Commissioned by the bishops of the United States, this team produced the booklet, *Spiritual Renewal of the American Priesthood* (1973). This publication reflected the ideals of the Second Vatican Council and offered an up-to-date spiritual doctrine for the clergy in contemporary North America. As a coeditor of this document, Father Larkin composed its final version.

In the fall of 1970 Father Larkin, with James Gill, S.J., traveled to Alaska, Japan, and the Philippines to present workshops for Air Force chaplains. Subsequently Father Larkin and Father Gill offered numerous programs to Carmelites and to diocesan priests. In 1974 Father Larkin spent two months teaching and preaching in Rome. From there he left for Australia where he lectured in that country's major cities. For five years during the 1970s Father Larkin coordinated prayer experiences for the men of his Carmelite province. During this decade, Father Larkin was much in demand as a retreat master and lecturer at various colleges, universities, and other institutions throughout the country.

For a time in the1970s Father Ernest was also involved as a participant and as a leader in the Charismatic Renewal. This experience was very formative and freeing for him. He has said that it helped him to develop a more personal relationship with Christ. After his involvement in the Charismatic Movement, Father Ernest found his own prayer moving in the direction of Centering Prayer.[10] This new interest in the practice of Centering Prayer would have a very important impact on his own life and on those to whom he ministered.

Back to the Midwest

The many far-flung travel commitments entailed in Father Larkin's ministry brought him to Chicago in 1981. He settled at the Titus Brandsma Carmelite House adjacent to the north shore campus of Loyola University where he had easier access to national and international air travel. From this Carmelite community Father Larkin spent the next six years on the road as a teacher and preacher. From 1981 until 1986 he was a regular teacher at the Carmelite

International Centre in Rome where ongoing formation programs for Carmelites from around the world were held. From 1980 until 1990 Father Larkin was a faculty member in the Summer Institutes of Retreats International that were held on the campus of the University of Notre Dame where he developed a close friendship with Father Thomas Gedeon, S.J., then director of Retreats International. From 1982 until 1986 Father Larkin taught a module in the Continuing Formation Program for Clergy, at that time located at Notre Dame but now situated at Catholic Theological Union in Chicago. From 1985 on, Father Larkin has taught regularly in the annual Summer Seminars on Carmelite Spirituality at Saint Mary's College, Notre Dame, Indiana. This program is offered by the Carmelite Forum of which Ernest Larkin was a founding member.

From 1980 until 1990 Father Larkin acted as a consultant for the spirituality section of *Concilium,* an international theological review that has brought to readers throughout the world scholarly studies of contemporary theological and religious interest. During that same decade Father Larkin acted as a spirituality consultant for the Center for Human Development in Washington, D.C.

Father Larkin's book, *Silent Presence: Discernment as Process and Problem,*[11] is an example of his gifts as a writer. This book is clear, crisp, and economical even though it deals with a theme that has often been given a complex exposition. Father Larkin has mastered the tradition of discernment and has studied carefully the pertinent contemporary scholarship on this subject. He has a unique gift for presenting the wisdom of the tradition in plain, readable language. *Silent Presence* also reveals a theme that pervades Father Larkin's thinking and writing— integration. In this book he integrates the themes of contemplation and discernment, too often treated as if contemplation and discernment had nothing to do with each other. For Father Larkin discernment is a matter of spiritual maturity that "enables us to be aware of the Silent Presence deep within oneself." Father Larkin considers Carmelite contemplative prayer as loving attention to the Lord fostered by an awareness of the presence of Jesus. Father Larkin is at work on a "wholesale" revision of *Silent Presence*. He has already published a summary statement on discernment that will appear as an epilogue in the second edition of *Silent Presence* (Dimension Books).[12]

Three years after the appearance of *Silent Presence*, Father Larkin published *Christ Within Us*, a title that reveals the author's focus on living and praying with a growing awareness of the presence of Jesus.[13] This book is a collection of monthly essays that he had written from 1971 until 1981 for *Alive*, a magazine of the diocese of Phoenix. Once again this book is eminently clear and accessible. Moreover, it shows that astute theological observations can be applied simply and with precision to the everyday lives of Christians. In the introduction to *Christ Within Us*, Father Larkin writes that these essays are "a record of my personal spiritual journey." Chapters in this book explore scripture, Christ, church, prayer, peace and justice, world hunger, the Charismatic Renewal, the relationship of holiness to wholeness, and so on. As a Carmelite is wont to do, Father Larkin also wrote about the Virgin Mary in this book. Carmelite men have long called themselves Brothers of Mary of Mount Carmel, a relationship that dates back to the thirteenth century chapel dedicated to Mary and which stood in the midst of the hermitages on Mount Carmel.

A Return to the Southwest

Father Larkin returned in 1987 to minister in the diocese of Phoenix where he resides to this day.[14] In addition he keeps up what he aptly calls his itinerant ministry. The Carmelites became itinerant ministers in the church when they moved from being hermits to friars in the middle of the thirteenth century. Ernest Larkin has been a traveling friar all of his adult life. During the 1980s and 1990s Father Larkin has taught and preached in Rome, Ireland, and Zimbabwe. He has also spoken frequently at cloistered monasteries of Carmelite nuns. During this time he returned frequently to lecture and to preach at favorite locations like Dubuque, Saginaw, New Orleans, and at Maggie Valley in North Carolina where his visits were eagerly awaited by the many who have been nourished by his teaching and preaching.

Like one of his favorite Carmelite mentors, John of the Cross, Ernest Larkin has been a trusted spiritual guide for many. He helps his directees grow in prayer, especially in contemplative prayer. Heeding the advice of this Spanish mystic, Father Ernest sees to it that those who come to him for spiritual guidance realize fully that their "principal guide is the Holy Spirit" (LF.3.46). Father Ernest's directees have experienced him as clear and direct, empathetic and challenging, always an understanding and accepting spiritual guide. A spirit of simplicity characterizes his spiritual guidance, which has been shaped by a profound knowledge of Christian spiritual traditions.

Contemplative Prayer and Carmelite Spirituality

Over the last two decades, amid his continued teaching and preaching, Father Larkin has been especially committed to studying and writing about contemplative prayer. Essays on contemplative prayer have been shaped by Father Larkin's own journey in prayer which he has characterized as a journey from observance to a contemplative openness to Jesus in the scripture, the liturgy, in creation, and especially to the presence of Christ within.[15] From his computer has come a steady flow of essays on this topic.[16] His contribution to this book of essays takes up the theme of contemplative prayer forms and their relevance to the Carmelite heritage of prayer: "Carmelite Tradition and Centering Prayer/Christian Meditation." He sees these contemporary forms of contemplative prayer as especially suitable for those who find themselves at home in the Carmelite tradition or who sense a call to pray more contemplatively. For some time he has shown a personal preference for Christian Meditation devised by

Father John Main, O.S.B. Father Larkin has discovered in the practice of Christian Meditation an affinity with the teachings of John of the Cross where prayer is an invitation by God to occupy the human heart with love. In Christian Meditation the recitation of a mantra like the Aramaic *marána tha* (Come, Lord Jesus) is not only "an echo of one of the oldest prayers used by Christians...,"[17] but it brings one in faith into the presence of Christ. The praying of this mantra, or a holy word like it, helps to develop within one what John of the Cross calls an emptiness, nakedness, or spiritual poverty. The work to be done in this prayer is God's work and aims at opening up one to union with God in love. Such a process of emptying one's mind and heart is an invitation to the Lord to do what needs to be done to bring one to a love of God and neighbor. God's love fills that emptiness with God's loving presence. It is prayer congenial to Teresa of Jesus and John of the Cross. It is a move to letting God take over one's heart. Perhaps more than at anytime in his life Father Larkin has become a theologian of contemplative prayer.

In a beautifully written essay, Father Larkin has shared his own experience of praying the mantra in Christian Meditation. In this essay he includes entries from his journal concerning his practice of Christian Meditation. The entries come from a five-week personal retreat at the Camaldolese Hermitage, Big Sur, California.[18]

Not surprisingly Father Larkin has been publishing essays on the spirituality of Thérèse of Lisieux for whom he has a special affection and whose prayer was eminently simple but truly contemplative.[19]

Concluding Comments

There is not space here to list the many writings of Father Ernest Larkin. A collection of these writings can be found in a special file in the Carmelitana Collection, Whitefriars Hall, Washington, D.C., 20017. His many audiocassettes and videos are also housed there and at the library of Kino Institute, Phoenix, Ariz. 85020. Moreover, his numerous writings have been collected by friends and are available on the world wide web.[20]

Special honors have come to Father Larkin during these latter days in Phoenix. In 1994, when the diocese of Phoenix celebrated its twenty-fifth anniversary, he was one of twenty-five honorees to receive the Diocesan Ministry Award. In 1996 Father Larkin celebrated with family, Carmelites, and friends the fiftieth anniversary of ordination to the priesthood. The homilist at the eucharistic celebration on this occasion was his brother, Father John Larkin, O. Carm. For his article, "Jubilee Spirituality," *Spiritual Life* 45 (Spring 1999) Father Ernest received the Catholic Press Association's first prize award in the category of spirituality. In June of 2000 the annual Carmelite Summer Seminar on Carmelite Spirituality, with the theme "Carmelite Prayer," honored Father Ernest Larkin as a pioneer in the study and dissemination of Carmelite Spirituality. The weeklong seminar concluded with a lecture by Father Ernest, a reception followed by a banquet at which family, friends, and Carmelites gathered to celebrate his life, ministry, and numerous contributions to Carmelite spirituality.

Father Ernest's friends have found it more than appropriate that the prayer cards for the celebration of his fiftieth anniversary of ordination and for the Seminar in 2000 carried the following saying from John of the Cross: "When evening comes, you will be examined in love" (Sayings 60). One quite easily detects in Father Ernest's writings and in his life an ever-growing appreciation for the importance of personal relationships, especially a pivotal relationship with Jesus of Nazareth. Father Ernest's family (his brothers Jack and Bob, Bob's wife, his sister Mary, and his three nieces) have a very special place in his heart. They and his Carmelite brothers and sisters, friends, and colleagues are unanimous in their appraisal of Ernest Larkin as a wise, warm, down-to-earth, no pretense, gentle man of prayer and love. That is why the essays in this book are dedicated with gratitude to this Carmelite priest who has personified the contemporary longing to develop through prayer an ever-deepening relationship with Jesus of Nazareth.[21] Dom Helder Camara, the late archbishop of Recife, Brazil, once said that "I can't imagine being anything but a priest....For me, being a priest isn't just a choice, it's a way of life. It's what water is for a fish, the sky for the bird."[22] No friend of Ernest Larkin can imagine him as anything but a Carmelite and a priest.

Notes

1. Declaration on the Relation of the Church to Non-Christian Religions (1965), #1, #2. *Vatican Council II, Constitutions, Decrees, Declarations*, rev. ed., ed. Austin Flannery (Northport, N.Y.: Costello; Dublin, Ireland: Dominican Publications, 1996).
2. Declaration on Religious Liberty (1965), #2. Ibid.
3. Dogmatic Constitution on the Church (1964), #40. Ibid.
4. E.g., *Satan* (New York: Sheed & Ward, 1952) and *Love and Violence* (New York: Sheed & Ward, 1954).
5. The Theological Faculty was first established at the Teresianum in 1935; it became a Pontifical Theological Faculty in 1963. The Pontificio Istituto di Spiritualità was established there in 1964. The Discalced Carmelite journal *Ephemerides Carmeliticae* began publication in 1947 and since 1988 the journal *Teresianum* has been its successor.
6. The Institutum Carmelitanum over the years has also published many scholarly monographs besides more popular publications. Ernest Larkin published an essay in the first issue of the Institute's scholarly journal: "The Ecstasies of 'The Forty Days' of Saint Mary Magdalen de' Pazzi," *Carmelus* 1, n.1 (1954), 29–71.
7. Rome: Pontificium Institutum Angelicum.
8. See Keith J. Egan, "The Divorce of Spirituality from Theology," *Theological Education in the Catholic Tradition*, eds. Patrick Carey and Earl Muller (New York: Crossroad, 1997), 296–307.
9. Four entries by Ernest Larkin were "Christian Spirituality," "Mary Magdalene de' Pazzi," "Mysticism in Literature," and "The Three Spiritual Ways." For volume 17, a 1979 Supplement to the *New Catholic Encyclopedia*, Larkin composed the entry "Priestly Spirituality."
10. See Art and Betty Winter, "Journey to Prayer: An Interview with Ernest Larkin," *Review for Religious* 42 (1983), 80–89. See a version of this article

as "Three Ways to the Center," *Stories of Prayer: Interviews with Leading Catholics on Their Experience of God* by Betty and Art Winter (Kansas City, Mo.: Sheed and Ward, 1985), 108–21.

11. Denville, N.J.: Dimension Books, 1981.

12. Ernest E. Larkin, "What to Know about Discernment," *Review for Religious* 60 (March-April 2001), 162–170, see 162.

13. Denville, N.J.: Dimension Books, 1984.

14. Father Larkin resides at Saint Agnes Priory, 1954 North 24th Street, Phoenix, Ariz., 85008-3556.

15. See note 10 above.

16. See especially "Today's Contemplative Prayer Forms: Are They Contemplative?" *Review for Religious* 57 (1998), 77–87; "Contemplative Prayer Forms Today: Are They Contemplation?" *The Diversity of Centering Prayer,* ed. Gustave Reininger (New York: Continuum, 1999), 77–87. "Contemplative Prayer as the Soul of the Apostolate," *Handbook of Spirituality for Ministers,* vol. 2, ed. Robert J. Wicks (New York/Mahwah: Paulist Press, 2000), 456–68.

17. Raymond E. Brown, *An Introduction to the New Testament* (New York: Doubleday, 1997), 795.

18. Ernest E. Larkin, "An Experience of Christian Meditation," *Review for Religious* 60 (July-August 2001), 419–31.

19. See *Spirituality* 4 (May-June 1998), 165–69; 4 (July-August, 1998), 231–34; 4 (September-October, 1998), 303–6; 5 (November-December 1999), 354–59; 6 (January-February 2000), 33-37; "The Little Way of St. Thérèse of Lisieux," *Review for Religious* 59 (September-October 2000), 507–17.

20. http://carmelnet.org/larkin/larkin.htm

21. For an interview of Father Ernest Larkin by a fellow Carmelite, see "Ernest Larkin, O. Carm., Looks Back," *Carmelite Review* 39 (May-August 2000), 1, 7–10.

22. Paul Dudziak, "Spirituality of the Diocesan Priest," *Church* 17 (Winter 2001), 30.

Contributors

Donald W. Buggert, O. Carm., is chair of the department of systematic theology at Washington Theological Union and resides at Whitefriars Hall, Washington, D.C.

Kevin Culligan, O.C.D., resides at the Edith Stein House of Studies affiliated with the Catholic Theological Union, Chicago, where besides his writing he practices the ministry of spiritual guidance and counseling.

Margaret Dorgan, D.C.M., is an author and lecturer who resides at John of the Cross Monastery, Ellsworth, in rural Maine.

Keith J. Egan, T.O. Carm., holds the Joyce McMahon Hank Aquinas Chair in Catholic Theology at Saint Mary's College, Notre Dame, Indiana, and is Adjunct Professor of Theology at Notre Dame University.

Constance FitzGerald, O.C.D., is the prioress of the Carmelite Monastery, Baltimore, Maryland., where she is engaged in the ministries of formation and spiritual direction besides her ministry as an author and lecturer.

Kieran Kavanaugh, O.C.D., is the prior of the Carmelite Friary, Lincoln Road, Washington, D.C., and the American translator of the writings of Teresa of Avila and John of the Cross.

Ernest E. Larkin, O. Carm., is an author, lecturer, and retreat master who resides at St. Agnes Parish, Phoenix, Arizona. See chapter 12 of this book for a biographical sketch.

Roland E. Murphy, O. Carm., was George Washington Ivey Emeritus Professor of Biblical Studies at Duke University and Adjunct

Professor at Washington Theological Union, Washington, D.C. He resided at Whitefriars Hall, Washington, D.C. Father Murphy died July 20, 2002.

Vilma Seelaus, O.C.D., is the former prioress at the Carmelite Monastery, Barrington, Rhode Island, where she is engaged in ministry as a writer and lecturer.

John Welch, O. Carm., past president of the Carmelite Institute, Washington, D.C., is a Carmelite Commissary Provincial and is professor at the Washington Theological Union, Washington, D.C. He resides at Whitefriars Hall, Washington, D.C.

All of the above contributors are members of the Carmelite Forum, or, like Margaret Dorgan and Roland E. Murphy, have been closely associated with the work of the Forum.

Index

Index